Politics, Participation & Power Relations

CRITICAL ISSUES IN THE FUTURE OF LEARNING AND TEACHING

Volume 4

This series represents a forum for important issues that do and will affect how learning and teaching are thought about and practised. All educational venues and situations are undergoing change because of information and communications technology, globalization and paradigmatic shifts in determining what knowledge is valued. Our scope includes matters in primary, secondary and tertiary education as well as community-based informal circumstances. Important and significant differences between information and knowledge represent a departure from traditional educational offerings heightening the need for further and deeper understanding of the implications such opportunities have for influencing what happens in schools, colleges and universities around the globe. An inclusive approach helps attend to important current and future issues related to learners, teachers and the variety of cultures and venues in which educational efforts occur. We invite forward-looking contributions that reflect an international comparative perspective illustrating similarities and differences in situations, problems, solutions and outcomes.

Edited by Michael Kompf (michael.kompf@brocku.ca - Brock University, Canada) & Pamela M Denicolo (p.m.denicolo@reading.ac.uk - University of Reading, UK)

Michael Kompf is Professor of Education at Brock University, Canada. Interests include developmental issues for adult learners and teachers; personal construct psychology; global policies and practices in higher education; and philosophies of inquiry. Recent writing and presentations have included exploring the nature of university corporatism, higher education success rates, individual and the social implications of distance learning, and Aboriginal education. A member of the International Study Association on Teachers and Teaching (isatt.org) since 1985, Michael has served four terms as Chair in addition to four terms as editor of the ISATT Newsletter. Michael is a member of several professional associations and serves as associate editor and reviewer on several journals. He is co-editor of six volumes of work in adult education and the various areas of teacher thinking. He has consulted, presented papers and given lectures throughout North America, the EU and Australasia.

Pam Denicolo is the Director of the Graduate School at the University of Reading and an active member of the University Committee for Postgraduate Research Studies. Her passion for supporting and developing graduate students is also demonstrated through her contributions to the UK Council for Graduate Education Executive Committee, the Society for Research into Higher Education Postgraduate Network, and other national and international committees and working groups which, for example, review and evaluate research generic skills training and the concordance of UK universities with the European Code and Charter, produce a framework of skills for researchers over their full career and consider the changing nature of the doctorate. As a psychologist working particularly in the fields of Professional and Postgraduate Education, she has supervised more than 50 doctoral students to successful completion, examined many more, and developed and led Research Methods Programmes for social scientists in her current and previous universities. She was honoured to be appointed an Honorary Member of the Royal Pharmaceutical Society for her contributions to the education of pharmacists. Her lifelong interest in student learning, and hence teachers' teaching, led her to become an active member of the International Study Association on Teachers and Teaching (ISATT) and serving member of the Executive Committee for many years. Her research has been oriented by a commitment to understanding the way participants in learning processes construe their roles, situations and activities, through the use and development of Personal Construct Theory approaches and methods.

POLITICS, PARTICIPATION & POWER RELATIONS

Transdisciplinary Approaches to Critical Citizenship in the Classroom and Community

Edited by

Richard C. Mitchell
Brock University, Canada

Shannon A. Moore
Brock University, Canada

SENSE PUBLISHERS
ROTTERDAM/BOSTON/TAIPEI

A C.I.P. record for this book is available from the Library of Congress.

ISBN: 978-94-6091-741-7 (paperback)
ISBN: 978-94-6091-742-4 (hardback)
ISBN: 978-94-6091-743-1 (e-book)

Published by: Sense Publishers,
P.O. Box 21858,
3001 AW Rotterdam,
The Netherlands
www.sensepublishers.com

Printed on acid-free paper

Cover Photo credit: This photo was taken by photographer Mario Garcia-Baeza and shows a group of American bankers assembled on a Chicago rooftop during their annual conference in October, 2011 while peering down on "Occupy Chicago" protesters. The photo originally appeared in the article "Community Groups, Labor and 'Occupy Chicago' Protest Mortgage Bankers Association, Seven Thousand Strong" by: Yana Kunichoff, an Assistant Editor with Truthout - an independent, web-based news organization - on 12 October, 2011.

The editors chose this photo as it represents a key dimension of the highly conflicted nature of contemporary capitalist relations and much of their corrupt underpinning being directly confronted by citizens in a free and democratic movement. These citizens are exercising their rights to assembly, to peaceful protest and to freedom of the press - acts of critical citizenship being debated in this text that many have died for in the recent "Arab Spring" uprisings.

All Rights Reserved © 2012 Sense Publishers

No part of this work may be reproduced, stored in a retrieval system, or transmitted in any form or by any means, electronic, mechanical, photocopying, microfilming, recording or otherwise, without written permission from the publisher, with the exception of any material supplied specifically for the purpose of being entered and executed on a computer system, for exclusive use by the purchaser of the work.

TABLE OF CONTENTS

1. Introduction: Politics, participation and power relations: transdisciplinary approaches to critical citizenship 1
   Richard C. Mitchell and Shannon A. Moore

2. School power and democratic citizenship education in China: Experiences from three secondary schools 9
   Wangbei Ye

3. Critical citizenship, popular theatre, and the social imagination of pre-service teachers 35
   Sandra J. Wolf

4. The corporatization of the university: Post neo-liberalism and the decline and fall of democratic learning 51
   Emery Hyslop-Margison and Josephine L. Savarese

5. Deliberative democracy, people's agency and education: A case of dialogic transformation of a school system 63
   Gaysu R. Arvind

6. Synthesizing participatory human rights education and critical consciousness in Australian schools: Possibilities and challenges for educators developing a model of human rights education 83
   Keith Heggart

7. Children's rights and teachers' responsibilities: A case study of developing a rights respecting initial teacher education programme 101
   Lee Jerome

8. Critical citizens or neo-liberal consumers? Utopian visions and pragmatic uses of human rights education in a secondary school in England 119
   Sam Mejias and Hugh Starkey

9. The politics of critical citizenship education: Human rights for conformity or emancipation? 137
   Helen Trivers and Hugh Starkey

TABLE OF CONTENTS

10. Writing community: Composing as transformation and realization 153
    Paul L. Thomas

11. Media representations of Muslim women wearing the
    burka: Criticism and implications 169
    May Al-Fartousi and Dolana Mogadime

12. Transdisciplinary approaches to young people's citizenship:
    From bystanders to action 183
    Shannon A. Moore and Richard C. Mitchell

Author biography 207

RICHARD C. MITCHELL AND SHANNON A. MOORE

INTRODUCTION

Politics, Participation and Power Relations: Transdisciplinary Approaches to Critical Citizenship

The notion of what constitutes an effective cultural or political expression of democratic citizenship in this post-millennial, post-colonial, even post neo-liberal moment is increasingly fluid as we write this Introduction for our second edited text on these themes (see Moore & Mitchell, 2008). As Hyslop-Margison and Thayer (2009, p. xv) have noted "these are extremely tenuous times for modern democratic states and for democracy more generally" as world society drifts dangerously towards "neo-liberal capitalist collapse" without the emergence of any viable alternative paradigms. This is so much more the case since our project was conceived that we're reminded of sociologist Zygmunt Bauman's (2005) "afterthought" that we live now in a time of "liquid modernity ... among a multitude of competing values, norms, and lifestyles without a firm and reliable guarantee of being in the right [that] is hazardous and commands a high psychological price" (p. 1095). We remain cautiously optimistic, in the sense that 20th century Brazilian educator Paulo Freire espoused, particularly as we observe the contemporaneous revolutions/revelations occurring in numerous Middle Eastern states- each one facilitated in their own geopolitical space through the phenomena of globalised social media. Recalling Freire's contributions Henry A. Giroux (2010b) reflects on this approach to pedagogy:

> What Freire made clear is that ... education is a political and moral practice that provides the knowledge, skills and social relations that enable students to explore for themselves the possibilities of what it means to be engaged citizens, while expanding and deepening their participation in the promise of a substantive democracy (para. 5).

This "substantive" approach to participatory democracy could be argued to possess at least a few common baselines. Parenthetically even the most optimistic of critical educators could not have forecast the new boundaries being created by populist uprisings in Egypt, Yemen, Bahrain, Syria, and Libya in the final months of this project. Indeed, even a short year ago any critique that decades-old military dictatorships and their frequently oppressive oil-based oligarchies would or could be toppled in a few weeks through such means would have been received as preposterous. Yet here we stand.

Two other recent scholarly contributions from a burgeoning literature on similar themes are noteworthy here (Earls, 2011; Rhoads & Szelényi, 2011). Each for the most part avoids any broad attempt to redefine American-style capitalist approaches to democratic citizenship - perhaps in both cases innocently enough by virtue of a cultural myopia. Written from eminent US-based academic institutions, the first comes from a 2009 Harvard symposium on 'child citizenship' with special editor Felton Earls of the American Academy of Political and Social Science (2011), and recounts a broad range of mostly astute international presentations marking the 20th anniversary the United Nations Convention on the Rights of the Child (1989). In a critical reflection on the citizenship of Guantanamo prisoner and former Canadian child soldier Omar Khadr, one of us has previously argued that this treaty represents a "transdisciplinary ... alternative model for citizenship education" (Mitchell, 2010, p. 38) by clearly marking out the new terrain children are travelling in this period from "rights to citizenship", as Earls (2011, p. 6) also rightly declares. One of numerous highly regarded contributors in their collection is British-based international legal scholar Geraldine Van Bueren (2011, p. 30) who theorises a "multi-generational citizenship" recognising children as both national and international citizens - perhaps the closest to many of the theoretical and political themes running throughout our anthology.

The second selection from scholarly literature is by Rhoads and Szelényi (2011) who address the influence of "Euro-American authored 'capitalocentrism' " (p. 4), but entirely omit the whole notion of children as active citizens or agents of change in this discourse and in the street. Drawing again upon a diverse group of international faculty and students from China's Guangdong University of Foreign Studies in China, University of California, Los Angeles, the University of Buenos Aires in Argentina, and Hungary's Central European University, these authors analyse "global citizenship" from the standpoint of the academy (Rhoads & Szelényi, 2011, p. 16). They view the role of the university in marking out this shifting terrain as a still dominant force for good, but start off with an observation that neoliberalism is "a confusing descriptor, since what we see today in terms of global economics is a near total victory of conservatism and the power of neoconservative geopolitical influence" (p. 13). This passage seems somewhat out of touch with their chapter from Argentina on that nation's resistance to neoliberalism as well as the current pitched street battles say in the ancient cities of Greece, coincidentally one of the ancient birthplaces of democracy. While their Argentine analysis goes some way in responding to Hyslop-Margison and Thayer's 2009 critique that too few alternative paradigms are being contemplated, in the end they make little of the sad overture being replayed in most of the international academy to accompany the bankrupt rearrangement of global capital's deck chairs. This same odious overture is heard throughout the Hollywood documentary *Inside Job* directed by Charles H. Ferguson (2010).

As co-editors, we envisioned some of the process for creating any viable alternative paradigm may be undertaken within the transdisciplinary framework of active, participatory and inclusive expressions of child and youth citizenship presented here. Despite criticisms valid and otherwise, we are still keenly interested in how to live and teach the participatory principles underlying democratic citizenship from the perspective of Freire. Thus, the volume began to take shape during our investigation of how 29-year-old Canadian activist Craig Kielburger - Nobel Prize nominee and 1995 co-founder of the international non-governmental organisation *Free the Children* at 13 years of age - defined and understood the concept in his work. With programs in 4,000 North American schools, the Kielburger brothers (older brother and Harvard-educated lawyer Marc is his co-founder/co-director) have built more than 500 schools in 16 countries, and employ more than 100 people in their Toronto-based charity (Kielburger & Kielburger, 2006). In 2009 they took in nearly $16 million in donations along with $8 million more in the US as part of what they identify as "the world's largest network of children helping children through education". Throughout their evolution and growth from an elementary school and home-based initiative, they have also quietly challenged the foundations of Canadian tax law related to charitable fundraising through their somewhat radical approach to social enterprise (Wingrove, 2010).

In line with some of the thinking espoused by democratic theorist Amartya Sen (see also Arvind, this volume), we present findings from an interview with Kielburger during that study along with selections from other mainly marginalised populations in Canada, England, India, Australia, the US and China while observing that the rise of democratic freedoms is certainly one of the principal developments of our time. We agree with Sen's (1999) assertion that in the distant future when people look back at what happened in the 20th (and early 21st centuries), they will find it difficult not to accept the emergence of democratic freedoms as the most striking development of the period. Certainly the still emancipatory, liberatory march of women, children and other minorities from chattel to rights-bearers forms a large portion of these new chapters in the story of global citizenship. Nevertheless, in contrast to the often sanguine tone taken by Rhoads and Szelényi (2011), we are concerned with this evolution in the same way as Henry A. Giroux (2010a) observes below:

> Imposed amnesia is the modus operandi of the current moment. Not only is historical memory now sacrificed to the spectacles of consumerism, celebrity culture, hyped-up violence and a market-driven obsession with the self, but the very formative culture that makes compassion, justice and an engaged citizenry foundational to democracy has been erased from the language of mainstream politics and the diverse cultural apparatuses that support it. Unbridled individualism along with the gospel of profit and unchecked competition undermine both the importance of democratic public spheres and the necessity for a language that talks about shared responsibilities, the public good and the meaning of a just society. (para. 2)

As in our first iteration, we respond to this capitalist hollowing out of public spaces in many democratic spheres by turning again in this anthology to a transdisciplinary collection of critical pedagogues for contemporary expressions of global and local citizenship. In this, we have also taken inspiration from thinkers such as Giroux, bell hooks, Ira Shor, Shirley Steinberg, Joe Kincheloe, Peter McLaren and others who declare mentor Paulo Freire as one of the most important educators of the 20th century. Paulo opened up new spaces allowing all of us to contribute to an "educational movement guided by both a passion and principle to help students develop a consciousness of freedom, recognise authoritarian tendencies, empower the imagination, connect knowledge and truth to power and learn to read both the word and the world as part of a broader struggle for agency, justice, and democracy" (Giroux, 2010b, para. 1). In thinking about this type of critical teaching for social change, Shor (1992) also cautioned that top-down "teacher-talk" alone along with attempts at "character education" cannot solve these problems since such traditional pedagogical approaches created these problems in the first place. "Teacher-talk" is a "frontal pedagogy ... [that] contributes to depressing the achievement and aspirations of nonelite students. It will continue to do so", he argues, "until teachers and students develop a type of mutual dialogue", and while such "dialogic education cannot change inequality in society or guarantee success in the job market", it can change student experiences by encouraging them "to develop the intellectual and affective powers to think about transforming society". Shor suggests this type of "critical dialogue opposes all mechanisms for sustaining inequality" (pp. 110–111).

As critical educators grounded in at least two disciplinary traditions - one in sociology (Mitchell, 2005, 2007, 2010) and one in counselling psychology (Moore, 2006, 2008; Moore & Mitchell, 2008, 2009), we attempt daily to contribute to Freire's mission (and Shor's above) though at times we have paid not a small price for our optimism. While transdisciplinarity is still an emerging concept, we agree with Albrecht, Freeman and Higginbotham's (1998) complex assessment that "politically, transdisciplinary thinking leads away from any form of authoritarianism, towards a politics of inclusion and an awareness that academics do not have a monopoly on wisdom. It is open *a priori* to all theories of knowledge, including those underlying indigenous beliefs....transdisciplinary thinking evolves reflexively as it assembles the meta-theory" (p. 58). As co-editors, we acknowledge and thank the contributors from six countries on four continents in total. The collection represents a robust expression of this overarching framework (see also Moore & Mitchell, 2008) while at the same time stands in solidarity with the reality of a struggle being fought by tens of thousands currently expressing a greater international thirst for a kind of globalised citizenship than ever previously known.

It is true that demonstrations and violent deaths have occurred daily for decades, and most likely over millennia, due to the lack of freedom of speech, freedom of the press, freedom of religion, orrights to peaceful assembly, to organised labour, to education, healthcare, and to democratically elected politicalinstitutions. In light of these struggles we make our contribution respectfully and cautiously, in contrast to Kiwan's rather forceful (2005, p. 37) argument that "human rights cannot logically be a theoretical underpinning for citizenship, regardless of how citizenship may be conceptualised". Indeed, the civil, political and social rights

INTRODUCTION

listed above are the simplyentry points for the critical framework woven throughout this collection.

These contributions include: An innovative case study from mainland China by Wangbei Ye, a lecturer in the Department of Politics at the East China Normal University, with findings from her doctoral research that looked into the Chinese Communist Party's (CCP) political control and involvement in citizenship education with data from the Special Economic Zone of Shenzhen City; a piece of narrative research from a Canadian Aboriginal setting by Sandra Wolf, an Ojibwe originally from North Dakota in Turtle Island and currently a northern Ontario-based teacher-educator who presents a chapter describing teams of pre-service teachers engaged in participatory social justice work; Emery Hyslop-Margison and Josephine L. Savarese, once again both Canadian-based teacher-educators from New Brunswick who present a theoretical analysis of post neo-liberalism in higher education and how current policies and trends undermine post-secondary education as a potential site of democratic learning; from Gaysu R. Arvind, an Indian teacher-educator from the University of Delhi, contributes a chapter drawing upon bottom-up case studies of school functioning while examining the education of marginalised children in the lowest strata of the traditionally unequal Indian society; from Australian educator Keith Heggart comes a chapter exploring the development of a model of human rights education in that nation that also addresses citizenship education.

From England, a troika of empirical studies are presented next: The first from teacher-educator Lee Jerome offers findings from a doctoral case study at London's Metropolitan University where a 'child rights respecting approach' has been incorporated; the second chapter is another doctoral study from Sam Mejias and Hugh Starkey of the Institute of Education, University of London presenting findings from an exploration of the partnership between the international non-governmental organisation *Amnesty International* and an English secondary school; and the third offering is a critical analysis by Helen Trivers of *Amnesty International* (co-authored again by Starkey) that focuses on the *Rights, Respect, Responsibility* initiative in Hampshire, England and the UNICEF UK *Rights Respecting Schools* project (notably both of these projects draw heavily upon a made-in-Canada model).

A contribution from US-based Paul Thomas of Furman University in South Carolina presents his theoretical reflection from the standpoint of growing up and teaching in the rural south arguing for the need of critical literacy, specifically in the writing curriculum, to foster critical citizenship; returning again to Canada for the final two chapters, one from Brock University colleagues May Al-Fartousi and Dolana Mogadime in the Faculty of Education who, in response to a 2009 Muslim Canadian Congress call to government to prevent Muslim women from covering their faces in public, present a critical study of media representations of Muslim women wearing the burka; and lastly, our Moore and Mitchell case study of a youth rally hosted at our southern Ontario university by international child and youth activist Craig Kielburger (which includes a heuristic model for critically engaging young people's citizenship) discussed above.

Also noted previously, we started and now end the project cautiously optimistic although with assumptions grounded in cultural and political perspectives (and upon many of our collaborators' positions as well) that these freedoms are being taken for granted in many contexts, and are clearly being eroded in the so-called democracies wherein the majority of us work. Nevertheless, the fact that these freedoms exist anywhere at all is an important feature of 'liquid modernity' as Bauman observes it, while offering some measure of the firm and reliable guarantee he opines as missing even as blood is spilled in geographies where they are absent. We humbly contend that with this constellation of theoretical and empirical contributions, and the often marginalised populations making up their subjects, our goal of making a thoughtful, critical, transnational contribution to democratic citizenship education has been achieved. This goal began in our Canadian lecture halls and classrooms, and has implications well beyond not the least of which are occurring in the streets and plazas of urban settings far removed from our own fragile democratic mosaic.

REFERENCES

Albrecht, G., Freeman, S., and Higginbotham, N. (1999). Complexity and Human Health: The Case for a Transdisciplinary Paradigm. *Culture, Medicine and Psychiatry* 22(1), 55–92.

Bauman, Z. (2005). Afterthought: On writing; on writing sociology. In N. K. Denzin & Y. S. Lincoln (Eds.), *The Sage Handbook of Qualitative Research* (3rd ed., pp. 1089–1098). London, Thousand Oaks, CA, & New Delhi: Sage Publishers Ltd.

Earls, F. (2011, January). *The child as citizen. Special Edition of The Annals of the American Academy of Political and Social Science*. Los Angeles, London, New Delhi, Singapore, & Washington, DC: Sage Publishers Ltd.

Ferguson, C., Marrs, A., Beck, C., Bolt, A., Damon, M., Volcker, P. A., Soros, G. (2010). *Inside Job*. Culver City, Calif: Sony Pictures Home Entertainment.

Giroux, H. A. (2010a, November 16). Living in the age of imposed amnesia: The eclipse of democratic formative culture. *Truthout/OP-ED*. [online]. Retrieved July 25, 2011, from: http://archive.truthout.org/living-age-imposed-amnesia-the-eclipse-democratic-formative-culture65144

Giroux, H. A. (2010b, November 23). Lessons to be learned from Paulo Freire as education is being taken over by the mega rich. *Truthout/OP-ED*. [online]. Retrieved July 25, 2011, from: http://archive.truthout.org/lessons-be-learned-from-paulo-freire-education-is-being-taken-over-mega-rich65363

Howe, R. B., & Covell, K. (2010). Miseducating children about their rights. *Education, Citizenship and Social Justice*, 5(2), 91–102.

Hyslop-Margison, E. J., & Thayer, J. (2009). *Teaching democracy – Citizenship education as critical pedagogy*. Rotterdam, Boston & Taipei: Sense Publishers.

Kielburger, C. & Kielburger, M. (2006). *Me to We: Finding Meaning in a Material World*. Toronto: Wiley and Sons.

Kiwan, D. (2005). Human rights and citizenship: An unjustifiable conflation? *Journal of Philosophy of Education*, 39(1), 37–50.

Mitchell, R. C. (2005). Postmodern reflections on the UNCRC: Towards utilising Article 42 as an international compliance indicator. *The International Journal of Children's Rights*, 13(3), 315–331.

Mitchell, R. C. (2007). Towards a transdisciplinary model within child and youth rights education. In A. Ang, I. Delens-Ravier, M. Delplace, C. Herman, D. Reynaert, V. Staelens, et al. (Eds.), *The UN children's rights convention: Theory meets practice. Proceedings of the International Interdisciplinary Conference on Children's Rights, 18-19 May 2006, Ghent, Belgium* (pp. 181–200). Antwerp, Oxford: Intersentia.

Mitchell, R. C. (2010). Who's afraid now? Reconstructing Canadian citizenship education through transdisciplinarity. *The Review of Education, Pedagogy, and Cultural Studies*, 32(1), 37–65.

Moore, S. A. (2006). Transdisciplinary approaches to critical multicultural pedagogy in Canadian higher education. In D. Zinga (Ed.), *Navigating multiculturalism: Negotiating change* (pp. 126–139). Newcastle, UK: Cambridge Scholars Press.

Moore, S. A. (2008). Social justice and education in a world fit for children? In J. A. Kentel & A. Short (Eds.), *Totems and taboos: Risk and relevance in research on teachers and teaching* (pp. 17–29). Rotterdam, Boston & Taipei: Sense Publishers.

Moore, S. A., & Mitchell, R. C. (Eds.). (2008). *Power, pedagogy and praxis: Social justice in the globalized classroom.* Rotterdam, Boston & Taipei: Sense Publishers.

Moore, S. A., & Mitchell, R. C. (2009). Rights-based restorative justice: Evaluating compliance wit international standards. *Youth Justice,* 9(1), 27–43.

Rhoads, R. A., & Szelényi, K. (2011). *Global citizenship and the university.* Stanford, CA: Stanford University Press.

Sen, A. (1999). *The value of democracy in development outreach by the World Bank Institute.* Retrieved July 25, 2011, from http://www.devoutreach.com/summer99/SpecialReport/tabid/839/Default.aspx

Shor, I. (1992). *Empowering education – Critical teaching for social change.* Chicago & London: University of Chicago Press.

United Nations (1989). *Convention on the Rights of the Child.* New York, Geneva: United Nations.

Van Bueren, G. (2011). Multigenerational Citizenship: The Importance of Recognizing Children as National and International Citizens. (pp. 30-52). In *The Annals of the American Academy of Political and Social Science - Special Edition - The Child as Citizen* edited by Felton Earls.

Wingrove, J. (2010, March 20). Marc and Craig Kielburger's do-gooding social enterprise. *The Globe and Mail* (pp. F1–F6). Retrieved July 25, 2011, from http://www.theglobeandmail.com/news/national/marc-and-craig-kielburgers-do-gooding-social-enterprise/article1506256/

Richard C. Mitchell
Shannon A. Moore,
Brock University, Canada

WANGBEI YE

SCHOOL POWER AND DEMOCRATIC CITIZENSHIP EDUCATION IN CHINA

Experiences from Three Secondary Schools

ABSTRACT

Numerous critical studies on citizenship have demonstrated that schools and teachers make a significant contribution to democracy. However, due to the Chinese Communist Party's (CCP) tight political control and the Chinese governments' deep involvement in citizenship education, the ways in which Chinese schools and teachers affect democratic citizenship education are under-researched. With reference to school-based curriculum development (SBCD, initiated in 2001), this chapter investigates the impact of Chinese schools and teachers on citizenship education, with particular attention to their influence in the three stages of SBCD: goal setting, content and pedagogy selection, and implementation. Data were drawn from studies in three secondary schools (Grades 7–9), 90 questionnaires completed by teachers and 23 individual interviews with government administrators, university experts, school principals and teachers from February to December, 2008. The findings indicate that Chinese school practices are congruent with critical pedagogy studies underscoring the emancipatory potential of schools and teachers: Schools can advance democratic citizenship education by de-politicising CCP-dominated citizenship education, decentralising curriculum decisions in order to take power from governments, and democratising school culture to better meet the needs of Chinese civil society. These practices do not, however, eliminate the CCP's and state's politically-motivated values, centralised control and non-democratic education management style in general. Therefore, this study suggests school power in China can best be understood by viewing the concept of school power as a semi-emancipatory relationship.

INTRODUCTION

Citizenship education has been introduced in many countries in recent years (Davies & Issit, 2005; Johnson & Morris, 2010; Torney-Purta & Barber, 2004), with the expectation that it would help to ease the political indifference and apathy caused by post-modern challenges (Terren, 2002). Reinforcing civic participation and stimulating social integration, therefore, is a major feature of recent efforts at promoting citizenship education in different countries (Keddie, 2008; Leenders, Veugelers, & Kat, 2008; Mitchell, 2010).

Schools and teachers, as suggested by numerous critical pedagogy studies, can contribute to a more active citizenship and a higher quality of democracy by reconstructing education to include the diverse voices, views and experiences of various societal groups, even "against the grain" (Giroux, 2003) of the inequities and injustices of the social world. Having a transdisciplinary nature, critical pedagogy studies suggest that schools and teachers realise their emancipatory roles from these comprehensive perspectives: Questioning and analysing the politics that pervade education, school practices and policies (Nieto, 2000; Oakes, 1995); incorporating diverse contents and critical conversation and dialogue pedagogies (Shor & Freire, 1987), rather than being informed by dominant social forces in curriculum content and pedagogy selection (Slattery, Krasny, & O'Malley, 2007); transforming the traditional bureaucratic approach to educational decision-making in curriculum, school structures, organisation and management into a form of social empowerment and a search for deeper understanding that leads to justice, compassion, and ecological sustainability (See Kliebard, 1986; Osler & Starkey, 2010; Slattery, 2006).

However, despite widespread international interest in schools' and teachers' emancipatory role in reconstructing democratic citizenship education, most studies have focused on Latin America and Western countries, and the efforts of Chinese schools and teachers have been under-researched. This article addresses this gap and provides an explanation of Chinese schools' and teachers' roles in pursuit of democratic citizenship education.

Due to the country's Confucian tradition, which stresses obedience and loyalty to the state (Sen, 1999), and its adoption of Marxist one-party governance (Held, 1992), citizenship education in China is characterised by strong political control (Hayhoe, 1993; Zhu & Liu, 2004). Since 1949, the ruling political party of the People's Republic of China, the Chinese Communist Party (CCP), has promoted citizenship education as a means to introduce communist ideologies based on Marxist philosophy (i.e., dialectical and historical materialism). Therefore, it has used the term citizenship education interchangeably with such terms as ideological education, political education, ideological-political education, ideological moral education, and moral-political education (Cheung, 1994).

Political control in Chinese citizenship education has been enhanced by centralised curriculum development, with the central government deeply involved in every aspect of education (Schneewind, 2006). Communist political knowledge is introduced at all levels of education in China: The Ministry of Education (MOE) follows CCP and state guidance in making education policies, the People's Education Press (PEP) follows MOE policies in creating national curriculum standards and national textbooks, and local education bureaus guide schools to follow the national guidelines relevant to citizenship education.

In this context, Chinese schools' and teachers' influences in citizenship education were quite limited. China's 1978 economic reform, however, witnessed the adoption of a market economic system, and an attendant emphasis on individual rights, interests and values, globalisation, mass media and the Internet, and the emergence of cultural diversity and pluralism in society (Li, Zhong, & Zhang, 2004), which have, collectively, made it difficult for the CCP and the state to maintain a centralised and authoritarian indoctrinating form of citizenship education. The CCP acknowledges this, admitting to the existence of a "crisis of three faiths"— faith in the Communist Party, in socialism and in the country (Domes, 1990). The country's youth are particularly cynical about Marxism-Leninism, urban intellectual enterprises care more about policies that materially benefit them than they do about ideology, and even CCP members are no longer motivated solely by Marxism-Leninism.

The CCP's need to win back the hearts and minds of its citizens and to nurture support for communism in an increasingly complex society has led to the emergence of decentralising decision-making, with Chinese schools and teachers gradually gaining some decision-making power over citizenship education since 1986. Following the CCP the principle of "one curriculum standard but various versions of textbooks" (*yi gang duo ben*) (Chinese Communist Party, 1985), schools adhere to a single national curriculum standard but gain the freedom to choose different textbooks, thus ending the PEP's monopoly over textbook creation. Since 2001, the promotion of school-based curriculum development (SBCD) has, for the first time, allowed schools to officially exercise some control over curricula. The policy allows secondary schools and teachers autonomy over 16–20% of school curriculum time (Ministry of Education, 2001), allowing them to reconstruct school curricula (including citizenship education) to better meet the diverse needs of the school, students and local community.

Therefore, China provides an interesting case for examining the issues and tensions involved in schools' and teachers' contributions to more democratic citizenship education against the background of tight political control and deep state involvement.

The following section presents the theoretical framework of the study and discusses theories of power in society and in schooling processes. Next, an empirical study based on the analysis of data from my doctoral study "Power and School-based Curriculum Development in Moral Education in China" will be introduced, key findings of which suggest that Chinese practices are congruent with studies conducted by critical pedagogues. The paper concludes with a discussion of, and conclusions regarding, theoretical implications for understanding school power as a semi-emancipatory relationship in the Chinese context.

THE THEORETICAL FRAMEWORK

This section introduces the theoretical framework the study will use to explore the complexity of and power dynamics inherent in the reconstruction of citizenship education in Chinese school through SBCD. It begins with an overview of relevant studies on power and school curriculum, then constructs the theoretical framework for describing and analysing school power in citizenship education through SBCD in China.

Power

According to Jary and Jary (1999, p. 513) power can be defined in four ways: first, as "the 'transformational capacity' possessed by human beings"; second, as "the probability that one actor within a social relationship will be in a position to carry out his own will despite resistance"; third, as "the reproductive or the transformational capacity possessed by social structures, which may be seen as existing independently of the wills of individual actors"; and, fourth, as Foucault (1982, p. 222) contends, as an "agonism" relationship characterized by simultaneous reciprocal incitation and struggle. Each of these definitions suggests that power can be interpreted as a form of social relationship and that power relationships fall into two broad categories: hard and soft power relationships.

In hard power relationships, power is the ability of someone or some agents to get someone or some agents to do something that they otherwise would not do (Cartwright, 1965; Dahl, 1957). Emerson (1962) echoes this, defining power as the ability to overcome the resistance of others: the power of actor A over actor B is equal to the amount of resistance on the part of B that can be potentially overcome by A. Hard power is characterised by superior-subordinate relationships, what feminist scholars categorize as either "power over" or "power to" (Woehrle, 1992). The former is coercive power based on superior strength, often in the form of physical strength or superior arms; the latter form relies on a variety of exchange and reward possibilities (Dugan, 2003). According to French and Raven (1959), rewards, punishment, legitimate right, knowledge and expertise can all be considered sources of power.

Soft power, according to Nye (2004), refers to one's ability to get what one wants through attraction, rather than coercion or payment. Unlike superior-subordinate power relationships, soft power emphasises collaborative endeavours (Woehrle, 1992), what feminist scholars call "power with" and others refer to as integrative or collaborative power. Dugan (2003) argues that power relationships should not be defined solely as one actor changing another; changes can be internal rather than external and a power relationship may consist of a combination of the two. Even in competitive power relationships, participants can be equal, with no party being either subordinate or superior; all players can be both influencer and influenced. Integrative power relationships are considered to be based on love, persuasion, integration, cooperation, communication or cooperation (Blades, 1998; Dugan, 2003); according to Foucault (as cited in Blades, 1998), power is derived from the complex network of relations between people and institutions.

Power and Curriculum

Power is a major concern in the field of curriculum, particularly when studying the curriculum decision-making process. Numerous scholars have noted and attempted to explain the diversities caused by power in curriculum decision-making (Deng & Luke, 2008). As Kliebard and Franklin (1983) conclude:

> [The study of power and curriculum] is the scholarly attempt to chronicle, interpret, and ultimately understand the processes whereby social groups over time select, organize, and distribute knowledge and belief through educational institutions... with... its focus on the question of what gets taught in schools, as well as (or perhaps especially) the ways in which "a settled body" of knowledge, the curriculum, undergoes or fails to undergo change. (pp. 138–139)

The literature suggests that power constructs our understanding of an array of concepts and notions – including teaching and learning, teachers and students, and achievement and failure – that mediate classroom interaction (Popkewitz, 1997). According to studies on power and curriculum, curriculum is shaped by both society and the education system. How curriculum shapes and is shaped by the hierarchical stratification of individuals in society has been widely discussed (Apple, 1990; Bowles & Gintis, 1976). Curriculum is shaped by numerous forces – technological, political, economic, cultural and educational – and the question of "whose knowledge is of most worth" is a key power-related problem in curriculum development (Apple, 1990, p. vii) and defines the differences between the main approaches to curriculum – functionalism, conflict theory, Marxism and critical education theory.

From a functionalist perspective, education and curriculum are tools to be used to unite society. As such, functionalists see that science and technology are important in determining curriculum (Karabel & Halsey, 1977); indeed, Spencer (1860) identifies them as the main determinants. Functionalism has, however, been criticised for exaggerating the role of technology and for underestimating the importance of conflict ideology (Bowles & Gintis, 1976), and is now widely in disrepute. According to Dahrendorf (1959), social reality is largely determined by conflict and flux, and not by the closed system envisioned by functionalism (p. 27).

Conflict theorists offer different perspectives on the relationship between power and curriculum at the macro level, identifying influential social groups (rather than technology) as main determinants. These powerful social groups, they maintain, use curriculum to socialise students and ensure that they will help to reproduce the existing social relations.

Economic force is central to Marxist traditions, which holds that all cultural and political institutions, relationships and activities, including education, reflect the economic relations of production. School knowledge and culture, therefore, serve the interests of privileged or (as Marx calls them) economically dominant groups (Hellrich, 1970). The question of power in schools is largely ignored beyond its role in reproducing "relations of domination and subordinancy through various school practices" (p. 150). More than a century after Marx, many scholars continue to see curriculum as a key social institution necessary for reproducing a society's existing economic relations. Young (1971) adds political forces to the list of factors shaping curriculum, while Mason (2007) concludes that curriculum is the site of political struggle and social stratification and Apple (1996) notes the influence of culture on curriculum, in that powerful societal forces and culture are interwoven. In schools, curriculum is expected to confer cultural legitimacy on the knowledge of specific groups, to "preserve and distribute what is perceived to be 'legitimate knowledge'—the knowledge that 'we all must have'" (Apple, 1996, pp. 61–62); in other words, school curriculum contributes to cultural reproduction.

Critical educational theory, however, questions the relationship between social power processes and educational processes (Masschelein, 2004), claiming that the relationship between curriculum and power is not so mechanical that only powerful societal groups determine school curriculum. Rather than interpreting curriculum as a kind of social control and trying to identify influential societal forces, some theorists employ Foucault's (1979) power-knowledge nexus, which suggests "[abandoning] the belief that... the renunciation of power is one of the conditions of knowledge. We should admit rather that power produces knowledge...; that power and knowledge directly imply one another" (p. 27) and claims that curriculum is not only a form of social control but also a form of emancipation. School itself plays an important emancipatory role affecting curriculum.

In the tradition of Dewey and Freire, critical pedagogy scholars advocate transformative practices directed at emancipation in schools and classrooms. Popkewitz (1997) proposes several strategies for empowering students and teachers to develop alternate pedagogical and curricular structures that offer students the opportunity to use lived experiences as a basis for acquiring language, literacy and critical thinking skills. Giroux (1983) argues that, for teachers, the relationship between authority and power is manifested not only in the legitimate exercise of control over students, but also in influencing the conditions under which they work. In this way, teachers can teach collectively, produce alternative curricula and engage in a form of emancipatory politics.

Connell (1993) goes further in describing the teacher's role in this new power-curriculum relationship. In his book *School and Social Justice*, he argues that, to advance social justice, teachers must invert hegemony and organise "[educational] content and methods that [build] on the experience of the disadvantaged" (p. 38). He further points out that "producing [social justice], and then generalizing it, requires constructive intellectual work. And this is not easy for disadvantaged groups to do, precisely because of their disadvantage: most of the tools of intellectual work are in other people's hands" (p. 41). Yoshiko (2006) suggests that Connell is hinting that teachers could help to produce and organise the knowledge of the socially subordinate (p. 78).

To summarise, the literature on power and curriculum offers an analytical framework for power and curriculum. Power is conceived of as a social relationship and can be defined in terms of control (hard power) or in terms of reciprocal struggle (soft power). Traditional curriculum theories take a hard power position, arguing that curriculum is shaped by powerful societal groups (i.e., macro-level technological, economic, political and cultural forces). The soft power view is the province of numerous critical educators, who argue that the power-curriculum relationship is not as mechanical as hard power advocates suggest, and that curriculum can work as a means of social emancipation.

The Three-stage Analysis Framework

This study proposes a theoretical framework that provides an overview of Chinese school power in citizenship education in the form of SBCD and reveals how schools interact with external sources of macro-level social power in the process.

This theoretical framework views power in school-based citizenship education reconstruction within a particular substantive area as a three-stage process. The first stage is a debate over curriculum goals and involves a wide range of actors – both influential social powers and curriculum makers and those with relatively little access to curriculum decision-making, such as academics, parents and the media – each of whom offers a different interpretation of what citizenship education should address, based on their particular values, views and interests.

Curriculum goal setting is mainly conducted by curriculum makers at the national, local and school levels, each of which negotiates (with varying degrees of success) for power and influence according to the resources they command, their inherent authority, their degree of participation and their overall role. Their actual agreed-upon goals (as opposed to their stated, published goals) influence and guide the next stage of the process. Some curriculum makers continue to exert influence over areas of school-based citizenship education reconstruction beyond the agreed-upon goals, in an attempt to realise what this study calls alternative goals; in changing situations, alternative goals may even replace agreed-upon goals.

The second stage is curriculum content and pedagogy selection. Contents and pedagogies are selected based on their perceived ability to effect the changes required; influential factors include the actors and forces involved in the first stage. While new materials, new organisation of contents, new presentations and new instruction methods are frequently adopted to address the agreed-upon goals, it should be noted that some old content and pedagogy may be retained for a variety of reasons. This study refers to this as "context": why, how and whom to select. Even the same content and pedagogy may, given a different context, result in a largely different school-based citizenship education programme.

The third stage, implementation, consists of interactions among curriculum makers as they attempt to rise above the restrictions of the previous two stages and exercise more influence over others. In turn, this stage may impact the previous two stages by altering the relationships shaped therein. This study divides the results of the interactions into two categories – victory implementation and alternative implementation. The solution that wins more agreement is successfully implemented, while the other may remain on the list to be implemented at another time.

This proposed framework examines both macro- and micro-level influential factors to better analyse school power in citizenship education reconstruction in SBCD in China. On a macro level, it identifies possible forces and explains their purposes in and mechanisms for affecting school curriculum; from the micro level, it describes the relationships among curriculum actors and their curriculum power zones. This theoretical framework forms the basis for case studies conducted by this research and is a template for describing and analysing empirical results.

THE STUDY

This paper is partly drawn from the author's PhD thesis "Power and School-based Curriculum Development in Moral Education in China", which utilised a multiple case study method to examine school and teacher power in citizenship education curriculum reconstruction in three stages of SBCD: curriculum goal setting; content and pedagogy selection; and implementation.

Case studies give a vivid and full description of what happens and are well suited to revealing the complex process through which schools and teachers influence citizenship education reconstruction. As Chinese economic reform is relevant to school citizenship education reform, the three secondary schools selected, in addition to having well-developed school-based citizenship education curricula, were located in Shenzhen City, a city that provides a window on Chinese economic reform.

Although case study is not a sampling research method, the cases in this study (hereafter Schools A, B and C) each had different external/internal power relationships, so as to maximise the range and quality of information gathered about Chinese school and teacher power in citizenship education. School A was a public nine-year school (Grades 1–9) that was greatly influenced by external authorities and competitive relationships among school staff in school-based citizenship education reconstruction. School B was a public junior middle school (Grades 7–9) and featured close collaboration with external groups (e.g., local communities and organisations) and more democratic relationships among school staff in developing a school-based citizenship education curriculum. Finally, School C was a private, foreign-run boarding school with elementary, junior, middle and senior sections and a foreign university foundation programme. It distanced itself from external authorities but showed deep interest in meeting parent and student needs, and had more open relationships among school staff in their school citizenship education reconstruction. School C was included due to the distinction between public and private Chinese secondary schools, with the latter having more autonomy in curriculum development, teacher recruitment and training, and students from a different social class than the former (Cheng & Delany, 1999; Lin, 1999; Ross & Lin, 2006); as of 2008, about 10% of Chinese students were enrolled in private schools (Law & Pan, 2009). This study focused on the citizenship education programmes at the junior secondary sections (Grade 7– Grade 9) in each of the three schools.

For triangulation purposes, 23 individual interviews were conducted with government administrators, university experts, school principals and teachers, and 90 questionnaires were completed by teachers, between February and December, 2008. The questionnaire was a relatively less expensive way to explore the views of informants, while the interviews allowed the researcher to clarify and examine the views of key respondents in depth (Cohen, Manion, & Morrison, 2007); the interview schedule was constructed based on existing literature on the subject. To ensure validity, all interviewees were asked questions about policies, perceptions and practices relevant to the three stages of school-based citizenship education curriculum reconstruction; at the same time, however, individual interview guides differed slightly to reflect the informants' different positions. Taken together, these actors reflect the conflicts of interest inherent in power relationships in school-based citizenship education curriculum development, and their differing responses combine to form a more complete, balanced picture of school and teacher power. Table 1 below shows the interviewees in the case schools.

Table 1. Interviewees in case schools

Type of Interviewees	School A	School B	School C
University scholars	1	0	0
Local education administrators	1	3	1
School principals	3	1	1
School middle leaders	0	1	4
Teachers	4	2	2
Total	9	7	7

Pilot interviews were conducted with two local education administrators and a university scholar to check for clarity, after which the wording of certain questions was changed slightly. The interviews, which were conducted in Chinese, were recorded, transcribed for closer examination and translated into English for this paper. Interviews with local education administrators lasted around 2 hours, compared to around 1 hour with other respondents; all were recorded on audiotape, with the permission of interviewees. Two teachers from School B preferred not to be recorded.

After the interviews, a questionnaire was administered to 90 teachers in the three schools to collect their opinions on school and teacher power in school-based citizenship education curriculum development; all 90 responses were effective. The questions covered: (a) their perceptions of the relationship between social context and citizenship education reconstruction; (b) the concepts, policies, procedures and mechanisms adopted by their school regarding school-based citizenship education curriculum development; (c) the design, implementation and evaluation stages of school-based citizenship education curriculum development; and (d) their reflections on the preceding. The response categories and corresponding codes are "strongly disagree" = 1, "disagree" = 2, "agree" = 3, "strongly agree" = 4, "no comment" = 5. The questionnaires administered in each case school differed slightly to suit the specific school context. A draft version of each respective questionnaire was sent to three teachers in School A, two teachers in School B, and one in School C for their comments on its relevance and wording. Based on this pilot test, the time required to complete the questionnaire was estimated at 40 to 50 minutes. To ensure reliability and to encourage greater honesty, the questionnaire was anonymous (Cohen et al., 2007). In addition, the internal consistency of the questionnaire was estimated using Cronbach's alpha (α). All versions were found to have high reliability, with Cronbach's alpha (α) = .9779 in School A, (α) = .9707 in School B and (α) = .9768 in School C's questionnaire.

To maximise the quality and quantity of information received from respondents, the researcher asked the school heads to help select, as far as was possible, teachers with different gender, age and subject backgrounds. Although most respondents in School A were female (73.3%), informants from School B and School C were roughly gender balanced. Most of the teachers answering the questionnaire were between 30 and 49 years old (80.0% in School A, 63.3% in School B and 70.0% in School C), and most held a bachelor's degree (80.0% in School A, 93.3% in School B and 60.0% in School C). Most of the informants from School A and School B had permanent teaching contracts (80.0% and 73.3% respectively), while most from School C held temporary contracts (93.3%). Finally, most respondents had more than 5 years teaching experience (86.7% in School A, 76.7% in School B and 70.0% in School C). Ethical procedures, such as obtaining consent and maintaining confidentiality, were strictly followed in accordance with established practice.

MAJOR FINDINGS

This section reports the empirical study's major findings on school power, which reveal features that emerged during the three stages in the cases' citizenship education programme development: schools deriving their goal setting power from centralised control in the goal setting stage; the growth of school power based on school resources and mechanisms in the content and pedagogy selection stage; and schools further enhancing their power by enlarging space, increasing commitment and including diverse voices in the implementation stage.

School Power in Goal Setting Stage: Goal Selecting and Making Power Grow from the Centralised Control

The analyses of school power in the three cases during the goal setting stage examined the kinds of goals set, who was involved, how they interacted in goal setting, etc. The findings indicate that schools gained their goal selecting and making powers from centralised educational authorities.

Despite the fact that since 2001, Chinese secondary schools have been allowed autonomy to decide curricula for 16–20% of school curriculum time, the CCP and various levels of Chinese governments continue to exert great influence over school-based citizenship education goal setting by assigning different statuses to national, local, and school curricula, by making government-determined curricula compulsory and by insisting that school citizenship education curriculum goals focus on improving existing government curricula. Their attempt is obvious in its policy.

> Schools should first accomplish national, local curricula, then they could allocate teaching time to school curricula, any levels of governments could supervise SBCD in schools directly (Ministry of Education, 2001).

School teachers in the survey acknowledge the lower status of school curricula as well (See Table 2).

Table 2. School teachers viewed school citizenship education as complementary curricula

	All Three Schools			Mean of Individual School			Difference in Means between Schools		
	No.	Mean	Std. Dev.	S.A M_A	S.B M_B	S.C M_C	M_A-M_B	M_A-M_C	M_B-M_C
School-based citizenship education curriculum in my school is a complement to the official curricula.	90	3.32	.91	3.50	3.37	3.10	0.13	0.40	0.27

In addition, the CCP and governments affect school-based citizenship education reconstruction by shifting funding and restrict goal innovation by defining the topics on which schools should focus. In School A, teachers attempted to improve official citizenship education by adding more aesthetic experiences; however, as its citizenship education programme was part of a nationally-funded project, macro-level bodies influenced goal selection. The university scholar leading School A's school-based citizenship reconstruction project suggests that the school

> had more freedom in the beginning. The central government funded our project... Later, the state decided the specific topics and we could only bid for it... As a result, we began to focus more on the topic dictated by the state (Interview with the university scholar, in Beijing, 2008).

Finally, the CCP and governments affect school-based citizenship education reconstruction by their promotion, over a number of years, of various education themes in informal citizenship education. School B and School C, for example, were urged to include such externally-determined goals as environment education and traditional virtue in their school-based citizenship education reconstruction.

Despite the level of control exercised by the CCP and governments, schools are nonetheless the selectors and makers of their school citizenship education goals. They have the power to select from a range of government-defined goals, rather than be forced to implement a predetermined set of goals. School A, for example, actively participated in nationally-funded projects, while School B addressed the non-compulsory theme of environmental education and School C focused on traditional virtues education, which was not, at the time, well reflected in education bureaus' policies.

Schools also have the power to reject goals suggested by the governments in favour of others that better reflect school needs. School A, while restricted to teaching the national and local citizenship education curricula, reorganised and improved these curricula to address school needs. School B's goals were based on national goals, but went beyond them to cultivate students' critical thinking in environment education, which they believed had been neglected by the governments. School C criticised government-dominant citizenship education as unattractive to students, and initiated a series of innovative citizenship education goals, including introducing character education from abroad and using foreign teachers.

Schools' individual interests guide their selection and creation of school-based citizenship education reconstruction goals, as can be seen in responses to the teacher questionnaire; most respondents agreed with the statement "To enhance school strength is one of the initiation reasons for our school-based citizenship education reconstruction" (83.3% agreed in School A, 96.7% in School B, 96.7% in School C). School A wanted, directly or indirectly, the resources, legitimacy, prestige and professional guidance government education authorities could offer; as such, its citizenship curriculum was designed as part of a nationally-funded project and accepted government-defined goals. School B, which wanted to enhance its ability to compete with other schools, focused on its strongest subject, environmental education. The private school, School C (which admits students based as much on the parents' ability to pay fees 20 times those for public secondary schools as on the student's academic performance) wanted to successfully compete with area public schools in a non-academic field, in order to enhance its reputation among those parents who wanted their children to have a fulfilling educational experience. As School C's principal noted:

> As an elite private school, we can afford good teachers and facilities but we do not have students as good as those in public schools. Therefore, there is no future for us in competing with public schools in student academic achievement (Interview with School C Principal for junior section, School C, 2008).

In short, in the first stage, schools have the power to challenge CCP- and state-suggested goals and select others instead.

School Power in Content & Pedagogy Selection Stage:
Growth Based on Strength in Resources and Mechanisms

This section presents the changes that took place in the three case schools in the content and pedagogy selection stage of citizenship education reconstruction. By examining the curriculum makers who were responsible for these changes, and the context (e.g., influences from the first stage) in which they were made, it can be seen that school power in this stage grew based on the strength of the schools' resources and systemic mechanisms.

First, external authorities exerted less influence over content and pedagogy selection stage than they had over goal setting. No direct CCP guidance was detected in this stage and, according to survey data, teachers in the three case schools showed less interest in political criteria.

Table 3. Political criteria and teachers' content selection

	All Three Schools			Mean of Individual School			Difference in Means between Schools		
	No.	Mean	Std. Dev.	S.A M_A	S.B M_B	S.C M_C	M_A-M_B	M_A-M_C	M_B-M_C
When choosing teaching materials for school citizenship education I would consider whether it is politically correct.	89	2.85	1.18	3.00	2.67	2.90	0.33	0.10	-0.23

The education bureaus, on the other hand, were seen as having a legitimate supervisory function to fulfill. However, they lacked the systemic mechanisms and resources necessary to exercise consistent guidance of content and pedagogy selection, with discrepancies existing between MOE departments and local education bureaus. For example, the National Office for Education Sciences Planning (NOESP) in MOE was responsible for overseeing the progress of the national project of which School A's school-based citizenship education programme was a part, but lacked the authority to supervise school performance – that fell within the purview of a different MOE department. The reverse was also true – the education bureaus in neither Shenzhen City nor Shenzhen District felt able to supervise School A's citizenship education programme, because it was part of a national-level project.

In addition, education bureaus in general lack the resources and experience necessary to supervise school-based citizenship education content and pedagogy selection. School A's programmes were supervised by a university scholar on behalf of the MOE, as the local education bureau was not deemed competent to do so. The MOE did issue several policy statements relevant to programmes in School B, but these were abstract and had little effect. Moreover, the teaching materials the MOE provided were seen by teachers as out of date. In the case of School C, the local education bureau lacked the time, ability and inclination to guide private schools in any endeavour, let alone citizenship education reconstruction. School C's district included 424 private schools and kindergartens in 2009, which served half of all registered students. When interviewed, the district's education bureau officer indicated they were simply too busy to supervise private schools:

> I have hundreds of public schools to oversee and visit in one school term... Sometimes I visit several public schools in one day to ensure I finish visiting all the public schools in my district. I really don't have time for private schools though I know citizenship education in private schools is also very important, perhaps more important than in public ones (Interview with the education officer in charge of citizenship education, in Bao An Education

Bureau, Shenzhen, 2008).

Unlike the external authorities, schools had the resources and flexible systemic mechanisms necessary to encourage teacher innovations, as well as the will to use them. Despite the differences in their programmes, each of the three schools pursued the same three main activities in content and pedagogy selection: adapting existing official citizenship education content; creating new content; and adopting innovative new pedagogies. Adapting content involved reallocating teachers and teaching time, creating new content required focusing on systematic curriculum content design, and pedagogical innovations required not only teacher innovation, but also financial support for teachers' professional training and pedagogical experiments (smaller classes, heavier teacher workload, higher salaries, increased activity space, etc.).

In all three case schools, school citizenship education programmes were initiated by the top school leaders and therefore received school-wide resource supports. Schools could, for example, devote time used for state-mandated ideological or political extracurricular activities (e.g., flag-raising ceremonies and class meetings) to their school citizenship education. Schools could also create separate classes for school citizenship education programmes or integrate them into other subject teaching time or and extracurricular time. This flexibility meant that school-based citizenship education involved not only teachers relevant to citizenship education but also many other staff in case schools. According to the teacher survey data, important school inputs such as these ensured the quality of their programmes.

Table 4. Teachers' criticisms about education bureaus' citizenship education curricula

	All Three Schools			Mean of Individual School			Difference in Means between Schools		
	No.	Mean	Std. Dev.	S.A M_A	S.B M_B	S.C M_C	M_A- M_B	M_A- M_C	M_B- M_C
The extent of resource input our school made was a criterion to assess the quality of our citizenship education programme.	90	3.13	.99	3.03	3.23	3.13	-0.20	-0.10	0.10

Significantly, all schools created a leadership team for school-based citizenship education reconstruction, and used professionalism and innovative ability as appointment criteria for leaders of the content and pedagogy selection stage – respected and popularly selected colleagues, rather than the school hierarchy, made the key decisions in this stage of citizenship education reformation. In School A, two school vice-principals, both specialists in citizenship education, made general recommendations to other teachers, while in School B, the Teaching and Research Office and the school-based citizenship education curriculum development team (which included experienced teachers) created the school textbooks, teacher handbooks and promoted basic principles. Schools encouraged teachers to innovate and provided mechanisms to absorb those innovations in a timely manner. Survey respondents from all three schools state that their school allowed them to communicate their ideas and opinions (mean = 3.12, standard deviation = .97). In School A, teachers' best classrooms practices were recorded in a scholarly article published nationwide. School C even decorated its school garden to show their appreciation of teachers' good ideas in school-based citizenship education.

Therefore, schools' increased power in the second stage can be seen in their enhanced control of internal school resources and mechanisms, and in the related power struggles with external authorities over content and pedagogy selection.

School Power in Implementation Stage: Enlarging Space, Enhancing Commitment, and Including Diverse Voices

School power in the three case schools in the implementing stage is examined by comparing the kinds of interactions that emerged, the curriculum actors who were involved and the influence they had on school citizenship education programme implementation. The findings showed enhanced school power in three aspects.

First, schools enlarged their school citizenship education programme operating space by seeking external supports and restricting the influence of education bureaus. The district education bureau supported School A's efforts to reconstruct citizenship education by reorganising teaching time and compulsory official citizenship education curricula contents, saying that "School A's citizenship education programme highlighted extant problems in citizenship education throughout the district". School B, with the permission of its local education bureaus, extended teaching time for school-based citizenship education, integrated the school programmes into all school activities and shared their experiences with other schools. In School C, parents, by virtue of the high tuition fees they paid, increased students' access to quality citizenship education (smaller classes in citizenship education programmes) and allowed the school to make extensive innovations while maintaining the continuity and enhancing the sensitivity of those innovations; moreover, through their tendency to send their children abroad for higher education, parents made it possible for School C to focus on citizenship education rather than on preparations for national university entrance examinations.

Education bureaus' influence over school-based citizenship education was restricted in two aspects: Their citizenship education curricula were criticised (See Table 5) and their supervision was regarded as poor. Schools felt that their school-based citizenship education programmes were an improvement over the education bureaus' weaker curricula or addressed areas the education bureaus had ignored. The fact that the school-based citizenship education programmes in the three schools had different foci than the education bureaus' citizenship education curricula made it difficult for the education bureaus to supervise them.

Table 5. Teachers' criticisms about education bureaus' citizenship education curricula

	All Three Schools			Mean of Individual School			Difference in Means between Schools		
	No.	Mean	Std. Dev.	S.A M_A	S.B M_B	S.C M_C	$M_A - M_B$	$M_A - M_C$	$M_B - M_C$
National citizenship education curriculum fully meets my students' needs..	90	2.49	1.03	2.63	2.37	2.47	0.27	0.17	.010
Local citizenship education curriculum fully meets my students' needs.	90	2.64	1.08	2.63	2.70	2.60	.0.07	0.03	0.10

By dismissing the education bureaus' supervision as inferior, schools were able to block attempts to make their school citizenship education programmes conform to local citizenship education curricula and ignore national education bureau policies. According to the survey data, most teachers from the three schools felt that education bureaus' supervision restricted their school citizenship education programme (mean = 3.17, standard deviation = 1.27).

Second, school administrators interacted in two ways to ensure school teachers' commitment to school-based citizenship education programme implementation. The first was to initiate internal interactions, such as competitions between middle-level leaders and those teachers participating in the school citizenship education programmes, thus encouraging the latter to display their knowledge of and commitment to the programmes. The second approach involved appointing school leaders and future teachers to ensure teacher commitment and continuity. As a private school, School C's owners had the right to select a chief school board member to represent their values, and gave her the power to select school principals and teachers.

In the implementation stage, teachers had autonomy over content and pedagogy selection and were not forced to implement school-decided content or pedagogies as given; rather, they had the freedom to add, delete or change them based on their judgment or to accommodate grassroots interests. Based on questionnaire responses, teachers in all three schools felt that they were mainly in charge of content selection (see Table 6).

Table 6. Comparison of school teachers' autonomy in school-based citizenship education

	All Three Schools			Mean of Individual School			Difference in Means between Schools		
	No.	Mean	Std. Dev.	S.A M_A	S.B M_B	S.C M_C	M_A-M_B	M_A-M_C	M_B-M_C
Teachers not only follow the school committee, they also have revision power	90	3.23	.77	3.23	3.37	3.10	0.013	0.13	0.27
When I have different opinions about the school decisions, I prefer to add some materials.	90	3.21	.84	3.20	3.17	3.27	0.03	0.07	0.10
Teachers mainly responsible for selecting teaching materials	89	3.12	.77	3.20	3.23	2.93	0.03	0.27	0.30

Table 7. Teachers' attitudes toward student, parent needs in citizenship education curricula

	All Three Schools			Mean of Individual School			Difference in Means between Schools		
	No.	Mean	Std. Dev.	S.A M_A	S.B M_B	S.C M_C	M_A-M_B	M_A-M_C	M_B-M_C
When choosing materials for school citizenship education, I would consider whether it meet student needs.	90	3.23	.72	3.43	3.37	3.20	0.07	0.23	0.17
When choosing teaching materials for school citizenship education, I would consider whether parents support.	90	3.08	1.03	2.93	3.10	3.20	.17	0.27	0.10

Third, this increased autonomy enabled teachers to allow student and parent voices to be heard in the implementation stage. Teachers from all three schools showed similar attitudes towards addressing student needs in selecting materials and could make adjustments autonomously to address parental concerns. Although some teachers in School A characterised parents as non-cooperative, others generally saw parents' understanding and support as important elements in programme implementation and evaluation (See Table 7).

The teachers made their own voices heard as well: School A's teachers enjoyed a high degree of lateral autonomy in the implementation stage; in School B, teachers unionised to share governing power and enlarge their power zones; and, teachers in School C exerted deep and broad influences during the implementation stage. Increased autonomy meant teachers could select materials from multiple diverse sources such as the Internet, books, etc., with interviewed teachers from all three schools reporting having done so.

In the implementation stage, therefore, it can be seen that the redistribution of power enhanced school influence on, commitment to and sensitivity in school-based citizenship education reconstruction.

DISCUSSION AND CONCLUSION: SCHOOL POWER AS A SEMI-EMANCIPATORY RELATIONSHIP

With reference to school-based curriculum development in citizenship education in three secondary schools in China, this study has examined the schools' and teachers' contributions to more democratic citizenship education in three stages: curriculum goal setting, content and pedagogy selection, and implementation. The study's findings indicate that Chinese schools' and teachers' practices are congruent with critical pedagogy studies, which underscore the emancipatory potential of schools and teachers in employing more democratic processes in schools and classes (Apple & Benne, 1995), incorporating diverse social groups' voices to improve existing education system inadequacies (Williams, 2009) and responding to the challenges brought by increased ethnic, cultural, linguistic and religious diversity in the society. At each stage of school citizenship education reconstruction, case schools in this study advance democratic citizenship education by depoliticising CCP-dominant citizenship education, decentralising curriculum decision-making power from governments, and democratising school culture to better meet the needs of Chinese civil society. Schools strategically select, develop, adapt or even ignore CCP and central government citizenship education based on their own perception of society's needs. They sensitively identify and help to address grassroots needs that may not be adequately reflected in CCP- or government-defined citizenship education. Furthermore, schools enhance the quality of citizenship education by reorganising school culture and mobilising resources to address societal needs; this helps to explain the influence of Chinese schools in reconstructing citizenship education during China's period of rapid social transition.

However, this does not mean the CCP's and the state's politically-motivated values, centralised control and non-democratic education management style has come to an end overall. The success of Chinese schools and teachers in attaining a limited degree of power suggests that school power in China can best be understood by the concept of school power as a semi-emancipatory relationship.

This view, as opposed to that shared by such progressive educators as Freire (2003), who sees schools as having the potential to work for radical democracy, addresses the tensions caused by state and political control over school citizenship education and depicts the schools' efforts to gain more influence: schools are partially integrated with political forces, but retain sufficient independence to influence curriculum and interact with external forces. This study has shown that schools enhance their independence in citizenship education reconstruction through collaboration with university experts, community organisations, parents, foreign investors and local governments.

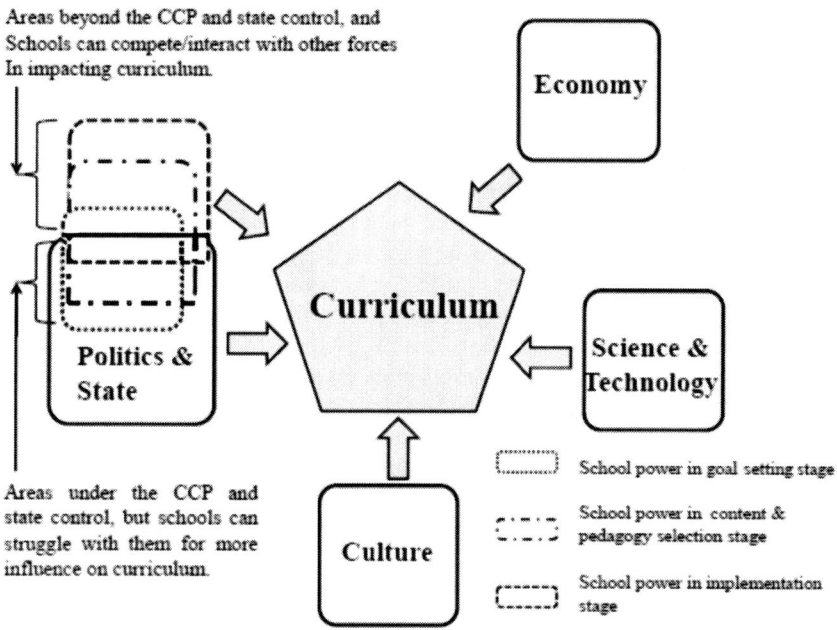

Figure 1. The Concept of School Power as a Semi-emancipatory Relationship in Different Stages of Chinese School-based Citizenship Education Curriculum Development.

Moreover, contrary to theories arguing that school power is radically emancipatory, the concept of school power as a semi-emancipatory relationship in the Chinese context holds that there are varied degrees of influence and independence at different stages of programme development. Schools' influence over curriculum and their interactions with the community or external social forces least influential, but still palpable, at the goal setting stage. Schools increase their influence in the content and pedagogy selection stage and are able to decrease CCP are intertwined, and vary at different stages in the context of China. School power is determined by the interactions among schools, the CCP, the state and other external social forces at different stages. Comparatively speaking, school power is and state control and support school decisions based on their control of local resources. School power extends even beyond curriculum development, by cooperating with external social forces, excluding CCP and state influences, and empowering school teachers (See Figure 1).

In addition, the concept of school power as a semi-emancipatory relationship has three implications for understanding the roots, mechanisms and sources of school power.

First, school power stems from the CCP's and the state's hard power. Although support for curriculum decentralisation is obvious in China's promotion of SBCD, the CCP and state retain ultimate control in some areas. Schools, by obeying the CCP's and the state's ultimate authority (power over) in some areas, and by using the powers and responsibilities assigned to them (power to) in others, initiate their struggle for more influence in citizenship education. This characteristic has shaped school power, and differs from the understanding that school power is emancipatory.

In "power over" relations, power is based on superior strength (Dugan, 2003). This study has found that the CCP and state have ultimate power over two areas: determining the basic communist values to be included in citizenship education and determining the curriculum status of SBCD. In these two areas, all other forces must obey their decisions. Since the official promotion of SBCD in 2001, the CCP and state (through curriculum reform policies) have clearly indicated their intent to continue to transmit communist values and to give SBCD a lower status than that afforded official curricula. Despite regulating the three school-based citizenship education stages differently in different schools, their status as the unquestioned rulers of China impels schools to accept their decisions without resistance. In particular, the CCP and state expect schools to improve weaknesses in the state's citizenship education curricula. Therefore, the CCP and state, by restating basic communist values and giving a lower status to SBCD, make schools serve their needs in citizenship education.

In "power to" relationships, power is based on a variety of exchanges, rewards, and punishments (French & Raven, 1959). This study found that the CCP and state, despite granting schools a measure of power, retained reward and punishment authority in three areas: making related policies; supervising schools' practices; and deciding school personnel, resources and survival.

This article has shown that the CCP and state allow schools a degree of flexibility in school-based citizenship education programmes, including the freedom to exchange various contributions – such as professional knowledge, expertise and resources – to improve the effectiveness of official citizenship education. Schools can invite prestigious university scholars to supervise practices, cooperate with non-education government sectors on their school curricula, or make use of school strengths to introduce citizenship education that differs from official citizenship education.

However, there is much evidence to suggest that the CCP and state, through their reward and punishment regulations and mechanisms, are the actual leaders in these areas. Their influence is the power to start, change or end funding and to evaluate school performance; thus, they can contract or stipulate schools' cooperation with non-education sectors.

Second, the concept of semi-emancipatory power implies that schools' involvement in conflict and collaboration with diverse external forces enhances schools' independent influence in citizenship education reconstruction. Schools initiate non-overt conflicts with the CCP and state over education regulations and lobby for greater freedom, a key feature of soft power relationships, according to Foucault (1982). One of the original CCP/state goals in promoting SBCD was to improve weaknesses in official citizenship education curricula to make them better fit the social transition period. The linkage among schools, citizenship education and changing social needs has influenced schools' conflict with the CCP and state supervision of school citizenship education reconstruction.

Schools challenge CCP- and state-dominated citizenship education curricula for not meeting student needs, for not being systematically designed (and thus difficult to apply to school situations) and for using outdated teaching materials and pedagogies that bore students. Moreover, they criticise education bureaus for not being professional and knowledgeable, and may choose not to implement education bureau policies fully when these policies do not fit their situation.

Thus, without changing their core requirements, schools revise official citizenship education curricula to respond to the demands of students, parents and society – incorporating and rearranging official citizenship education curricula to suit student and school needs, replacing teaching materials provided by the official citizenship education curricula with updated materials reflecting local community needs, experimenting with new pedagogies not included in official citizenship education curricula, addressing student and parent needs and developing citizenship education themes attractive to community and parents but ignored or under-developed in official citizenship education curricula.

Schools began to collaborate with external forces to enhance their independence in citizenship education and emancipate themselves from the "pastoral power" of the CCP and state. Collaboration was believed to be a source of soft power (Blades, 1998), with which schools could challenge the state's supreme power.

In the case of Chinese school-based citizenship education reconstruction, collaborations with external forces provide schools a greater range of resources and consultants, thus supplanting the CCP and the state as the sole resource providers and consultants and making schools more independent. As pointed out by Booher and Innes (2002), collaboration between interests groups of diverse backgrounds broadens the exchange and sharing of resources relevant to their tasks. Schools involve agents from education and non-education sectors (e.g., university scholars, district governments, district-level education bureaus, environment protection bureaus, and parents) in school citizenship education programmes, thus gaining professional insights, supports and resources from a variety of sectors rather than from the CCP and state alone. Collaboration with external forces helps schools to succeed in school citizenship education reconstruction, bringing them recognition, rewards and fame, non-measurable gains that enhance their ability to resist CCP and state regulation.

Third, the concept of school power as a semi-emancipatory relationship shows that the sources of this power are complex but not chaotic networks. To ensure the success of school citizenship education reconstruction, schools redistribute internal power to engage more school staff and units, thus forming complex networks and changing traditional top-down school personnel relationships into multi-engaged relationships that continuously drive semi-emancipatory relationships in school citizenship education.

School subunits relevant to citizenship education (e.g., Moral Education Office, Teaching and Research Affairs Office, School Vice-principal Office, Student Affairs Office, Subject Team, Teachers' Union) engage in school citizenship education reconstruction, decreasing CCP and state restrictions on school citizenship education programme implementation and facilitating schools' independence by providing more teaching time, teachers and space, and by making better use of their unique advantages to increase success.

Teachers relevant to citizenship education (such as moral education teachers, class teachers, grade headteachers, and other subject teachers) combine to make school-wide decisions regarding school-based citizenship education programmes, create materials and pedagogies and to teach school citizenship education subjects and other subjects and activities.

By engaging various subunits and teachers, schools can create space for and generate additional resources to reconstruct citizenship education. Rather than implementing SBCD in the roughly 16–20% of curriculum time allocated by the CCP and state, schools in this study embed school citizenship education into other school subjects and extracurricular activities. School teachers bring professional knowledge, detailed information about student and parent needs and continuous sources of innovation to school citizenship education programmes, thus increasing opportunities for success.

This study has found that in-school networks, despite their complexity, are structured rather than chaotic, and that they further the commitment to school-based programmes. Two mechanisms are used to organise these complex networks: empowerment and changes in leadership styles.

Empowering individual teachers is a key feature of soft power (Connell, 1993; Popkewitz, 1997; Yoshiko, 2006) and is believed to be important to teacher commitment (Bogler & Somech, 2004; Gaziel, 2009; Wu & Short, 1996). In this study, teacher empowerment is a similar phenomenon across the case schools, with teachers enjoying a high degree of influence in school citizenship education programmes. Some participant teachers are empowered with school-wide curriculum decision-making powers and all enjoy a high degree of autonomy in implementing school-made policies, selecting content and pedagogies and influencing school-wide policies and practices. Empowerment helps teachers to shape their identification with and commitment to school citizenship education programmes.

Changes in school leadership styles are important for schools' commitment to school-based citizenship education reconstruction. Managing the conflicting interests among diverse participants in decision-making is an important challenge. This study notes that conflicts of interest can exist between different school subunits, or between individuals, as they struggle to gain influence. Schools may make use of these conflicts to gradually shape common goals or to select leaders, teachers strongly committed to school-based citizenship education programmes.

To conclude, this study provides an account of school power in citizenship education reconstruction by examining the effect of school power in three stages of SBCD, advancing the concept of semi-emancipatory school power, and accounting for the roots, mechanisms and sources of this type of power in the Chinese context.

As a multiple case study, this empirical work has some limitations. The three case schools in the study were located in one open, economically developed city (Shenzhen) in mainland China. The choice of study site allowed this study to explore important relationships and issues associated with school power in citizenship education reconstruction and, in particular, to investigate various interactions among different forces in an urban and open region. However, China is a country that has experienced not only rapid economic growth, but also increased differences among regions – rural and urban, coastal and inland. Due to the case study site and the limited number of cases, the study results cannot be generalised to the wider context of China, particularly its less economically developed areas. Different regions of China have distinctive education traditions, reflecting their unique social, political and economic natures. For purpose of generalisation, a large-scale survey of comparable schools based on the insights from this study would be helpful.

ACKNOWLEDGEMENTS

This study was supervised by Dr. Wing-Wah Law, without whose participation the current paper would not have taken shape. The author also expresses her thanks to Dr. Hugh Starkey for the helpful information he provided.

REFERENCES

Apple, M. (1990). *Ideology and curriculum.* New York: Routledge.
Apple, M. (1996). *Cultural politics and education.* New York: Teachers College Press.
Apple, M., & Benne, J. (Eds.). (1995). *Democratic schools.* Alexandria, VA: ASCD.
Blades, D. W. (1998). *Procedures of power & curriculum change: Foucault and the quest for possibilities in science education.* New York: Peter, Lang Publishing.
Bogler, R., & Somech, A. (2004). Influence of teacher empowerment on teachers' organizational commitment, professional commitment and organizational citizenship behavior in schools. *Teaching and Teacher Education, 20*(3), 277–289.
Booher, D. E., & Innes, J. E. (2002). Network power in collaborative planning. *Journal of Planning Education and Research, 21*(3), 221–236.
Bowles, S., & Gintis, H. (1976). *Schooling in capitalist America: Educational reform and the contradictions of economic life.* New York: Basic Books.

Cartwright, D. (1965). Influence, leadership, control. In J. G. March (Ed.), *Handbook of organizations* (pp. 1–47). Chicago: Rand McNally.

Cheng, H. J., & Delany, B. (1999). Quality education and social stratification: The paradox of private schooling in China. *Current Issues in Comparative Education, 1*(2), 48–56.

Cheung, Y. P. (1994). *Changes in the conception of moral education in China in the post Mao period.* Hong Kong: The University of Hong Kong.

Chinese Communist Party. (1985). *Zhong Gong Zhong Yang Guan Yu Jiao Yu Ti Zhi Gai Ge De Jue Ding [Committee of the Communist Party of China's decision on the reform of the educational structure].* Beijing: Author.

Cohen, L., Manion, L., & Morrison, K. (2007). *Research methods in education.* London: RoutledgeFalmer.

Connell, R. W. (1993). *School and social justice.* Toronto: Our Schools/ Our Selves.

Dahl, R. A. (1957). The concept of power. *Behavioral Science, 2*(July), 201–218.

Dahrendorf, R. (1959). *Class and class conflict in an industry society.* Stanford, CA: Stanford University Press.

Davies, E., & Issit, J. (2005). Reflection on citizenship education in Australia, Canada and England. *Comparative Education, 41*(4), 389–410.

Deng, Z.,& Luke, A. (2008). Subject matter: Defining and theorizing school subject. In F. M. Connelly, M. F. He & J. Phillion (Eds.), *The Sage handbook of curriculum and instruction* (pp.66–87*).* Thousand Oaks, CA: Sage.

Domes, J. (1990). Ideology and politics. In F. Michael, C. Linden, J. Prybyla, & J. Domes (Eds.), *China and the crisis of Marxism-Leninism* (pp. 174–203). Boulder, CO: Westview Press.

Dugan, M. (2003). *Integrative power: Beyond intractability.* Retrieved March 15, 2007, from http://www.beyondintractability.org/essay/Power/

Emerson, R. M. (1962, February). Power-dependence relations. *American Sociology Review, 27*(1), 31–41.

Foucault, M. (1979). *Discipline and punish: The birth of the prison.* New York: Vintage.

Foucault, M. (1982). The subject and power. In H. L. Dreyfus & P. Rabinow (Eds.), *Michel Foucault: Beyond structuralism and hermeneutics* (2nd ed., pp. 208–226). Chicago: The University of Chicago.

Freire, P. (2003). *Pedagogy of the oppressed.* New York: Continuum.

French, J. R. P., & Raven, B. (1959). The bases of social power. In D. Cartwright (Ed.), *Studies in social power* (pp. 150–167). Ann Arbor: University of Michigan Press.

Gaziel, H. (2009). Teachers' empowerment and commitment at school-based and non school-based sites. In J. Zajda & D. T. Gamage (Eds.), *Decentralisation, school-based management, and quality* (Vol. 8, pp. 217–229). Heidelberg, London, New York: Springer Science + Business Media B. V.

Giroux, H. A. (1983). *Theory and resistance in education: A pedagogy for the opposition.* South Hadley, MA: Bergin & Garvey.

Giroux, H. A. (2003). Public pedagogy and the politics of resistance: Notes on a critical theory of educational struggle. *Educational Philosophy and Theory, 35*(1), 5–16.

Hayhoe, R. (1993). Political texts in Chinese universities before and after Tiananmen. *Pacific Affairs, 66*(1), 21–43.

Held, D. (1992). Democracy: From city-state to a cosmopolitan order? *Political Studies, XL*(Special Issue), 10–39.

Hellrich, G. (1970). Some educational implication of Karl Marx's communism. *Education Forum, 34*(4), 471–478.

Jary, D., & Jary, J. (Eds.). (1999). *Dictionary of sociology* (2nd ed.). London: Unwin Hyman.

Johnson, L., & Morris, P. (2010). Towards a framework for critical citizenship education. *The Curriculum Journal, 21*(1), 77–96.

Karabel, J., & Halsey, A. H. (1977). Educational research: A review and an interpretation. In J. Karabel & A. H. Halsey (Eds.), *Power and ideology in education* (pp. 1–85). New York: Oxford University Press.

Keddie, A. (2008). Engaging the 'maximal' intentions of the citizenship curriculum: One teacher's story. *Cambridge Journal of Education, 38*(2), 171–185.

Kliebard, H. M. (1986). *The struggle for the American curriculum, 1893–1958*. London: Routledge & Kegan Paul.

Kliebard, H. M., & Franklin, B. (1983). The course of study: History of curriculum. In J. H. Best (Ed.), *Historical inquiry in education: A research agenda* (pp. 138–157). Washington, DC: American Educational Research Association.

Law, W. W., & Pan, S. Y. (2009). Game theory and educational policy: Private education legislation in China. *International Journal of Educational Development, 29*(3), 227–240.

Leenders, H., Veugelers, W., & Kat, E. D. (2008). Teachers' views on citizenship education in secondary education in The Netherlands. *Cambridge Journal of Education, 38*(2), 155–170.

Li, P., Zhong, M., & Zhang, H. (2004). Deyu as moral education in modern China: Ideological functions and transformations. *Journal of Moral Education, 33*(4), 449–464.

Lin, J. (1999). *Social transformation and private education in China*. Westport, CT: Praeger Publisher.

Masschelein, J. (2004). How to conceive of critical educational theory today? *Journal of Philosophy of Education, 38*(3), 351–367.

Manzon, M. (2007). The necessary and the contingent: On the nature of academic fields of comparative education. *Comparative Education Bulletin, 9*, 5–22.

Ministry of Education. (2001). *Ji Chu Jiao Yu Ke Cheng Gai Ge Gang Yao (Shi Xing) [Guidelines for basic education curriculum reform (trial version)]*. Beijing: Author.

Mitchell, R. C. (2010). Who's afraid now? Reconstructing Canadian citizenship education through transdisciplinarity. *The Review of Education, Pedagogy and Cultural Studies, 32*(1), 37–65.

Nieto, S. (2000). Placing equity front and center: Some thoughts on transforming teacher education for a new country. *Journal of Teacher Education, 61*(3), 180–187.

Nye, J. S. (2004). *Soft power: The means to success in world politics*. New York: Public Affairs.

Oakes, J. (1995). *Keeping track: How schools structure inequality*. New Haven, CT: Yale University Press.

Osler, A., & Starkey, H. (2010). *Teachers and human rights education*. Stoke on Trent, UK: Trentham Books.

Popkewitz, T. (1997). The production of reason and power: Curriculum history and intellectual traditions. *Journal of Curriculum Studies, 29*(2), 131–164.

Ross, H., & Lin, J. (2006). Social capital formation through Chinese school communities. In B. Fuller & E. Hannum (Eds.), *Research in the sociology of education* (Vol. 15, pp. 43–69). Bradford, UK: Emerald Group Publishing Limited.

Schneewind, A. (2006). *Community schools and the state in Ming China*. Stanford, CA: Stanford University Press.

Sen, A. (1999). Democracy as a universal value. *Journal of Democracy, 10*(3), 3–17.

Shor, I., & Freire, P. (1987). What is the "dialogical method" of teaching? *Journal of Education, 169*(3), 11–31.

Slattery, P. (Ed.). (2006). *Curriculum development in the postmodern era* (2nd ed.). London: Harper & Row Publishers.

Slattery, P., Krasny, K., & O'Malley, M. P. (2007). Hermeneutics, aesthetics, and the quest for answerability: A dialogue possibility for reconceptualizing the interpretive process in curriculum studies. *Journal of Curriculum Studies, 39*(5), 537–558.

Spencer, H. (1860). *Education: Intellectual, moral and physical*. New York: D. Appleton and Company.

Terren, E. (2002). Post-modern attitudes: A challenge to democratic education. *European Journal of Education, 37*(2), 161–177.

Torney-Purta, J., & Barber, C. (2004). *Democratic school participation and civic attitudes among European adolescents: Analysis of data from the IEA Civic Education Study*. Strasbourg, France: Council of Europe.

Williams, A. D. (2009). The critical cultural cypher: Remarking Paulo Freire's cultural circles using hip hop culture. *International Journal of Critical Pedagogy, 2*(1), 1–29.

Woehrle, L. M. (1992). *Social constructions of power and empowerment: Thoughts from feminist approaches to peace research and peace-making.* Syracuse, NY: Syracuse University Press.
Wu, V., & Short, P. M. (1996). The relationship of empowerment to teacher job commitment and job satisfaction. *Journal of Instructional Psychology, 25*(1), 85–89.
Yoshiko, N. (2006). Riding tensions critically: Ideology, power/knowledge, and curriculum making. In L. Weis, C. McCarthy, & G. Dimitriadis (Eds.), *Ideology, curriculum, and the new sociology of education: Revisiting the work of Michael Apple* (pp. 69–89). New York: Routledge.
Young, M. (1971). *Knowledge and control: New directions for the sociology of education.* London: Collier Macmillan.
Zhu, X. M., & Liu, C. L. (2004). Teacher training for moral education in China. *Journal of Moral Education, 33*(4), 481–494.

Wangbei Ye
Lecturer, Department of Politics,
East China Normal University

SANDRA J. WOLF

CRITICAL CITIZENSHIP, POPULAR THEATRE, AND THE SOCIAL IMAGINATION OF PRE-SERVICE TEACHERS

We, as humans with current and genetic memory, are historically situated beings. The implications of this assertion for teachers lie in the ways that curriculum is organised, the ways that discipline in enacted, and the ways that diversity and equity are represented in speech acts and social practice within individual classrooms and in schools as institutions. Further, responses of teachers as individuals to remembered grand cultural and historical narratives about Aboriginal history and Aboriginal people may determine the extent to which teachers feel that opportunities exist for their efficacious exercise of personal agency toward social justice. If teachers feel that oppression is a generalised, naturalised and eternalised manifestation of life in the "civilised world" in the 21st century, they are unlikely to struggle with oppression in their own classrooms (Sears & Cairns, 2010, p. 124). In this chapter I will describe the ways that small teams of pre-service teachers from various disciplines engaged in participatory social justice work in an Aboriginal education course at Lakehead University in Ontario, Canada. Teacher education students selected a topic and then used primary source historical documents and other artifacts to construct a 20-minute one-act play representing an event in Aboriginal history about which little was previously known.

I am an Aboriginal educator with over 30 years of experience teaching in classrooms for Aboriginal children and adults, from pre-school to graduate school. I am the fourth generation of Ojibwe Métis people in my family to be born in North Dakota, a short distance south of the US/Canadian border. Prior to that, my family lived in what is now Manitoba and Saskatchewan. I come from a long line of storytellers and those who have been critical of mainstream social policy. Thus, I am a storyteller and a critical educator. It's in my DNA. I could not be any other way. My students in the Aboriginal education class were non-Aboriginal, in large majority. However, a small number of Aboriginal students also enrolled in the class and identified themselves as Aboriginal. I was always delighted to welcome them. Theremay have been others who did not self-identify. As always, the ethnicity of my students did not change what I taught or how I taught the class since I was already teaching from an Aboriginal perspective, which involves broad principles of inclusion and respect, and an Aboriginal application of universal design in instructional planning. Aboriginal people have historically viewed children and students, even adult students, as "holy little ones," (Black Elk, as cited in Neihardt, 1988, p. 77) a gift to be treated with great care. So it was with my students in the Aboriginal education course.

Pre-service teachers typically arrived at the Faculty of Education enlivened and enthusiastic about their hopeful future as a teacher. They were willing to engage with content that was new to them as long as they could see that mastery of the content would contribute to accomplishment of their career goals. Many also came to the classroom full of gratitude to the nation of Canada for the benefits of Canadian citizenship that they enjoyed, and rightly so. As Canadians, they were able to travel around the world and expect to be welcomed. They enjoyed the high regard of other world citizens, respected for the role Canada has taken in peacemaking on a global scale. Students shared with me that while travelling, they carefully sewed patches bearing the Canadian flag on their backpacks and clothing, which guaranteed acceptance and welcome.

Many of the pre-service teachers who entered the Professional Year travelled extensively around the world. However, many have not travelled in Canada north of, for example, North Bay in Ontario, which is considered to be "the North," though the city lies far to the south of Thunder Bay. Prior to their entry into the Lakehead University education program, conceptualising "the North" had meant enjoying winter sports, wildlife, and the life-changing challenge of surviving the cold for the nine months of the Professional Year. During conversations or activities in class, non-Aboriginal students indicated that they have few personal relationships with Aboriginal people. They have grown up knowing only what they learned from the media about Aboriginal people. They commonly reported having no knowledge about the history of residential schooling for Aboriginal people in Canada. Some expressed scepticism that such a practice could exist in Canada. If such a thing happened, why was it not taught in their history classes? Since the apology of Prime Minister Stephen Harper on June 11, 2008, to the Aboriginal people in Canada who experienced residential school trauma, those arguments diminished. Students were, nonetheless, surprised to find that their course of study to become a teacher would include conversations and research about the experiences of Aboriginal people who historically occupied "the North." This is not the north of North Bay, Ontario. This is the north that extends from the area around Thunder Bay and Sioux Lookout to the south shore of Hudson Bay in Ontario and the edge of the Arctic Circle in other provinces.

Some students in the course articulated alarm and, to some extent, resistance in emails and face-to-face communication. They questioned the rationale for their enrolment in the class. "I'm from southern Ontario. We don't *have* Indians in southern Ontario," one student shared. Another informed me, "Maybe you have not noticed, but I'm white. I think I'm in the wrong class." I consistently assured them that they were not in the wrong class. I responded to this effect: "Yes, there are Indians in southern Ontario. You have not learned to see them yet, but you will." And, "No, I did not notice that you are white. After so many years of teaching, I really don't notice that about students. But in any case, whether you are white or Native or something else, you are Canadian, and this is Canadian history. You did not have a chance to learn this history the first time around, but you have a chance to learn it now. We'll learn it together, so let's get started."

How my Professional Year students and I go about approaching change and growth, developing critical citizenship, and exercising social imagination is as important as the new content that they will encounter. I consider it less important that they walk away with a set of facts in their scholarly repertoire than it is that they construct new knowledge about the experiences of First Nations, Métis, and Inuit people in Canada. I would much prefer that they develop the beginnings of empathy and wisdom than that they acquire decontextualised information about Canada's Aboriginal people.

CANADIANS LEARNING CANADIAN HISTORY

Young Canadians learn Canadian history with varying levels of resulting expertise. A 1997 survey conducted with young Canadians by the Dominion Institute indicated that two out of five survey respondents thought that Canada had fought France, Great Britain, and Russia in the two world wars and that Canada had bombed Pearl Harbor, for example. Results of similar surveys conducted in the United States by the Reagan administration and in Great Britain by the Thatcher government revealed a similar lack of historical knowledge in those countries. What possible explanation could there be for this phenomenon? Lowenthal (1998) argues that what we offer to our young people as "history," a study of the past, is actually "heritage," what we have made of the past. Thus, we are not teaching history, we are teaching an interpretation of history. "The past does not change, but its interpretation can alter radically" (Morton, 2006, p. 23).

The teaching of history, as originally framed within the early 19th century Common School movement in both Canada and the United States, was organised as part of a public education system "designed to create loyal, dutiful citizens" (Morton, 2006, p. 26). During that period when both Canada and the United States were earnestly at work building a cohesive and like-minded citizenry, public schools served as a foundry for nationalistic loyalties as they trained young men and young women in civic ideals. "Properly trained young men would be patriotic conscripts in the ranks of national armies, and patriotic women would cheer their son's departure to the latest national war" (Morton, 2006, p. 26). Problem-recognition and self-critique were not elements of public school curriculum in any discipline and large blocks of past historical events have typically been omitted from public education, including Aboriginal history. But wait, is the kind of knowledge that would support accurate responses to the Dominion Institute Survey the kind of knowledge that we want our students to have? Surprisingly, it is not. Critical citizenship requires understanding beyond dates, locations and a simplistic view of allies and enemies.

We need to set higher standards than this. … I do not simply mean that students need to know more facts, or get more of them right. Rather, we need to acknowledge that contention over meanings of the past is an ongoing feature of an ongoing contemporary culture and that it might even be constructive if citizens had ways to participate knowledgeably and thoughtfully. (Seixas, 2006, p. 14).

Critical citizenship requires participation in the critical interpretation of the past beyond the inculcation of master narratives. I would argue that critical citizenship requires the ability to resist the master narrative through study of primary sources, application of secondary concepts of historical consciousness, and the public participation in storytelling about historical events that influenced the state of Aboriginal education today.

"Without an accurate knowledge and understanding of history, we are doomed to be victims of manipulation at best, and subjugation, at worst" (Osborne, 2006, p. 103). It would be possible to teach about Aboriginal education without extensive discussion of Aboriginal history, but the content of such teaching would be shallow, incomplete, and decontextualised. That's not the kind of teaching in which I can (successfully) engage. I believe that Aboriginal education, as with other aspects of education, in general, is best taught within the context of the social, historical, and cultural contexts in which that discipline developed. My students and I research and study applied history. This investigation of applied history is in search of several of the secondary concepts organised in Seixas' typology (2006, p. 18). I did not require students to memorise dates and events. I asked them to develop an understanding of evidence, significance, continuity and change, empathy/perspective-taking, and agency. Agency is the capacity of "particular groups to shape and reshape the course of events in history, as they come up against the structural constraints that have been handed down from the past" (Seixas, 2006, p. 19). With a rich source of historical records available to us in the Northern Studies Resource Centre of Lakehead's Paterson Library, my students and I began our search for Canadian history, not learned before, at that site. I will discuss this repository of primary sources in slightly more detail later in this chapter.

I do not take a narrow view of how Canadian history has affected educational outcomes for Aboriginal people in Canada. Every historical event impacts those immediately involved as well as those only remotely aware of those events. An Indigenous concept integral to social relationships among Indigenous people is expressed by the Elders as, "The hurt of one is the hurt of all, the honour of one is the honour of all" (Four Worlds Development Project, 1984, p. 74). The collective nature of social relationships within Aboriginal culture was an aspect of our study that students occasionally struggled to comprehend. The Canadian ideal of individual effort and merit was challenged by that concept and by the amount of small group work that students were expected to complete during the term. Students occasionally asked, "Can't you just tell us what you want us to know and give us a test and we're done?" "No," I told them, "I can't." Then I would tell them a story about how I learned when I was a child, and how what I learned, and how I learned, applied to them. Some of them smiled or chuckled when I told them that. Those smiles and chuckles let me know that some of them were starting to understand the implications of the Indigenous social practice, a foray into collectivity, they would experience for the next nine weeks.

CRITICAL CITIZENSHIP, POPULAR THEATRE, AND THE SOCIAL IMAGINATION
CALLING ON THE POWER OF STORIES TO EFFECT CHANGE

During our nine weeks of classes for the course, my students and I engaged in the practice of listening to stories, reading stories, researching stories, and ultimately reconstructing stories that reflected the lived experience of Aboriginal people in Canada. Our investigation was conducted through the transdisciplinary study of history and storytelling. Stories are an Indigenous art form, and are endemic within all cultures. They embody small universes. Stories have tremendous power as a medium of communication and cultural transmission; they have the power to create or destroy. They can wound or engender healing. How can stories do all of that? First, stories have a powerful impact on the processes of human cognition. We think in story form. We construct stories to provide explanation for events that occur in our lives. We construct stories as a means of speculating what will happen if we make one choice over another choice. We are, in fact, "hard-wired" to learn most effectively from stories (Haven, 2007).

In addition, stories have the capacity to evoke a powerful impact on learning because they tap into the natural human tendency to crave human interaction. Humans are, thus, social animals who crave relationship with one another.. Stories provide a medium through which humans are able to communicate guiding principles for human interaction that encourage communication and strengthen relationships.

What do I mean by asserting that stories can create or destroy? Clearly stories allow us to create order from a series of disparate events, sequencing occurrences and describing cause and effect. In addition, we can recreate remembered events when we recall those events and weave them into a story. But the destructive power of stories may be less obvious. Let's take a look at a particular kind of story, the master narrative, for clarification. The stories of societies that engaged in domination of other societies take the form of master narratives that explain and justify the domination. Master narratives are stories of grand scale that provide the meaning and value within which people position their social and national identities. Master narratives are produced when public memory supplies historical accounts that make it seem normal, natural, and common sense that certain events or traits, and not others, have come to represent national identity. "When the master narratives to which we are exposed and from which we are expected to learn in school are those told from the perspective of the colonizer, master narratives may constrain our actions and limit our freedom" (Mehl-Medrano, 2007, p. 123).

Early during each term, my students and I explored their perceptions of the master narratives about Indigenous people in both Canada and the United States. We typically found a somewhat stark contract in those respective master narratives. In the United States, the master narrative about Native people is that "Indians are dangerous." That narrative is both represented and reinforced in stereotypes that take the form of film and television portrayals, Western fiction, advertising, and mascot names of sports teams. However, in Canada the master narrative about Canada's indigenous people is that they are incompetent.

Centuries of myths about Aboriginal racial inferiority have laid the foundation for negative stereotypes of Aboriginal people that are used to justify domination today. The *incompetent Indian* is one of the most harmful stereotypes of Aboriginal people because it is used to justify policies such as the *Indian Act*. It implies that Aboriginal people are incapable of competing in a modern society and therefore need special legislation that allows governments to control and intervene in their affairs. Exposing the role that myths and stereotypes play in conflict, past and present, is critical to the reconciliation process. (Rice & Snyder, 2008, p. 54)

The Canadian national narrative regarding Aboriginal people is that they are unable to seize control of their lives, families, and governments. Thus, it was a natural, normal, and a common sense thing to do for the Canadian federal government to pass the Indian Act, which controls so much of the lives of Canadian Indigenous people. After all, Canada did not need to pass an Italian Act, nor a Finnish Act, the master narrative asserts, because Italian and Finnish people in Canada have been able to manage their lives as immigrants, we are asked to believe.

Countering the Master Narrative

Stories told from an Indigenous perspective serve as counter-narratives (Mehl-Medrano, 2007) to the Canadian national narrative of reasoned domination of Aboriginal people for their own good. Indigenous stories resist the power of master narratives to define and thus determine and limit, our actions, identifies and personal agency. Processes of telling and hearing counter-stories serve to support social relationships (Haven, 2007) and activate or reactivate an alternative historical memory (Stanley, 2006). These processes also constitute acts of collective resistance to colonial influences of the governments of North America that sought to obliterate Indigenous history, language, and culture. In the Aboriginal Education course that I teach, my students and I studied and constructed stories that affirmed the capacity of Indigenous people for healing, courage, and well-being.

Experiencing Indigenous Stories

Pre-service teachers in the course who did not grow up hearing Indigenous stories learned the form of Indigenous stories as they listened to Elders in the classroom and on film. I told stories, but I also gave students extensive visual support for the concentrated oral language involved in storytelling. I was careful to provide my students with both the contextual background and the potential application for the content they learned in class. I alerted my students early during the term that everything I do in the classroom is an expression of Indigenous pedagogy. Everything I did was intended to serve as a model for them of the critical, respectful, and inclusive pedagogy, which included written text and technology that was appropriate for classrooms and teaching in the 21stcentury. My use of humour, sometimes self-deprecating humour, was also an aspect of Aboriginal pedagogy. I teased myself. I acknowledged that I was not an expert on either Canadian history or Canadian Aboriginal history, and that I was grateful for the opportunity to learn that content with them. I never failed to thank my students for their attention and for the expertise in the respective fields that they brought to the classroom.

Pre-service teachers learned the cadence, the scope, and other elements of storytelling through first-hand experience in class, but they learned the content of Indigenous stories as they researched and studied primary sources, including documents, maps, photos, diaries, and others. My students and I had access to the Northern Studies Resource Centre, the repository for a huge collection of historical documents and other resources, including Hudson's Bay post records and RG - 10 (Record Group 10) records of Indian and Northern Affairs Canada (INAC), the federal agency in charge of many aspects of the lives of Indigenous people in Canada. INAC records were also available dating from a time when that agency was the Indian Bureau. My students also conducted ethnographic interviews with community Elders regarding their experiences, for example, of residential school or military service.

In their quest for primary source documents and other historical resources, pre-service teachers explored one of four broad themes that articulated the lived experiences of Indigenous people in Canada. Each term during which I taught the class, my students and I graphed an array of topics that might fall into what we considered to be the most prominent aspects of Indigenous life in Canada related to education. The graph constructed during winter term in 2010 included the following:

CLASSROOM-BASED EVENTS

- Loss of Native Language
- Harsh discipline
- Misunderstandings between students and teachers
- "Common school" curriculum

SCHOOL-BASED EVENTS

- Harsh living conditions
- First days: haircut, clothing burned, bathed in turpentine
- Abuse, physical, emotional, and sexual
- Children running away from school
- Children segregated from one another by gender (growing up not knowing how to behave around persons of the opposite gender)
- Siblings separated from one another
- Half-day academic, half-day work assignments

FEDERAL OR PROVINCIAL EDUCATION POLICY-BASED EVENTS

- Church and government collusion to assimilate children at any cost
- Sixties swoop, children taken from homes, sent to homes across Canada and Europe (stated purposes were for improved educational opportunity)

- Prime Minister Stephen Harper's apology to residential school survivors – Who encouraged this apology? Who actually wrote the apology? How did people respond?
- Effects of enfranchisement as Canadian, and loss of Indian status, of Aboriginal people who chose to go to college

EVENTS REPRESENTING ABORIGINAL RESISTANCE TO THE CANADIAN NATIONAL NARRATIVE

- Passage and enforcement of the Indian Act
- Effects of enfranchisement as Canadian, and loss of Indian status, of Aboriginal people after serving in the Canadian Armed Forces
- Pass laws, denial of the right to freely travel without permission of the Indian Agent
- Voting rights, enfranchisement, granted in 1960 without concurrent loss of Indian status
- Grassy Narrows fight for environmental justice
- James Bay Cree forced relocation
- Métis Resistance to encroachment upon land
- Elijah Harper's refusal to vote in favour of the Meech Lake Accord
- Cultural maintenance activities that allowed the cultures to be sustained, though underground
- Effects on Aboriginal communities when children were taken away
- Flooding of Lac Seul and Sand Point First Nations by Ontario Hydroelectric
- Events at Oka, Ipperwash, Via Rail Blockade
- Kitchenuhmaykoosib Inninuwug (**KI**) leadership jailed

Theatre, the Natural Next Step

After collecting primary source documents, including maps, newspaper articles, interview transcripts, governments reports, for example, pre-service teachers used the primary source materials they had researched to construct a one-act play about an event in history. Their reconstruction of an event in history was based partially on the historical resources they found and partly on their interpretation of those resources. Students questioned how they might be expected to accurately portray an event in history based on sometimes scant evidence. I assured them that I was considerably less interested in accuracy than I was hopeful that other standards such as adherence to the "truth" of the evidence, the significance of the event, the extent to which their script demonstrated the capacity to take the perspective of another person, and the degree to which they had represented the presence of agency. Who was making decisions during the event in history that they were portraying? I asked the students to think of the stories that they would construct as a metaphor. If we, the audience, could understand the metaphor, the scriptwriters had done a good job. Students worked in small groups of between three and six members to write a script, rehearse that script, locate minimal props and costumes, and present their one-act play to their classmates. Student actors kept their scripts with them so they would not undergo the pressure of memorising lines and fearing that they would forget lines. They kept their scripts handy and occasionally referred to them.

Why is theatre the natural next step? The history of theatre as a social movement provides some explanation. Historically, theatre as a vehicle for social justice has included:

- Epic theatre, the dialectical theatre of Bertolt Brecht (Conrad, 2004, p.13);
- Popular Theatre, Theatre of the Oppressed, of Augusto Boal, influenced by Paulo Freire (Conrad, 2004, p.14);
- Currently, and in Canada, the work of Diane Conrad (2004), with Indigenous youth in northern Alberta
- Indigenous theatre forms, across time, utilised to teach history and important lessons about relationships and world view

Theatre is participatory and thus, social. Theatre is performative and thus, engaging of learners. Theatre presents alternative ways to engage participants in research (See Conrad, 2004).

ENGAGING THE SOCIAL IMAGINATION OF PRE-SERVICE TEACHERS

Perezhivanie is the "intensely-emotional-lived-through-experience" that occurs for humans when they inhabit the literary, and I would argue theatrical, space of another person (Ferholt, 2010). Perezhivanie allows us to participate and "witness how a lifeless construction is transformed into a living organism" (Vygotsky, 1971, p. 150). Recently, two actors explained how they inhabit the entity of another person when they are engaged in drama. First, James Earl Jones, who has stuttered since childhood, explained how it is that he does not stutter while he is acting. He said, "I'm not myself anymore. I'm that security guard or that inmate. If the character were to stutter, I'd have to come up with a way to stutter, but when I am acting, and the character I am playing does not stutter, I don't stutter" (CNN Connect the World, January 7, 2010).

More recently, actor Lambert Wilson was interviewed by Terry Gross on NPR regarding the success of his latest film, "Of Gods and Men." The film depicts the last days of seven Trappist monks in Algeria. When faced with the necessity to leave the monastery or possibly be killed, the monks choose to stay. Commenting on the scene in which the monks cast their votes, Gross asked Wilson about the expressions on the faces of the actors/monks, "How did you manage to achieve and sustain the look of utter submission to destiny?" Wilson responded, "We knew the men whose lives we were depicting and we felt deeply for their fate. We weren't acting anymore" (NPR, Fresh Air, February 22, 2011). Wilson and his colleagues "weren't acting anymore". I would venture that for many of the Professional Year students who were beaten as children, though only in the context of the one-act play they had helped to craft, or the First Nations leader arguing that the hydroelectric dam must not proceed because the water was flooding the village at

Lac Seul, Sand Point, James Bay, and other places, they also were not acting anymore. Perizhivanie, the capacity to inhabit the lived experience of another through the arts, had allowed them to argue convincingly and, occasionally bring their student colleagues to tears in doing so, because it was their land at stake, or their pain being experienced.

History Takes to the Stage

The theme of citizenship was prominent in the dramas developed by students. Students frequently chose to study events in the lives of Aboriginal people that highlighted differential benefits and kinds of citizenship. Over several years, students prepared and presented dozens of dramas depicting Canadian history. In this discussion, I will highlight two of those dramatisations that focused on events in the life of Métis leader, Louis Riel. I chose these dramatisations to discuss because they both exemplify creativity in telling a good story and using humour, intentionally or unintentionally. Within Indigenous stories, humour is often used by a Trickster figure to teach important lessons. Both of the dramatisations I will describe taught important lessons. Trickster is not concerned with mastery of the content. Trickster wants to know that the listener/observer walks away changed, having grown from the experience.

Each term, several groups of students studied and enacted events in the life of Louis Riel, the Métis leader who led resistance to the colonisation of the ancestral lands of the Métis and their Cree allies and relatives. Riel is considered by Aboriginal people in Canada to be the founder of the Province of Manitoba. I'd like to think that Riel was of keen interest to the students because of the complexity of the issues of citizenship, indigeneity, change, and Canada's colonial past engendered in Riel's life story. I also recognise that the ready availability of abundant primary sources on-line may also have influenced the choice, and that is perfectly acceptable. The Métis and other Aboriginal people, refer to the events that took place from 1869 to 1885 as the Métis Resistance, not as "rebellion." Rebellion implies revolt from within a population. Resistance implies opposing forces. The Métis did not consider themselves to be British subjects. They held themselves to be citizens of their own nation. Riel formed a Provisional Government in 1869, which included some of my ancestors, and began the process of actively governing both land and social processes. Resistance to encroachment on Métis territory eventually led to the execution, by Riel, of a member of an opposing faction. Riel then travelled to Montana where he taught in a small Catholic school near the present city of Cascade. Many of the Métis, in the meantime, relocated to Saskatchewan and set up the community of Batoche.

Métis Resistance of Batoche In the fall of 2008, a group of students sought to depict the struggle that eventually took place at Batoche. They had researched the events that led to the point when Canadian troops stationed at Winnipeg amassed for an attack on a village of Metis men, women, children, and elders. In their depiction, the students wanted to highlight the number of Canadian troops and the weaponry, including a Gatling gun. In order to do so, they chose to develop their drama in the form of stick-puppet theatre. They constructed a small model of the church at Batoche and several miniature horse-drawn wagons carrying weapons, as well as a scale model Gatling gun with moving parts and sound effects. The students mounted plastic military figures, "toy soldiers," on small wooden platforms and painted their jackets red. Similar groups of Métis resistors were mounted and painted brown. Additional stick puppet depicted the Cree allies who fought with the Métis. The students created a replica of the field in which the fighting took place with slots through which the students could operate their stick puppets as groups of the military and groups of the Métis advanced and withdrew. Their final set preparation was a stage with curtains that could be drawn or opened.

The dramatisation, *Métis Resistance at Batoche*, began when a narrator introduced the setting, the time period and a brief history that led to this event. Then the battle began. Threads attached to some of the Métis figure stick-puppets allowed them to fall to the ground. As the fighting continued, more and more Métis men fell.

The narrator of the drama interjected details from time to time to inform the audience what was happening with the women, children and elders. Much of our knowledge about what happened among the Métis at Batoche came from testimony provided by Gabriel Dumont, second-in-command to Louis Riel, who was present at Batoche, having been convinced to return to his people in Saskatchewan.

The students who had prepared the drama included the recorded sounds of weapons and men shouting. In spite of the serious, even tragic, nature of the dramatic content and the care with which preparations for the dramatisation were made, there was an inescapable comic effect to the puppetry. Quiet muffled giggles began to emerge from class members viewing the puppet theatre presentation. The steady low sound of chuckles grew in volume. I began to think to myself, "Sandra, these are your relatives being killed. And now the students are giggling and chuckling at this event. What are you going to do? How are you going to respond?" I recognised that the students depicting the Métis resistance at Batoche had gone to great effort to research the event. I believed that they meant no disrespect. I began to hear students whispering, "Is Sandra going to be angry?" The drama continued to the conclusion of the fight and the narrator provided a tally of the dead and the living. Then the curtain was drawn. I stood up, smiled, and applauded for a long time. Several class members stood with me and applauded. I told the class how proud I was that the team of researchers had prepared so well for their presentation. I had stood and applauded for a long time, first, because I wanted the entire class to see me and know that I was appreciative of the presentation. Second, I had provided an opportunity for students in the audience who could not suppress laughter to express that laughter while it was muffled by applause.

Later, in the hallway, I could hear team members speaking to one another as they packed their stage and characters into a cardboard box. One of them said, "I didn't expect that people would think the skit was funny, but I guess that it reminded them of a Punch and Judy show." Another said, "Yes, but Sandra liked it anyway. She liked it so well that she gave us a long standing ovation!" I was pleased that the team members felt affirmed and complimented. They had done what I asked them to do. The theme of "resistance in the face of overwhelming odds" was evident throughout their presentation. They deserved appropriate credit for their work.

The Execution of Louis Riel After events at Batoche, Louis Riel surrendered to the Canadians. He was eventually tried for treason and found guilty. In the fall of 2009, a group of students depicted the execution of Louis Riel in Regina. Their drama took the form of a "drama-within-a-drama." On the stage, three actors sat at a table. There were stacks of books, journals, and other documents in front of them. As the drama began, the actors read from the texts of several of the documents. One actor pointed out, "With all of the information available about Louis Riel and his life and death, it's hard to know where to start and what to believe." As the actors seated at the table began to read descriptions of the execution of Louis Riel, three other actors entered from the other side of the stage. One was dressed as a priest. One was the executioner, wearing a hood over his face. The actor playing the part of Louis Riel was handcuffed. Some actors were men and some were women.

Another actor seated at the table read from a textbook, "After saying his prayers, Louis Riel was shot by an executioner as the priest looked on." With that, the actors standing on the other side of the stage depicted Louis Riel being anointed with holy water, the priest making the sign of the cross, the executioner holding a gun to Riel's head and firing. With that, the actor playing the part of Riel fell to the ground.

Then, one of the actors seated at the table held up a document. He argued, "No, that is not what happened. I know that it says that in the textbook, but in the RG-10 I found a primary source, a report that indicates that Louis Riel was hanged. He was not shot. He was hanged. The textbook got it wrong." With that, the actors dressed as the priest and the executioner lifted the actor playing the part of Louis Riel to a standing position, dusted him off, and apologised. The actors "broke character." One said to the Riel character, "Hey, sorry, man, we depended on textbooks." The other said, "Yeah, man, it won't happen again." Then, the Riel character shrugged and responded, "That's OK. That happens to a lot of people, man." They led him to the rear of the stage where a noose was silhouetted against the back wall. Members of the audience could then see, in silhouette, the noose positioned over Riel's head to his neck and Riel being hanged.

The actors seated at the table gathered up their papers and books, packing them into backpacks. One actor said to the other, "You can't always trust textbooks. Sometimes textbook authors just use other textbooks for sources. Primary sources are the places to look for evidence." Another said, "Yes, and if the textbooks and historians don't tell the truth about Louis Riel's execution, then what else about Louis Riel could they have gotten wrong?" The others agreed that not everything taught as history might be true. The actors at the table walked off stage chatting and gesturing with one another. The curtain closed. Applause filled the auditorium.

Engaging the Social Imagination

The relationship of critical citizenship, popular theatre and the engagement of the social imagination of pre-service teachers is one of reciprocal and concurrent influence. Engaging the social imagination occurs when pre-service teachers construct counter-narratives that will support the presence of a critical agenda for their classrooms. Social imagination is the capacity to envision what might have been and what could be in the present and future for the cultures and societies that we inhabit.

Within the context of their work toward social justice, social imagination suggests to pre-service teachers that oppression is not a generalised, naturalised and eternalised manifestation of life in the "civilised world" in the 21st century. Social imagination further suggests that their struggle with oppression in their own classrooms will serve a meaningful purpose as master narratives are refuted and denied power.

Schools in Canada currently exist within an environment strongly influenced by conservative political thought. Even in provinces in which less conservative leaders currently hold office, the conservative critiques of schools as institutions lacking accountability appear to determine how initiatives (that are not new) are structured. Within the classrooms with which I am familiar, I see intensifying reliance on competition to motivate students; intensifying expectations for individualisation, as peer support is less available to them in a high-stakes environment; and intensification of an environment of survival of the fittest, not unlike those that characterised ineffective school reform in the first Bush Administration in the US. My colleagues and I engaged in the struggle for social justice could not have imagined that we would continue to witness the same intensification strategies not working, but still popular, in the second decade of the 21st century (See Berliner & Biddle, 1995, pp. 181–189, for a well-framed critique of intensification and other aspects of the first Bush Administration's assault on US schools).

Repeated calls for the re-visioning, re-purposing, and re-humanisation of public schooling continue to be heard. Eisner's (2002) call for a revitalisation of the arts in school affirms my choice to employ theatre as a form of critical inquiry:

The sense of vitality and the surge of emotion we feel when touched by one of the arts can also be secured in the ideas we explore with students, in the challenges we encounter in doing critical inquiry, and in the appetite for learning we stimulate. In the long run these are the satisfactions that matter most because they are the only ones that insure, if it can be insured at all, that what we teach students will want to pursue voluntarily after the artificial incentives so ubiquitous in our schools are long forgotten. It is in this sense especially that the arts can serve as a model for education.

Others have repeated the call for education to reframe narrow curricular constructions and expand perspectives. "Learning has to do with the capacity to interact creatively and constructively with problems. In most of our current pedagogical practices throughout the minority and majority worlds such problems are often concealed or ignored altogether" (Moore & Mitchell, 2008, p. 10).

Students in the Aboriginal Education course occasionally communicate with me well after the end of the course, but particularly so when they are in the process of completing their student teaching. One student slipped a note under my door to tell me, "I can't think of a medium more suited than Drama to deepen understanding and create empathy. I think that Drama techniques, while much easier to use in an

English class, are, in fact, far more valuable in an History class, where true understanding and empathy are crucial for our understanding of our world today and how it came to be that way." If it is possible to nurture the capacity in humans for the experience of empathy, perizhivanie-laden theatre may be a way for that to happen. As pre-service teachers inhabit, briefly, the lives of Aboriginal people, the strength and the struggle of the people become their own.

REFERENCES

Berliner, D., & Biddle, B. (1995). *The manufactured crisis: Myths, fraud, and the attack on America's public school.* Reading, MA: Addison Wesley.

Conrad, D. (2004). Exploring risky youth experiences: Popular theatre as a participatory, performative research method. *International Journal of Qualitative Methods, 3*(1), 12–24.

Cable News Network. (5 January, 2010) *Connect the World Interview with film actor James Earl Jones.* Available online at: http://connecttheworld.blogs.cnn.com/2010/01/05/thursdays-connector-of-the-day-james-earl-jones/

Eisner, E. W. (2002). What can education learn from the arts about the practice of education? *The encyclopedia of informal education*, Available online at: www.infed.org/biblio/eisner_arts_and_the_practice_or_education

Ferholt, B. (2010). A synthetic-analytic method for the study of perezhivanie: Vygotsky's literary analysis applied to playworlds. In M.C. Connery, V. P. John-Steiner, & A. Marjanovic-Shane (Eds.), *Vygotsky and creativity: A cultural-historical approach to play, meaning making, and the arts* (pp. 164–179). New York: Peter Lang.

Four Worlds Development Project. (1984). *The sacred tree.* Twin Lakes, WI: Lotus Light Publications.

Haven, K. (2007). *Story proof: The science behind the startling power of story.* Westport, CT: Libraries Unlimited.

Lowenthal, D. (1998). *The heritage crusade and the spoils of history.* Cambridge, UK: Cambridge University Press.

Mehl-Medrano, L. (2007). *Narrative medicine: The use of history and story in the healing process.* Rochester, VT: Bear and Company.

Moore, S. A., & Mitchell, R.C. (2008). Introduction: Power, pedagogy and praxis – towards common ground. In S. A. Moore & R. C. Mitchell (Eds.),*Power, pedagogy and praxis:Social justice in the globalized classroom* (pp. 1–18). Rotterdam,Boston & Taipei: Sense Publishers.

Morton, D. (2006). Canadian history teaching in Canada: What's the big deal? In R.W. Sandwell (Ed.), *To the past: History education, public memory, and citizenship in Canada* (pp. 23–31). Toronto: University of Toronto Press.

National Public Radio (22 February, 2011) *Fresh Air – Terry Gross Interview with film actor Lambert Wilson re: "Of Gods and Men".* Available online at: http://www.npr.org/2011/02/22/133278072/lambert-wilson-of-gods-and-men-and-james-bond

Neihardt, J. G. (1988). *Black Elk speaks: Being the life of an Oglala holy man.* Lincoln: University of Nebraska Press. (Original work published 1932)

Osborne, K. (2006). "To the past": Why we need to teach and study history. In R.W. Sandwell (Ed.), *To the past: History education, public memory, and citizenship in Canada* (pp. 103–131). Toronto: University of Toronto Press.

Rice, B., & Snyder, A. (2008). Reconciliation in the context of a settler society: Healing the legacy of colonialism in Canada. In M. Brant Castellano, L. Archibald, & M. DeGagné (Eds.), *From truth to reconciliation: Transforming the legacy of residential schools* (pp. 45–61). Ottawa: Aboriginal Healing Foundation.

Sears, A., & Cairns, J. (2010). *A good book, in theory. Making sense through inquiry.* Toronto: University of Toronto Press.

Seixas, P. (2006). What is historical consciousness? In R.W. Sandwell (Ed.), *To the past: History education, public memory, and citizenship in Canada* (pp. 11–22). Toronto: University of Toronto Press. Stanley, T. (2006). Whose public? Whose memory? Racisms, grand narratives, and Canadian history. In R.W. Sandwell (Ed.), *To the past: History education, public memory, and citizenship in Canada* (pp. 32–49). Toronto: University of Toronto Press.

Vygotsky, L.S. (1971). *The psychology of art.* Cambridge, MA: MIT Press.

Sandra Wolf
Lakehead University

EMERY HYSLOP-MARGISON AND JOSEPHINE L. SAVARESE

THE CORPORATIZATION OF THE UNIVERSITY

Post Neo-Liberalism and the Decline and Fall of Democratic Learning

INTRODUCTION

When capitalism suffered its major international swoon in the late 1970s citizens of industrialized countries were advised that welfare state interventions in *laissez faire* economics were entirely responsible. Rather than blaming the structural flaws of capitalism, corporate captains argued the general economic decline and series of recessions were caused by state interference in the market. Corporate leaders and their government allies moved quickly to convince the public through mass media manipulation, or what Althusser (1989) describes as the ideological state apparatus, that the blame for economic collapse rested with those who interfered with unfettered market logic.

The message conveyed by the ideological state apparatus suggested the solution to restoring economic wealth required large-scale dismantling of social safety net mechanisms and state policies designed to mitigate the savage inequities of capitalism. In Canada, these various welfare state programs were designed over a period of several decades to protect citizens during periods of job loss, health crisis and general economic decline. In exchange for passively accepting massive cuts in program spending and labour deregulation, the public was promised improved economic opportunities in the form of more and better jobs, enhanced consumer conditions and generally stronger economic growth. The dismantling of the welfare state combined with market deregulation and globalization to create the neo-liberal values that have dominated Canadian society for the past thirty years.

The recent G20 events in Toronto vividly illustrate the precarious state of contemporary Canadian democracy in the face of neo-liberal policies and the repressive state apparatus employed to enforce them. Neo-liberal capitalism has launched a frontal attack on freedom of speech and assembly, as well as undercutting public discursive spaces such as universities. The 1.4 billion dollar security price tag for the G8 and G20 meetings, the arbitrary arrest and detention of independent journalists and a thousand other passive observers and protesters, and the point blank firing of rubber bullets into the bodies of young women who were simply retreating from armoured, charging, baton wielding, police officers painted a troubling portrait of the changing Canadian political landscape. Neo-liberal capitalism now requires police state enforcement of its policies.

In this chapter we explore how current neo-liberal policies and trends undermine post-secondary education as a potential site of democratic learning and social change. We argue that concerned academics no longer have the luxury of intellectual isolation and political inaction but must instead confront the present situation in manifest ways. This requires openly challenging government meddling in university governance, the massive under-funding of higher education, and removing the institutional control of the managerial class over universities. We begin by examining neo-liberalism and review the current shift from the ideological to repressive enforcement of its policies. We then discuss the impact police enforcement of the corporate state is having on human rights and education.

THE SHIFT TO POST NEO-LIBERALISM AND THE REPRESSIVE STATE APPARATUS

A range of scholars have commented on some of the central ideological tendencies of neo-liberalism. In this section, we review this scholarship to lay the groundwork for our investigation into the delivery of higher education in a post neo-liberal climate. We use the term post *neo-liberal* to designate the shift toward police state enforcement tactics. The commentators we examine emphasize the market's prominence in dictating economic, social and political life. Neo-liberal ideology directs citizens towards individualism and consumerism, rendering more superficial and cursory their involvement in public policy debates and decision making. The naturalization of neo-liberal capitalism is prevalent throughout society from media representations to post-secondary curricular imperatives.

Dale and Hyslop-Margison (2010) define neo-liberalism as "an economic, moral, and social system designed to advance global capitalism" (p. 6). Harvey (2005) explores the economic and social policies fostered by prosperous and powerful nations that promote deregulated, liberal markets. He emphasizes the centrality of the marketplace along with the requirement that social institutions conform to economic policies. Conteh-Morgan (2006) shares this perspective by observing that, "Neoliberalism is the primary discourse of globalization. Within neoliberalism is the emphasis on a system of ideas, beliefs and values presented as the only credible economic and political system, and therefore the most normal" (p. 4).

For Springer (2010), neo-liberalism refers to "a political, economic and social arrangement emphasizing market relations, minimal states, and individual responsibility" (p. 1). Springer works to foster awareness of what he calls "the larger imperatives of capitalism" (p. 2). He tracks the development of neo-liberalism from a "marginalized ideal" to its present status as "the primary economic doctrine of our age" (p. 2). Critical analysis is essential to ensure that this "particular transitory moment" does not serve as the "end of history" (Springer, 2010, p. 2). Robbins (2008) brings forward similar themes in *Emergency! Or How to Learn to Live with Neoliberal Globalization*. He describes "neoliberal globalization" as "capitalism Mark II where economic power and politics are disconnected to the extent that national governments and transnational corporations operate in separate spheres" (p. 4). This state of affairs results in the "globalization of power and the localization, if not asphyxiation, of politics" (Bauman, as cited in Robbins, 2008, p. 4).

While these trends may seem far removed from local school and educational policies, Robbins reinforces points made by other scholars including Dale and Hyslop-Margison (2010) who identify the influence neo-liberalism exerts on school policies. Students are increasingly viewed through a market generated lens that silences dissenting opinions that might undermine capitalist driven objectives by promoting beliefs and values that contradict those neo-liberalism embraces. According to Robbins (2008):

> Public education is persistently whittled away by market-based initiatives, leaving students with teachers-turned salespeople or teachers-turned-prison guards. Simply, citizens are left with few social venues that provide non-commodified, public, and democratic languages and experiences. The cultural politics of the consumer society promotes highly competitive and individualistic languages and modes of social interaction. (p. 6)

Robbins concludes that, "The 'I' has colonized the 'we' in social organization" (2008, p. 6).

In contrast to the calls of progressive educators and in exchange for an opportunity to imagine and engage in genuine resistance and reformation, university students are typically invited to express their views on micro topics that have little to do with the structural factors that influence the delivery of education. They evaluate their professors through private surveillance systems such as Rate My Professor or comment on their institutions in private surveys that imply the quality of campus food and the effectiveness of teaching "strategies" are important markers of quality education. The reduction of student involvement to micro-issue discussion diverts attention from the broader socio-economic framework that influences higher education policies. Neo-liberal platforms strain institutions of higher education by justifying spending reductions, eliminating humanities while increasing human capital disciplines, and by fostering obedient student and faculty bodies distanced from democratic and collegial forms of governance. Hill (2004) captures this point when he maintains:

> Business wants education fit for business - to make schooling and higher education subordinate to the personality, ideological and economic requirements of capital, to make sure schools produce compliant, ideologically indoctrinated, pro-capitalist, effective workers. (p. 38)

Dale and Hyslop-Margison (2010) respond to these factors by promoting resistance to socially and economically regressive policies. They voice commitment to social justice as an imperative to undermine these negative trends:

> Within a post neo-liberal context, the goals of the marketplace, and its methods of operation are increasingly reflected in the organization of education. This relationship ensures that students are indoctrinated into a monolithic worldview devoid of social critique or alternative social visions. (p. xi)

These developments are especially evident in the two case studies we discuss in a later section of the chapter. We believe these examples nicely illustrate the tension between democratic, human rights oriented approaches to education and post neo-liberal ideology.

THE IMPACT OF POST NEO-LIBERALISM ON HIGHER EDUCATION

The naturalization of neo-liberal ideology is widely evident in the prevailing discourse surrounding higher education. This discourse typically describes present structural circumstances to students in terms that suggest either their inevitability or their desirability. Neo-liberal ideology removes the economic sphere from moral or social discussion by portraying these latter realms of discourse as dependent on the former. All other spheres of life, including higher education, are correspondingly designed to address the needs of the naturalized marketplace and any interference with market logic becomes historically unimaginable.

Habermas (1996) suggests we are witnessing the complete corporate invasion of what he describes as the *life world* through the creation of false needs and the rapid destruction of public spaces such as universities. The life world for Habermas consists of those fundamental human experiences and interactions that generate a sense of inner peace or individual well-being and provide the necessary community space for democratic discussion. These public spaces include our institutions of higher learning but, in particular, require specific programs such as history, philosophy and politics to foster social analysis and critique.

Higher education reflects the corporatization consistent with neo-liberal policies more generally as evidenced by the growth of research chairs based entirely on corporate sponsorship. Universities are increasingly adopting an unbridled faith in the corporate values of human capital preparation and micro-level accountability as the means to correct all possible educational ills. In spite of their traditional, if somewhat romanticized, role as the gatekeepers of intellectual freedom, universities have drifted rapidly toward serving the instrumental demands of the marketplace. Faced with huge public financing reductions, universities increasingly focus on technical training programs and ubiquitous credentialising rather than on creating informed and engaged democratic citizens.

Concordia University in Montreal, for example, is presently marketed under the slogan "real education for the real world," a mantra that effectively reduces higher education to social efficiency precepts by implying there is a real social world beyond that shaped by human decision-making (Hyslop-Margison & Sears, 2008). Such sloganizing glosses over the important distinction between a constructed social reality and a naturally occurring one, ideologically undermining student agency in the process. In the U.S. and Canada, a significant number of research chairs are entirely corporate sponsored with the attending obligation to direct research agendas toward studies that pay corporate dividends.

Universities increasingly view their relationship with students within a business model framework, with students now frequently described as clients or customers of the university rather than as members of a scholarly community. A recent article appearing in a University of Toronto publication extolled that institution's new focus on students as "customers" who deserved good service as a smart move, not for delivering quality education but for nurturing long term alumni loyalty — and, of course, the corresponding financial contributions (Hyslop-Margison & Sears, 2008). The commodification of education not only appears in marketing and customer service campaigns directed at students, parents and alumni, but in an increasing focus on universities as providers of commodities (under the guise of credentials) rather than education. Forty years ago social critic Ivan Illich (1971) argued that Western educational institutions had substituted credentialing for educating, an observation far more salient today than even he might have imagined.

The reduction of public funding for universities creates intense competition between faculty for available private and public grants. The ability to attract funding into the university is now typically viewed as a fundamental tenure requirement. The research funded by these grants often poses little challenge to the neo-liberal structure because it either neglects society as a primary unit of analysis or manifestly embraces prevailing human capital objectives. The focus of this research is often grounded far more in the idea of prevailing social and economic utility than in fostering democratic critique. The idea that a university experience is about intellectual growth, social debate and democratic dialogue has been largely usurped by the neo-liberal objectives of customer service, credentialising, technical training and instrumental learning. In the current university milieu, faculty are reduced from their potential democratic role of public intellectual and social critic to that of entrepreneurial researcher or clerical proletariat labour.

Neo-liberal culture is naturalized to students in public and higher education as an unchangeable social reality rather than critiqued as an ideological movement imposed by special corporate interests on citizens of industrialized democratic societies. Outside the strictures of the global market, education in the neo-liberal order conveys to students there are simply no longer any meaningful choices to be made. Throughout contemporary education, and in a variety of ideologically manipulative ways, students are expected to prepare for an uncertain occupational future and are discursively convinced that such conditions are beyond the scope of their own political agency. Pedagogical tools of social critique such as critical thinking, lifelong learning and literacy are all reshaped by neo-liberal assumptions to become mere tools of instrumental instruction. As a result, schools fail to prepare students as democratic citizens who possess the necessary knowledge, understanding and dispositions to decide politically between various social possibilities. Instead, students are portrayed as mere objects in history and inculcated with a consumer driven worldview devoid of imagination, hope or alternative social visions.

Consistent with post neo-liberal motives, a managerial class of administrators has assumed increasing control over various university decision-making processes. Universities were once places of collegial governance where faculty and, to a lesser extent, students helped shaped the type of programs and policies that governed the institution. Over the past decade in particular, this approach has been replaced by travelling mercenary managers who tend to spend a few years at one institution and then, after making a series of unpopular decisions, move on to ply their trade elsewhere. The irony of the managerial class is that in spite of being retained for their supposed administrative expertise, they have driven Canadian universities into serious financial crisis. The university managerial class affords a clear example of what happens when individual interest trumps the community good, a major marker of contemporary neo-liberal capitalism.

Universities confront numerous fiscal challenges caused by significant reductions in public funding that impact directly on the structure of contemporary academic life. The growing number of technical training programs at many universities, the generally declining stature of the humanities, and research agendas chiefly dependent on various forms of external funding, all impact deleteriously on the academic independence of faculty. The Utopian ideal of the university as a bastion of intellectual, academic and political freedom now seems largely an anachronism. Instead, the bureaucratic, increasingly authoritarian administrative practices of Canadian universities encourage widespread political passivity among contemporary academics. The university, largely removed from public political influence, is now a subsidiary instrument in the virtually uncontested drift toward economic globalization and widespread technological jingoism.

The institutional demands of contemporary faculty experience are especially damaging to the agency and political activism of young academics. Junior faculty members readily learn the significance of publishing in intellectually obscure, inaccessible and uninteresting scholarly journals, largely irrelevant to most of the general public. Academics are frequently sequestered in their office, working primarily in isolation while writing scholarly articles, compiling accountability notebooks, teaching dossiers, or accumulating other evidence of their institutional worthiness. To achieve tenure at recognized research universities, academics require a research agenda, which typically constitutes a narrowing of knowledge, understanding and social influence. The entire peer-review process often becomes a bureaucratic mechanism to force academic deference to the prevailing conservative institutional culture.

Although rewarded by promotion and tenure committees, this academic milieu renders faculty largely innocuous to hegemonic political interests by diverting the former from socially influential scholarship and politically engaged activities. The increased standardization, accountability and use of technology on university campuses centralize administrative control over course content, teaching and assessment practices. These administrative forces limit the control university faculty exercise over their courses and threaten their traditional role as autonomous professionals. Faculty who resist the reduction of academic work to clerical proletariat labour risk being marginalized or blackballed as political troublemakers. The contemporary academic, then, becomes trapped within a cyclical ordeal of production, publishing, and collegial and institutional suspicion, hence never achieving any lasting measure of personal gratification or professional security. The anxiety emerging from this chronic uncertainty creates academics often far more comfortable in relationships marked by political compliance to university administrators than by political activism.

THE CORPORATIZATION OF THE UNIVERSITY

SNIFFER DOGS, THE G20 AND THE SUPREME COURT OF CANADA

To illustrate our concern about the influence of neo-liberalism on democratic processes and higher education, we highlight two case studies in this section of the chapter. We argue that police interventions in both of the case studies showcase some of the ways that students as docile bodies are being produced. Youth are discouraged from seeing themselves as able to mount resistance to market interests and instead are being controlled to comply with capitalist ideals. As Belsey (2002) observes:

> In the postmodern, globalised era, from the viewpoint of the market, youth are consummate consumers. The market logic penetrates ever more deeply. From the early 1980s we have witnessed multinational corporations targeting niche marketing to specific age/interest groups that are labeled in various ways - e.g. pre-teens, tweenies, kidults, generation X, rappers, hip hoppers, homies, surfers etc. - and focussing on their multiple identities, differences, desires and buying- power. The central idea here is the way the market infiltrates the social fabric, probing into sensitive zones, from youth to preschool, to the barely linguistic in order to 'train' young market populations in the habits and disciplines of consumerism. Now, more than ever, kids find their identities and values in the marketplace, rather than in traditional sources such as the family, church, school that comprise a locality, and moreover, that marketplace is an increasingly globalised one.

The first case study we review is *R. v. A.M.* decided by the Supreme Court of Canada in 2008 (1 S.C.R. 569). In that case, the court was asked to consider the legality of police "sniffer" dogs in high schools to detect the presence of illegal or street drugs. The majority of the court held that trained police dogs could only enter schools to search for drugs when there was a "reasonable" or objective suspicion, not on the basis of a hunch or at random due to generalized knowledge of drug use among the student body. The court reasoned that searches in school contexts were governed by the s. 8 of the *Canadian Charter of Rights and Freedoms* because students retained privacy rights in their possessions even while at school. The court compares student backpacks to the briefcases of business people, ironically revealing the influence of neo-liberal doctrine on conceptions of individual rights. Justice LeBel commented:

> No doubt ordinary businessmen and businesswomen riding along on public transit or going up and down on elevators in office towers would be outraged at any suggestion that the contents of their briefcases could randomly be inspected by the police without "reasonable suspicion" of illegality. Because of their role in the lives of students, backpacks *objectively* command a measure of privacy. (Supreme Court of Canada, 2008, para. 62)

While the decision is often considered an example of the higher court's balanced approach to surveillance (MacKinnon, 2007), the decision is rife with references to schools as appropriate sites for law enforcement. Control and quality education are interconnected throughout the decision. For some members of the higher court who concurred in the majority judgment, it was seen as important that schools not become "safe havens for juvenile drug dealers" (para. 47). In their view, this would be "unacceptable". In his dissent, Justice Deschamps voiced similar concerns:

> The presence of drugs in our schools is a very serious social problem. Schools must be substantially free of illegal drugs to promote a safe and productive learning environment for the benefit of students and staff. (Supreme Court of Canada, 2008, para. 100)

While the focus of the decision was on drug searches in high schools, we maintain that the court's acceptance of attenuated social control as a necessary component of the school environment has implications for our work as educators in sites of higher learning. Students learn to see themselves and others as in need of regular surveillance to enforce compliance with policies that operate beyond question. They are trained to question and scrutinize the morality of their fellow students and/or professors who may be law or policy breakers. There is limited if any encouragement to resist the rules and policies that contain the assumption of a dangerous youth subculture gone "wild" through illicit drug use. Neither is there encouragement to question school environments often rife with bullying and authoritarianism that make escape through drug use an attractive and perhaps even necessary option.

In his dissenting decision, the judge stated in *A.M.* that the illicit drugs, presuming to include the bags of marijuana and the small quantity of "magic" mushrooms found in A.M backpack, could render harm equivalent to weapons. Justice Deschamps queried:

> Schools are places of education, but will that education consist of enlightenment for the betterment both of students and of our free and democratic society, or will schools become places where students become ensnared by drugs, gangs, violence and anti-social behaviour? (Supreme Court of Canada, 2008, para. 146)

In answer, he stated:

> Our criminal law, education legislation and school board policies recognize that students are particularly vulnerable to the dangers posed by illegal drugs, dangers which are so immediate and grave as to be indissociable from the social risks posed by, for example, weapons. The introduction of drugs into a school is tantamount to the introduction of a toxic substance into an otherwise safe environment. Not only are drugs literally, and directly, toxic, but they are indirectly toxic as well in light of the harm and violence that attend the production, trafficking and consumption of drugs. (Supreme Court of Canada, 2008, para. 146)

The irony is that the need for police action suggests that teachers could not pinpoint behavioural problems associated with drug use, making the use of sniffer dogs a necessity. Otherwise, the misconduct said to flow from illicit drug use could have been handled through standard school disciplinary policies. It appears that the problematic behaviour was modest and even undetectable, necessitating law enforcement efforts to identify the drug users that were proclaimed to be rendering unstable the delivery of middle education.

The second case study we discuss outlines details on the G20 protest in Toronto that occurred during the summer of 2010. The G20 refers to the Group of Twenty (G20) that serves to provide global governance in finance and related fields (Kirton, 2005). While certain commentators praise this arrangement, we suggested in the chapter introduction that they have ushered in greater social economic inequality and have undermined important democratic rights. In the report released in December 2010, *Caught in the Act,* Ontario Ombudsman André Marin critiques some of the practices engaged in by police who were providing security during the G20 protests. In his view, confusion was created with officers on the street who believed that they had extraordinary police state powers to detain and search protesters due to a misinterpretation of special provincial legislation (Marin, 2010).

Additional investigations into allegations of police misconduct are also underway. A police oversight body is currently investigating the statements of a police officer who was videotaped telling Paul Figueiras, a protester who refused to turn over his backpack for a search during the Toronto G20 summit, "This ain't Canada right now" (Baute, 2011). The video caught the verbal exchange between Paul Figueiras and York Regional Police officers patrolling in downtown Toronto, about a block from the security perimeter. In an interview, Figueiras stated that the officer's comment that Canada had virtually disappeared implied to him that the officer was saying, "As far as I am concerned, you don't have civil rights" (Baute, 2011). This exchange occurred after he agreed to leave when it was made clear that he would have to open his pack. Figueiras was turning away when he was assaulted. The officer indicated that he did not "get a choice" on whether or not his pack was searched. A complaint over this incident, one of many similar incidents, was filed with Ontario's Office of the Independent Police Review Director.

It is conceivable that the G20 protests in Toronto and elsewhere were fostering the bottom-up resistance that may be required to destabilize and redirect harmful neo-liberal advances. Neo-liberalism's proclaimed support for individual freedom, and equality, as well as its stated commitment to widespread affluence and development, are quickly being revealed as abject falsehoods. In Harvey's (2005) view, the insights that flow from moments of clarity on the limitations of neo-liberalism "will foster a basis for a resurgence of mass movements voicing egalitarian political demands and seeking economic justice, fair trade, and greater economic security" (p. 204). We maintain that institutions of higher learning are most effective when they promote the critical resistance and democratic dialogue that might undermine the escalating repressive state apparatuses reflected in these case studies.

RECLAIMING HIGHER EDUCATION AS A PUBLIC DISCURSIVE SPACE

Robbins (2008) asserts that democratic ideals and human rights are still worth struggling for even though their influence is obscured by the current market driven political landscape. De Feyter (2005) connects the neo-liberal policies that have sway over global markets with the general collapse of human rights. His goal is straightforward; he "investigates whether human rights can assist people abandoned by globalization in achieving human dignity" (p. 1). He argues that human rights must be applied in flexible ways "that can address new threats to human dignity" (p. 30). De Feyter lists "economic globalization" as a challenge to human rights and favours a return to ideals that promote diversity and grassroots collaboration as well as individual agency. Because we are interested in similar ideas, we suggest that De Feyter's findings can be linked to the delivery of higher education to encourage educators and students to endorse "the revolutionary spirit of a transformative pedagogy based on freedom" (Dale & Hyslop-Margison, 2010, p. 3).

In his *Notebooks*, Gramsci (1971) encourages the working class movement to develop its own organic intellectuals to counteract conservative ideologues and transform the structural conditions reproducing the social inequality of capitalism. He suggests the struggle to achieve social change cannot be limited to simple consciousness-raising, but demands direct political activism — in other words, the creation of an active political movement created and edified by socialist organic intellectuals. Gramsci (1971) explains: "the mode of being of the new intellectual can no longer consist in verbal eloquence but in active participation in practical life, as constructor, organizer, permanent persuader, and not just a simple orator" (p. 10). The organic intellectual affords a model for faculty to adopt who are concerned with neo-liberal post-secondary education policies and the repressive political practices we identify.

Knight Abowitz (2002) considers Cornell West the epitome of a contemporary academic who has successfully translated scholarly influence into the public political realm. She argues that West transcends the institutionalized confines of the university to "creatively address some deeply rooted social problems related to human oppression in America" (p. 293). Knight Abowitz also worries, however, that public politics as practiced by West risks commercial appropriation by "a market driven, entertainment-orientated culture" (p. 298) more interested in character exploitation and marketing than the message. She warns that West's confrontation with the past neo-conservative president of Harvard and top economic advisor in the Obama administration, Lawrence Summers, and the former's eventual departure from that institution, also highlights the occupational hazards academics assume when they pursue public philosophy in lieu of politically benign, university sanctioned activities.

Aronowitz (2001) traces the career of C. Wright Mills to highlight the personal qualities that characterize a university professor acting as public intellectual: "Mills exemplified a vanishing breed in American life: the radical intellectual who is not safely ensconced in the academy" (p. 239). Aronowitz views the public life of Mills as especially relevant during a period when corporations and their various political allies are seriously undermining the quality of university experience for many students. Mills (as cited in Aronowitz, 2001) was highly contemptuous of the idea that academic investigation is somehow "obliged to purge herself of social and political commitment" (p. 239). Rather than hiding behind declarations of political neutrality, the archetypical, dangerous and fraudulent mantra of the social sciences, he openly advocated freedom and emancipation as primary political goals, and worked to establish the foundation for a radically democratic society through public and university life.

Academics acting as public intellectuals seek to propel society toward social transformation through their direct political engagement. Similar to Gramsci's vision of the working class organic intellectual, academics acting as public intellectuals utilize their privileged position to raise public consciousness about social inequities that impact on schooling, and make manifest the political ideologies and policies that give rise to these conditions. Public intellectuals enter the political realm by expanding the content of their discussion, rejecting the chimera of political neutrality and the moral inertia it typically generates, and by pursuing public forums to communicate with a non-academic constituency. When acting in this fashion, academics have the capacity to initiate meaningful structural change both within the confines of post-secondary institutions and in society more generally.

CONCLUSION

We hope this chapter provides post-secondary faculty and teachers at all levels with the incentive to counter the neo-liberal policies that threaten to turn our remaining public democratic university spaces into realms of instrumental human capital preparation and ideological control. As academics our responsibility is daunting. We must accept our inter-generational obligation to students and to future citizens, and work to protect the rapidly fading higher education principles at the heart of a meaningful democratic society. We believe the choice before us is a relatively simple but critically important one for the future of our democratic societies: Do we create students as future citizens who view themselves as mere objects in history, or do we create learners who view themselves as dynamic political agents of personal and social improvement? From a higher educational perspective that respects the principles of intellectual and political freedom, the answer is abundantly clear and our charge as academics exceptionally compelling. We must mobilize the voices of dissent and we must begin the process of university, social and political transformation immediately.

REFERENCES

Althusser, L. (1989). Ideology and ideological state apparatuses. In L. Athusser (Ed.), Lenin and Philosophy and other Essays (pp. 170–186). London: New Left Books.
Aronowitz, S. (2001). *The last good job in America*. Lanham, MD: Rowan and Littlefield.
Baute, N. (2011, January 20). G20 officer: 'This ain't Canada right now'. *Toronto Star*. Retrieved March 01, 2011 from www.thestar.com/news/torontog20summit/article/925742-g20-officer-this-aint-canada-right-now.
Belsey, A. (2002, September). *Hybridised world kids: Youth cultures in the postmodern era*. Paper presented at the European Conference on Educational Research, Lisbon, Portugal.
Conteh-Morgan, E. (2006). Globalization, State Failure, and Collective Violence: The Case of Sierra Leone. *International Journal of Peace Studies, 11*(2), 87–104.
Dale, J., & Hyslop-Margison, E. (2010). *Paulo Freire: Teaching for freedom and transformation*. Dordrecht, The Netherlands: Springer Publishing.
De Feyter, K. (2005). *Human rights: Social justice in the age of the market*. London: Zed Books.

Fukuyama, F. (1992). *The end of history and the last man.* New York: The Free Press.
Gramsci, A. (1971). *Selections from the prison notebooks of Antonio Gramsci.* London: Lawrence and Wishart.
Habermas, J. (1996). *Between facts and norms: Contributions to a discourse theory of law and democracy,* studies in contemporary German social thought. Cambridge, MA: MIT Press.
Harvey, D. (2005). *A brief history of Neo-liberalism.* Oxford, UK: Oxford University Press.
Hill, D. (2004). Educational perversion and global neo-liberalism: A Marxist critique. *Cultural Logic: An Electronic Journal of Marxist Theory and Practice, 7.* Retrieved February 23, 2011, from eserver.org/clogic/2004/2004.html
Hyslop-Margison, E. J., & Sears, A. (2008). The Neo-liberal Assault on Democratic Learning. *University College of the Fraser Valley Research Review, 2*(1), 28–38.
Illich, I. (1971). *Deschooling society.* New York: Harper & Row.
Kirton, J. (2005, March). *From G7 to G20: Capacity, Leadership and Normative Diffusion in Global Financial Governance.* A paper prepared for a panel on "Expanding Capacity and Leadership in Global Financial Governance: From G7 to G20". International Studies Association Annual Convention, Hawaii, United States.
Knight Abowitz, K. (2002). Heteroglossia and Philosophers of Education *Educational Theory, 52*(3), 291–302.
MacKinnon, W. (2007). Tessling, Brown, and A.M.: Towards a Principled Approach to Section 8. *Alberta Law Review, 45*(1), 79–116.
Marin, A. (2010). *Caught in the Act.* Investigation into The Ministry of Community Safety and Correctional Services conduct in relation to Ontario Regulation 233/10 under the Public Works Protection Act. Toronto: Office of the Ombudsman. Retrieved January 10, 2011, from www.ombudsman.on.ca/media/157555/g20final1-en.pdf
Robbins, C. (2008). Emergency! Or How to Learn to Live with Neoliberal Globalization? *Policy Futures in Education, 6*(3), 331–350.
Springer, S. (2010). Neoliberalism and geography: Expansions, variegations, formations. *Geography Compass 4*(8), 1025–1038.
Supreme Court of Canada. (2008). *Her Majesty the Queen vs. A. M.* (1 S.C.R. 569, 2008 SCC 19). Ottawa, ON: Author.

Emery Hyslop-Margison
University of New Brunswick,

Josephine l. Savarese
St. Thomas University

GAYSU R. ARVIND

DELIBERATIVE DEMOCRACY, PEOPLE'S AGENCY AND EDUCATION

A Case of Dialogic Transformation of a School System

Abstract: This chapter briefly looks into the ways of invigorating democracy by constructing deliberative decision-making spaces in access to school and its curricular and governance practices. The theoretical framework is largely informed by works of Amartya Sen on democracy and social justice, Archon Fung on empowered participatory governance (EPG), the Brazilian experience of the Citizen School Project, and the structural provisions made in the Indian Constitution for local governance. Drawing on case studies of bottom-up approaches to strengthen school functioning, the chapter examines an array of innovative forms of people-based participatory governance practices that emerged in diverse settings to make the state more responsive and accountable for the education of marginalized children in the traditionally unequal Indian society. These practices also enabled a fuller realization of peoples' rights, as even citizens drawn from the lowest strata of the society experienced empowerment by influencing larger state institutions and policies that affect schooling and life options of their children. These people-centric efforts gain further significance as they emerged against the backdrop of enduring inequalities and asymmetries embedded in the mainstream social and educational system. The article ends on a cautionary note, warning that in the absence of an enabling context, in existing neo-liberal times the emerging practices of school transformation and social justice run a risk of either withering away, or degenerating into piecemeal measures for crisis intervention, leaving neither a legacy of empowerment nor a hint of systemic change.

THE PRESCRIPT

The 1950 Constitution of Indiaaimed for free and compulsory education for all children until they complete the age of 14 years and this national commitment was to be realized through a more egalitarian, inclusive and equitable public education system. Yet, the goal to universalize elementary education (UEE) continues to be elusive, both in qualitative and quantitative terms, in spite of much-publicized education reform programs of the 1990s. According to the Annual Status of Education Reports (ASER) of 2006 and 2007, an independent survey conducted by Pratham (2007), nearly 14 million children are out of school, 52% to 55% of these out-of-school children are girls, and most children leave government primary schools without gaining basic skills of reading, writing and arithmetic. The broad contours of this pattern continue to be reiterated in more recent annual ASER reports.

It is not difficult to discern the identity of these children: They are children of communities that are at the bottom of the socio-economic ladder, largely located in rural or poor urban tracts. The 2003–2004 Educational Statistics (Government of India, 2006) reveal that non-enrolment and discontinuation of education gets more pronounced by social group and location. Rural girls belonging to disadvantaged groups like Scheduled Castes or *Dalits*[1] and Scheduled Tribes or *Adivasis* are the worst off with a staggering 50% and 56% respectively having dropped out. Male-female differences are highest among the poorest quintiles of our population in both rural and urban areas. The situation with respect to the spread of education among Muslims is also quite disappointing. Social and Rural Research Institute (SSRI) Surveyestimates that 9.97% of Muslim children are out-of-school and this figure climbs to 12.03% in rural contexts, making it the highest among all social groups. Thus Dalits ('untouchable' castes), Adivasis (tribal groups) and Muslims (religious minorities) represent the poorest and most disadvantaged section of the Indian society, with social and spatial identity as the central axis of their exclusion (Kabeer, 2006).

Govinda (2008) delineates three major levels at which exclusion from school occurs: non-availability of school is the first level; dropping out at initial years of schooling without gaining basic literacy and numeracy skills is the second level; and the acquisition of basic competencies but with an inability to transit from a lower primary to an upper primary stage constitutes the third level of exclusion. Other silent forms of exclusion include: underinvestment in resources for elementary education, the socially reproductive nature of educational provisions, discriminatory school practices, disjuncture between the socio-cultural ethos of home and school, and institutional arrangements that lack accountability and responsiveness (Jeffery, 2005). Expanding and deepening community participation in the state's actions appears to be a promising strategy to shore up this institutional deficit. Part of the challenge is to move away from a centralized, bureaucratic mode of governance to a more inclusive, participatory form of governance through which the traditionally excluded social groups gain a sense of agency by articulating their voice in decision-making practices that shape the school and life options of their children.

At this juncture, the chapter[2] intervenes in three ways. First, it lays down a framework of participatory governance for reconfiguring the relationship between state and people in a manner whereby ordinary people, the most subordinated, can experience empowerment by effectively participating in and influencing institutional arrangements affecting their life options. The framework is largely informed by works of Amartya Sen on democracy and social justice, Archon Fung (2004) on empowered participatory governance (EPG), the Brazilian experience of the Citizen School Project, and the structural provisions made in the Indian Constitution for self- governance. Second, it seeks the realization of this framework in the context of real educational settings. The transformative potential of education is seen as linked to the imperatives of critical democracy, a way to experience empowerment for the vast majority in a socially unequal society. The emerging meta-theoretical perspective, evolving from integrating critical strands in education and polity discourses provides a rich theoretical backdrop for understanding the relationship between democracy and school governance practices. Third, the chapter claims the possibility of realizing social and educational changes under a system of governance in which particularism rather than universalism is a guiding factor in providing education.

LOCAL DEMOCRACY, EGALITARIAN DIALOGUE AND LEARNING COMMUNITIES:

Evolving a Theoretical Framework

It is a well-established fact that the social and institutional practices frame and reproduce systemic inequalities in power relationships based on gender, class, caste and other location characteristics. Democracy is then envisioned as a way of organizing a state so as to evolve a more egalitarian social formation that redresses the compounded forms of social, political and economic inequities and exclusionary processes emanating from it. However, persistence of inequities, in spite of a democratic form of governance being in place, has led social scientists to critically examine the very conceptualization, construction and quality of realization of 'conventional' democracies and their intended transformative potential.

The ballot-centric form of democracy is largely entrapped in the state's rigid institutional structures and practices that are falsely premised on the essentialist assumption about the universal nature of human beings and their societal contexts. In this centralized framework, there is no space for the plurality of perspectives, differentiated identities, and irregularities that constitute a nation. Consequently, it fails to meaningfully realize the espoused emancipatory agenda of liberating people from social circumstances that dispossess and marginalize them (Gaventa, 2006).

In the Indian context, for democracy to be an empowering experience, it should be located at the grassroots level. For Jayal, Prakash, and Sharma (2006) local democracy is a way of enabling people to genuinely participate in and influence policies that affect their life options. It is premised on the belief that quality of public life will be substantively transformed only when people "collectively debate and deliberate on issues of common concern, and are provided with decision-making powers to give effect to their shared concerns". This is a much deeper and more direct form of democracy than the rather minimal conception of it as implied in the idea of elections (Jayal et al., 2006, pp. 2–3). The underlying vision is that the innate problem-solving capacity residing in common people can be nurtured and distilled through a localized network of socially connected communities, which collectively attempt to achieve their 'common emancipation' by inventing indigenized solutions to their problems.

In a socially stratified and culturally diversified Indian society, it becomes imperative that a more localized, inclusive and participatory form of democracy is practiced for building critical consciousness and a sense of empowerment in the historically marginalized people. Tracing the roots of democracy in distant Indian history and culture, Amartya Sen points out the Emperor Ashoka in the third century BCE created a civic tradition of public reasoning and debating for accomplishing wider social collectivity and ownership in arriving at a political consensus. The right to participate in public deliberations was conferred equally on all people, including women and slaves (Sen, 2005, pp. 13–16). Rightfully apportioning the space among women, dalits, tribal and other socially disadvantaged social groups in *Panchayats*, the constitutionally[3] mandated local structures of self-governance, is then a way to take forward the historically held values of self-governance and social justice. The *Gram Sabha* or the Village Assembly, comprising all citizens eligible to vote, is the base of the local democratic structure and the ultimate forum of accountability.

The Indian project of participatory democracy, as obtained through the self-governance practices, gets somewhat displaced by the World Bank and the IMF directed discourse on decentralization. The terms local governance and decentralization are often used interchangeably in recent academic writings. However, they are not coterminous. Jayal et al., (2006) also note that there is "more to local governance than a focus on decentralization alone allows us to apprehend" (p. 1). In the context of India, the notion of 'localism' as implied in the concept of self-governance is not ideologically congruent with role and scope of 'local' as invoked in the neo-liberal developmental discourse. One is more people-based while the other is statist. In the language of globalization, 'local' is primarily conjectured up to signify a way of deregulating and decentralizing state bureaucracy by devolving responsibility to local, lower tiers of the administrative set-up. This view is minimalist in its conception and design and is generally enacted by the state through legal decrees for gaining institutional efficiency.

Localism as embodied in the self-governance structures signifies a way of nurturing and strengthening the self-steering ability inhered in the masses to seek optimal solutions through collective action. From this ideological perspective, the grassroots movements initiated by peasants, tribal groups, dalits and women are instances of the collective transformative capacities of people to challenge the existing social order and state practices for claiming their rights and basis of existence. The ongoing environmental movement against the construction of *Sardar Sarovar* dam in the Narmada Valley is a rural people's struggle for non-compliance to a centralized model of development planning that fails to take into account concerns and interests of local people. Through such social movements, rural people have begun to articulate their demand for space and voice in government's decision-making practices. Kothari regards this relationship between state and society as a "non-party political process" (as cited in Fuchs & Linkenbach, 2003, pp. 551–552).

Sheth and Nandy are also of the view that a more empowering form of democracy can be constructed by spearheading a collective struggle against society's blind subservience to the state, and installing "institutional alternatives that may deepen democracy"as a Gandhian way of indigenizing social transformation not as "an apolitical activity, but a *lived* political agenda for democratizing all forms of organizations and consciousness in the society" (Sheth & Nandy, 1996, as cited in Bhattacharya, 2001, p. 674, emphasis mine).

Amartya Sen's work on 'Social Choice Theory' holds that for realizing social justice in a sizeable and stratified society, people, especially the disadvantaged should be regarded as situated agents, and scope of their inclusion and participation in the state's decision-making governance structures should be enhanced. Critically reflecting on his work, Fukuda-Parr (2006) holds that for Sen, people are not simply beneficiaries of economic and social progress in a society, but are active agents of social change. Sen's idea of agency in human development is about demanding rights in decision-making practices so that people can live in freedom and dignity, with greater collective agency, participation and autonomy. The collective action is an important force that can pressure changes in policies and bring about transformative change. Democratic governance through institutional practices that expand the participation, power and voice of people, and ensure the accountability of decision-makers, is an important way for gaining empowerment. These collective choices can then be realized through "a process of forming associations, making alliances, and generating public debates" (Fukuda-Parr, 2006, p. 337).

"Social Choice Theory is the study of systems and institutions for making collective choices, choices that affect a group of people". [NOTE: quote from where?] Such groups of people are generally structured by gender, class and other forms of social hierarchies. From this perspective, the ultimate success of a disadvantaged group then hinges critically on the institutional framework available for equally participating in and exercising power for advancing their welfare and for resolving interests conflicting with the other dominant societal traditions. This framework is necessary for reconciling with the existing "diversity of preferences, concerns, interests, and predicaments of the different individuals *within* the society" (Sen, 2006, p. 370, emphasis original). At the level of the state, this means that institutional ways should enhance people's choices and not serve as instruments of arbitrary domination.

Empowered Participatory Governance (EPG) is one such way "in which ordinary people can effectively participate in and influence policies which affect their lives… They are participatory because they rely upon the participation and capacities of ordinary people, deliberative because they institute reason-based decision making, and empowered since they attempt to tie action to discussion" (Fung & Wright, 2003, p. 5). EPG can be realized by reconfiguring the space between people and formal state structures through creating intermediaries that have the potential to actualize people's participation in decision-making practices. These intermediaries can emerge in the form of public forums or social associations, the bottom-up structures that are designed to enable local people to marshal their ingenious understanding and resources to respond to local exigencies such as a failing school, rather than relying on the uniform solution prescribed by a centralized top-down system. Equality of participation, informed deliberations and actualizing change through a concerted action are the defining principles of these forums. Parent-teacher associations, village education committees, school development committees, and mothers' groups are some of the more productive forms of associations for realizing the value of EPG. For Fung, these associations construct a more dynamic form of democracy in practice than the static configuration of conventional political representation and bureaucratic administration (Fung, 2003, p. 340).

Creating spaces for empowered participatory governance then approximates to the Habermasian notion of the 'public sphere'. This public sphere is a pluralist civic space constructed away from the state, in and out of civil society. It is the space in which people deliberate about common issues and concerns; it is a site of production and circulation of discourse that can, in principle, be critical of the state. The public sphere is not absorbed into the state, but addresses the state and the "sorts of public issues on which state policy might bear" (Pinto, 2006, p. 206). The 'public sphere' can then be regarded as a countervailing force to the state's 'official space' that according to Fine (1997) rests on, in fact is constituted by a number of significant exclusions (p. 461). In the context of government schools, these exclusions have been embodied by parents, communities and the larger public interest.

A critical perspective of education provides a more inclusive philosophical vision by constructing governance alternatives in terms of needs and experiences of specific social groups, the ones whose contexts and voices have traditionally been excluded from the mainstream theorizing and practices. The aim is to radicalize education as a transformative process that has potential to evolve a more equal and just social order. The more egalitarian and participatory spaces can be created within the education system for realizing the shared vision for real empowerment, meaningful social change and equality. It is largely a dialogical process as it is characterized by collective participation and acceptance of interchangeability and mutuality in the roles of ordinary people and the state.

The emerging meta-perspective further gains ground as, in the neo-liberal times, the impact of institutional failure is likely to be experienced most severely by poor people since they lack meaningful alternatives. For instance, purchasing good quality private education is well beyond their meagre economic and cultural capital. In such a scenario, organizing people into reflective bodies to harness their social capital seems to be a positive way of contesting the inertia of the state. Schools, as public spheres, provide the contexts in which shared visions, textured solidarity, and ongoing struggles can be realized to re-experience democracy.

The 'Citizen School', in Porto Alegre, Brazil, is perhaps one of the best examples where the intellectual and creative potentiality of ordinary people living in *favelas* (shantytowns) was harnessed in a concerted fashion to influence administrative, curricular and organizational practices that affect schooling and life options of their children (Apple & Au, 2009; Gandin, 2010). The Citizen School signifies the importance of a more inclusive and participatory framework of democratization, of access to schools, knowledge and governance as a robust way of re-constructing democracy as a 'lived' experience, one that encourages the possibility of practicing democracy on a continuing basis. The people experienced empowerment by raising concerns, holding the state accountable, setting agendas, building social capital and evolving indigenous solutions. These people-centric efforts further gain significance as they emerge against the backdrop of enduring inequalities and asymmetries embedded in the mainstream educational and social system. Drawing on the Brazilian project of transforming school into a learning community, Flecha (2010) observes that social transformation could be realized by constructing democratic spaces for egalitarian dialogue among all the concerned stakeholders. The dialogue emerged as an effective way of overcoming school failure and improving learning performance by bringing in the experiential knowledge of the community on educational issues (Flecha, 2010, p. 344).

In India, Hoshangabad Science Teaching Programme (HSTP), Kerala Shastra Sahitya Parishad (KSSP), Bihar Education Project and Lok Juumbish (LJ), are largely non-governmental projects that stand out as 'people's collective' initiatives to revitalize the education system by harnessing the potential of the community to make schools more participatory and responsive and, in the process, the community's own development in terms of its quality of life also gets advanced. These projects drew upon the community's ingenious knowledge and resources to evolve curricular and pedagogic practices organically linked to children's socio-cultural context. By involving community in the process of school mapping and micro planning, the people's collective was initiated into the 'democratic culture' of decision-making and self-determination. The guiding assumption was that capabilities for self-management among the community members would evolve through lived practice rather than prescription. Thus, these projects demonstrated the possibility of building a system of local governance for primary education from below – the grassroots level. Community empowerment is not, then, a notional idea. Rather, it aims at building social synergy and cohesion by drawing all stakeholders into a process of informed decision-making that is tied to an action. *Sarva Shiksha Abhiyan* (SSA)[4], the erstwhile District Primary Education Programme (DPEP) is a nation-wide state interventionist programme that is fashioned to reform the school system by involving a community as an equal partner in decision-making practices.

A marked increase in enrolment, retention, learner achievement, gender parity, social equity and other educational and social gains as realized through these participatory practices are viewed with skepticism by a many educational theorists. Ramachandran and Saihjee (2006) are of the view that in spite of the constitutional provisos, the dominant social groups continue to hold sway in everyday management of the local government school[5]. Govinda and Diwan (2003) also question the sustainability of these short-term, project-based efforts in bringing about enduring systemic changes in the traditionally governed mainstream system. However, discernable positive shifts in bureaucratic mindsets and the emergence of participatory spaces in the state's structures also point to the potential of these initiatives as harbingers of change processes to transform the existing system of school governance (Govinda & Diwan, 2003, p. 27).

G.R. ARVIND

THE DIALOGIC TRANSFORMATION OF SCHOOL SYSTEM

In this article, three projects of community involvement[6] are discussed: Rundko (rural context); *Rana Basti*, Jaipur City; and Janathanagar, Hyderabad City (urban context). Each case reflects the hard work of NGOs, social activists, parents, the community, teachers, and practitioners for strengthening people's presence inside the school and around concerns of education. Village education committees, parent-teacher associations, school management and betterment committees, mothers' groups, school-basti committees and other community-based organizations are a few instances that afford a rural community the context to experience empowerment by participating in activities that support schools, generally hierarchically governed institutions. However, as these artifactual instances were purposively selected to look for the likely possibility of social and educational gains stemming from the project initiative, the emerging conclusions are to be held with caution. As substantiated below, education created a context for realizing 'collective empowerment' spreading across a diversified network of stakeholders.

The Government Primary School, Village Rundko, Block Deeg

Rundko is a remote habitation in Deeg block of Bharatpur district in Rajasthan. It is largely inhabited by Meo-Muslim. Meo-Muslims are an ethnically unique tribal community that practices both Hindu and Islamic customs, traditions and beliefs. After embracing Islam in the 14th century AD, the community retained its distinctive Hindu heritage and lineage. Once a warrior tribe, they now are marginal farmers with nominal land holdings. Over the years, closely knit Meos became socially alienated from the larger, mainstream society that itself is marked by distinct caste, religious and ethnic fault lines. The social alienation and economic deprivation[7] has led to an abysmally low literacy rate in Meo-Muslims, less than 10% of whom can barely read and write.

A mismatch between historically held religious traditions of Meo-Muslims and the formal school's ways of organizing curricular experiences was pushing up the non-enrollment rate, especially in Meo girls to an alarming level. According to official estimates, it is less than 1% in Mewat region. The educational character of school – especially singing, dancing and pictorial representation of certain phenomenon – was perceived as anti-Islamic. The influential local clergy advocated *din-ki-taleem*, the study of religion as the only form of education that was permissible for girls. Afsana, a 14-year-old never-enrolled girl shared with me that *Maulvi*, the local clergy, advised her, "*don't go to school, say your prayers and learn Urdu for reading Quran*". Her parents complied with *Maulvi*'s dictate. The non-availability of an all-girl school and women teachers further exacerbated the state of educational deprivation.

Both, the community and the school were encased in their own self-constructed framework of reference and thus failed to see each other's perspective. The local community-based organization (CBO) intervened to break the deadlock. It dialogued with local religious leaders and the Muslim intelligentsia on one hand; on the other, it appealed to official machinery to take a more informed view on the issue.

Consequently, a 'Stakeholder Forum' was created for convergence of the state officials, PRIs, government teachers, parents, the community, local religious leaders and social activists. Through this monthly platform, all the key stakeholders exchange information, break barriers, understand and appreciate each other's views on school practices and evolve informed choices through deliberative processes. Muslim women were also envisioned as critical stakeholders in enabling girl child education.

I was the participant observer in one such 'stakeholder forum' meeting that happened during the field visit. A series of issues were examined: data of select schools was analysed in terms of enrolment, retention and quality of educational outcomes; the framework of a forthcoming teacher training program was presented; monthly plans of action were finalized; and the dynamics of cultural resistance to education in some 'hard to reach' habitations were discussed. Khushiram, the Block Resource Centre Facilitator (BRCF) concedes that, *"educational structures and practices are not always supportive of desirable educational outcomes. The system should have in-built flexibility to be responsive to varying contextual needs and aspirations"*.

Staggering the government school timing to enable children to attend religious education in local Madarsa, making classroom practices more culturally relevant and appointing female teachers were some of the measures that were initiated to bring the children back into the fold of education. The Meos' rich oral history and traditions were integrated in school's pedagogic discourse. A meaningful interface between religious and formal school education was created wherein both systems of education were seen as more complementary than adversary to each other. As a result, an appreciable gain in student enrolment and retention, especially among girls in the government school of Rundko was realized. According to school records, about 56% of girls from 6 to 10 years of age and 72% of boys of the same age group are currently enrolled. It is a healthy gain considering that resistance to girls' education is stubbornly ingrained in the community's social fabric. The change would not have been possible without the support of Maulana Mir Quasim of Meel ka Madarsa, a respected religious figure in Deeg.

Sahib Singh, the community coordinator reminiscences that gaining an entry into a closed community and realizing change in a traditionally held mindset was a daunting task. Keeping in view the contextual reality, a multi-pronged strategy evolved. At one level, women were mobilized around the issue of the reproductive health of pregnant and lactating mother and child; and on the other level, men were organized into self-help groups for undertaking vocational training. With such practices, trust of the community was won and an enabling context was created for building the consensus on schooling of children (especially that of the girl child) in changing times. Motivated Meo youths, progressive clergy and educated Muslim women were taken on board for realizing a wider ownership of the process. *"It is painfully a slow process; a wrong move can derail all the efforts that have gone in it till now"*.

A School visit affirmed the gains of education. A group of 20 young girls were playing 'Pattu', a game for promoting numeracy skills. A huge flower petal containing various number combinations was drawn on the floor. The teacher was randomly announcing numbers, and a girl child had to identify the correct answer and hop onto the petal containing that specific number. Observing those girls singing, jumping and talking confidently was indeed evidence of the freedom of expression they were enjoying. The girls told us with great pride that they commuted by bicycles and were keen on pursuing higher studies, even if they had to travel far. Little Saira can't say how old she is, but clearly articulates, "*I want to grow up to be like you, a teacher*". They had begun to envision career options in their limited lived realities. Nagma, mother of Saira, musingly says that her familial dynamics have changed since the day all four of her children started going to school. Abdul, her functionally literate husband, comes back early to oversee the children's studies.

The *Rundko* case raises the possibility of resolving conflicting perspectives in a reasoned way. In a culturally diversified society, the interests and concerns of the indigenous ethnic groups are likely to be either overlooked or subsumed in the state's uniform practices. From the perspective of Social Choice Theory, collective decision-making emerging from a process of democratic deliberations is a more constructive alternative to any generalized prescription. Sen (1999) characterizes this value of democracy as, "the practice of democracy gives the citizens an opportunity to learn from each other, and to re-examine their own values and priorities, along with those of others,… guaranteeing of open discussion, debate, criticism and dissent are central to the process of generating informed and reflected choices" (p. 3). Thus, both the state agencies and communities had to learn together how to construct new mechanisms more responsive to the needs, aspirations and cultural ways of the community.

The Government Primary School, Rana Basti, Jaipur City

With shrinking of agrarian economy and frequent crop failure, Jaipur City, the state capital of Rajasthan, is experiencing an unprecedented influx of migrants who are descending on the state capital in search of better livelihood opportunities and life options. In absence of well-intended social welfare policies, the incoming mass of the dispossessed people settles down on any available vacant stretch of state land. Their settlements are built without valid permission, without infrastructure, and without any modicum of planning. From the state's perspective, these migrants are illegal inhabitants and hence cannot claim the basic entitlements that are being conferred by the state on its people. Consequently, there are no specific policy directives or provisions to address the schooling needs of the children dwelling on the encroached state land. This official posturing contravenes the constitutional mandate that any child is entitled to education irrespective of spatial location.

Rana Basti slum is an instance of one such unauthorized slum settlement. Against this exclusionary backdrop, the people organized themselves into a slum-level association – 'the Basti Committee' – and resolved that school is the basic right of children and children should not be denied education on account of their spatial location. The 'Basti Committee' presented an application to the Principal Secretary,

School Education and Commissioner, Jaipur Development Authority, for constructing a temporary structure for a government school in their Kacchi Basti, an informal slum settlement. The local municipality granted some *de facto* rights to the residents by allotting land for constructing a makeshift school and appointing a government teacher to run the school. In the foundation-laying ceremony of the primary school, also attended by the author, the local political representative, state functionaries, government teachers, parents, local social activists and community members converged on a single platform to mark the occasion.

With the setting up of a government school, a state institution on an unauthorized tract of public land, a heightened sense of empowerment was visible in the community that until now had perceived itself merely as an 'electorate mass'. The community experienced a shift from the 'representative democracy' as exercised through voting as a periodic elector to the 'participatory democracy' where the system took into account the local people's needs and aspirations as the basis for action. In such an expanded framework of collaborative partnership that cuts across various levels of the power structure, there is a 'wider ownership' of the school and its practices. This process of setting up a school has being initiated in some 324 slums in Jaipur City.

As of now, the government school is functioning from a temporary makeshift structure. The teacher has started the process of enrolling and orienting children to the basic schooling competencies. The case of Rana Basti symbolizes a struggle to seek identity, social justice and equitable entitlement by those excluded from the state's misplaced development policies. In the process, the assumptions perpetuated by the dominant development discourse – that subalterns are neither cognitively able to articulate their own world view nor validly interpret their own oppression – also gets dismantled. Thus, the school emerged as a primary site for deepening the meaning of democracy as an ongoing struggle by people collectively, for dealing with the other government agencies concerned with health, food, alternative housing and livelihood security.

Transformation in Rana Basti could be realized because of a visible shift in the mindset of policy planners, bureaucracy and state officials. The rigid government system is 'opening-up' to give space to local, community-based initiatives. It clearly emerged in a discussion with Akhil Arora, Director, SSA, Rajasthan Council of Elementary Education. He opined that "*till now the social disadvantage image was limited to the rural sector; urban marginalized never figured prominently in the state's planning exercises...the government has now realized that rather than prescribing a universalistic strategy, it will be more meaningful to partner with local people to strengthen the school system*".

The Government High School, Janathanagar, Hyderabad City

In large urban areas, especially in the old industrial cities like Hyderabad, the state capital of Andhra Pradesh, spatial dispossession as concentrated in tracts of slums and squatter settlements is the most visible and evident form of social exclusion[8]. For a slum-based community, material impoverishment, social dislocation, and exclusion from society's strategic resources – in particular the school – is an inscribed way of life. The landless and marginal farmers, local artisans, weavers, potters, and other dispossessed groups who have been unwittingly subsumed in the industrial economic order constitute the social fabric of a typical urban slum.

An education survey was conducted by the state government in 2006-2007 in select child-labour intensive slums or Basti in Balanagar Mandal of the Hyderabad City. The survey found that many slums lacked basic schooling facilities, while others were served by an under-resourced school system that was largely dysfunctional in terms of quality of schooling and other stimulating experiences, teachers' pre-constructed stereotypic beliefs about the academic abilities of these children, and a limited horizon of realizable social and occupational mobility as seen by parents and children. Madhusudan, Additional Project Coordinator (ACP) of the State Education Program further informed us that, *"Though enrolment is over 95%, but only 27% of children in class five can read and write. The major challenge is to improve quality of schooling experiences so as to retain children and raise level of their academic competencies"*. He visualized an active civic society support in realizing education targets and educational outcomes.

At every point, both inside and outside the formal education system, there are social forces that systematically create a context for children to disengage from school and to get appropriated into the dynamics of an informal labour economy. Rolling of beedis (a local cigarette), making incense sticks, manually moulding iron stripes into safety pins, working in liquor shops, auto repair workstations, bootlegging and domestic helpers are some of the occupational destinations of school drop-out children. Children are highly vulnerable to physical and mental health hazards.

The civil society was an active partner in implementing and owning the state's educational outcomes. With support from a local NGO, 'The School Development Committee' (SDC) was constituted as a forum for multiple stakeholders – children, parents, families, communities, local social and political activists, teachers and government officials – to converge on a common platform to engage in a continuous process of collective reflection, decision-making and evolving action to revive a failing neighbourhood school. For an enduring change to occur, all of them were visualized to be strategically equal partners in the process. SDC was envisioned as an innovative participatory approach for rallying people's collective around the common agenda of owning the neighbourhood schools. SDC was constituted in each of the some 44 elementary and high schools in the Balanagar Mandal by an official order.

The Government High School in Janathanagar is one such school that figured near the bottom of annual academic league tables published by the state education department. One of the major tasks of the School Development Committee of Janathanagar was to stabilize school attendance. The Community Volunteers (CVs) played a crucial role in ensuring students' regularity. Every day, after the roll call is over, they collect a list of absentee children from the headmaster, make a hurried visit to these children's homes, try to sort out their problems, if any, and then persuade the children to come to school with them. For Laxmi and Swarnalatha, the CVs attached to the school, *"sibling care, storing drinking water, seasonal illness, and the family's economic uncertainties are some of reasons for missing school"*. On the day of the field visit, the Community Volunteers were able to bring back five out of 14 absentee children.

SDC emerged as a pressure group for liberating children from their workplaces and reinstating them in school, and for influencing the larger society and local political or administrative systems. As Ramesh, an SDC Member at Janthanagar articulates, *"I used to employ children in my flour mill as it was a form of cheap labour. With the intervention of SDC, I have not only stopped the practice but feel morally responsible for education of Bala and Suresh, child labourers and his former employees"*. Ramesh got both children enrolled in the Janthanagar School and is taking care of their educational needs. He is actively campaigning against child labour as a member of School Development Committee. At the same time, SDC involved teachers actively in the social transformation process – they were encouraged and supported to improve their pedagogic practices – instead of merely holding them responsible for all the problems in education.

In a well-attended SDC meeting, I observed that over 20 members assembled in the principal's room, listened to each other, questioned, argued, and systematically worked out solutions for a range of issues such as: fixing malfunctioning flushes in toilets; requisitioning the zone education officer to release the grant for procuring text-books; deciding to retain poor performing students for an extra year in the primary school before they reach the examination-oriented senior classes; finalizing modalities for selecting para-teachers; reviewing the impact of a book reading club; and an after-school programme for improving students' literary competency. The community in Janathanagar is today positioned as the primary decision-maker concerning education. However, it has yet to cover considerable ground as the material power is still held by the central administration. Nevertheless, school reform practices in Balanagar Mandal provide a framework of collective resolve and synergy between the state administration and the civil society to resurrect a failing government school.

PROSPECTS AND DILEMMAS FOR CHANGE

This chapter examined some of the possible ways, both theoretically and practically, through which the potential of ordinary people drawn from the lowest strata of the society was harnessed in a concerted fashion to influence larger institutional practices affecting the schooling and life options of their children. The strength of these participatory efforts lie in their artifactual nature; that is, 'derived *Samudayaik Bethak*' or Community Meeting, 'Stakeholder Forum', 'Mother Group', '*School Basti Committee*' were largely the informal people-collective arrangements that evolved naturally in different ways in response to exigencies of the local situation rather than passively relying upon a top-down institutional arrangement that fails to take into account contextual needs and specificities. An additional benefit was that people who were initiated into deliberative culture through these intermediaries have started demanding that the same consultative mode be practised in formal, state bodies like village education committees, school management committees and other social or political arrangements.

The intrinsic value of these constructive efforts, though of modest scale, is inhered in their potentiality to: re-construct a school as an organic extension of a local community, the hub around which all social activities and formations get formed; hold state officials accountable to a given community; and accord an active role to the community to ensure the school's effective functioning. These concerted efforts gain significance against the backdrop of the state's traditional framework that conceptualizes school as a stand-alone, fixed, rule-bound system that is alienated from the rural community's social realities, where the school is managed by controlling teachers through an inspectorial supervisory system and the community's participation is limited to a 'tokenist' nomination in largely defunct state bodies.

The concluding section draws out a web of possibilities that emerged during the study for reforming school and social practices. These possibilities assume an added significance as in neo-liberal times, the Indian State is struggling to meaningfully resolve dilemmas such as the choice between centralization and decentralization, institutional and local context of education, regulatory and participatory forms of school governance, bureaucratic structure and democratic culture, and singular and collectively evolved vision. It is a challenge as selecting or deselecting a 'choice' can further marginalize or empower the ordinary people, specifically the most subordinated.

DIALOGICAL RELATIONSHIP BETWEEN STATE AND PEOPLE

The governance of education is largely envisioned as a state held welfare activity. The Indian state is the central actor in any claim to the right to education: It is the guarantor, the policy framer and the prime implementer. However, the state's conventionally assumed role is changing in response to emerging economic and political compulsions. In neo-liberal statecraft,[9] decentralization is widely promoted as a major instrument for deregulating and disaggregating a state's functioning by opening up the space for multiple other actors, primarily the market, the state's own 'delivery agency' model of public education and the others to intervene. Krishna Kumar (2008) cautions that a neo-liberal perspective is often whipped in the education discourse to cover up the inefficiency of the Indian State in providing an equitable quality of education to all children. He argues that an instrumentalist notion of the state "poses a grave risk for the role of education in harnessing the intellectual and creative potential of society" (p. 10). The author portends that in a traditionally unequal, rural and sizable society like India, the space vacated by the state does not necessarily translate into genuine people participation. Rather, in absence of a strong alliance between state and rural community, chances of it being usurped by market forces are amplified. From this viewpoint, a more nuanced theory of the state is needed than is usually available from the liberal state-versus-market debate.

In order to fulfill its constitutional mandate of providing free and compulsory education to all children until they attain the age of 14 years, the Indian State needs to be positioned in a way that it is strong (literally speaking) enough to offset the impact of supranational forces on the one hand, while on the other, it strives to evolve a framework of governance in which all stakeholders feel sufficiently empowered as their concerns and interests are systemically addressed. To realize the intended transformative potential of education, it is then imperative that the state-society relationship should be reconfigured in a manner where the state continues to be the major provider of an equitable quality of education to all children, builds a democratic culture of public participation and deliberation in education, provides some coordination in the face of externalities across social locations, and organizes the field of possibilities for maximal accrual of social and educational gains. The task of everyday conduct and governance is devolved to people for strengthening a local school's functioning. It is envisioned that synergy between a strong state (not necessarily decentred) and an empowered community would have the potential to move towards universalizing elementary education, to ensure equitable distribution of institutional resources across different strata of the society, and to keep the market forces at bay.

These findings also gain significance as a dysfunctional school is likely to impact poor people with greater force as they lack meaningful alternatives. With their meagre economic and cultural capital, the choice of purchasing private schooling does not exist. With privatization of education getting an active push in policy discourse, in the context of the present study constituting vibrant public culture within the state's schooling system emerged as a viable countervailing strategy. An interlinked observation is that if governance space is reconfigured from people's perspective, then community emerges as a decisive force by virtue of the self-steering ability inhered in it. The emerging reflective community is not a residual, an adjunct to state or market as is being assumed by many political theorists.

Making the Institutional Context of Education more Inclusive and Participatory

The institutional context determines, to a lesser or greater extent, a group's or an individual's capacity to make informed choice, and then to transform those choices into desired actions and outcomes. There is a burgeoning literature to support the observation that compliance to a regimental culture of bureaucratic arrangements or to a dominant social ideology does not enhance school functioning. Rather, it stifles the inherent ability of teachers, parents, communities and other social actors to innovate in challenging conditions.

The effective schools in the present study were those that either evolved active public spaces or energized the existing institutional and social forms by infusing them with a collegial culture of democratic decision-making. These concerted efforts ranged from creating or invigorating deliberative forums at the level of community, local government institutions, or state. At the most inclusive end of the spectrum, people were able to influence the decision to set up a school in *Rana Basti*, and make pedagogical practices more contextually relevant in *Rundkho*.

These participatory efforts set into motion a chain of *change* processes, albeit slowly: Collegial and deliberative culture was established in school to improve its functioning; a more inclusive community-school forum created an avenue for strengthening social building; an enabling familial context was created for girl children to attend school; and state machinery became more responsive and accountable. These change processes were realized by instilling a habit of deliberative decision-making tied to action among those common people who have been hitherto tuned to a system of top-down decision-making. In this dynamic process, a more critical consciousness and sense of agency was gained by women, landless labourers, dalits and other social groups that are often locked into a cultural framework in which they perceive their disempowerment to be a 'naturalized' and just social act. With the emergence of these empowered social identities, the state and society's mental space in constructing and reproducing educational and social inequalities also get desilted.

To conclude, mere constitutional promulgation does not necessarily translate into genuine community empowerment as envisioned by the 73rd and 74th Amendments. A set of enabling conditions have to be created for institutionalising the practices of self-governance; otherwise, common people will flounder due to lack of capacity, knowledge, or internal conflict. The holding assumption is that capabilities for self-management among the community members evolve through practice rather than prescription. This belief concurs with SSA's perspective that community ownership is vital to ensure accountability and needs to be cultivated by assigning responsibilities in grassroots level initiatives.

Building a Wider Ownership of the School

The constitutional mandate of the independent India envisioned education as a vehicle for personal progress and empowerment on one hand, and as a site for seeking social equity and justice on the other. However, exclusionary tactics of the bureaucracy stifled the realization of any such intended transformative possibility of education by rejecting or undervaluing the vision and voices of women, landless labourers, marginal farmers, tribal, dalits, and other social groups – historically the most subordinated. The centrally imposed vision, singular voice and paternalistic culture, all an integral part of the administrative machinery, countermanded any process, whatsoever of changing and improving school. With the recent constitutional amendments and policy initiatives, a space has been created for building a collective vision and a wider ownership for reforming the school governance practices. The challenge lies in ultimately choosing between enhancing genuine empowerment and solidifying administrative control.

In the context of present study, active civic engagement, collaborative working relationships, joint problem-solving capacity, shared decision-making and interpersonal trust emerged as the core values for supporting the school governance practices. These efforts then tend to entail Putnam's notion of social capital: the capital that is embodied in a trusted and shared relationship among persons in any social network, social organization or structure that enables its members to leverage a far wider range of resources than are available to a stand-alone member in a community (Putnam, 2000). An effective marshalling of the community's social capital has led to enhanced teacher commitment, reduced probability of dropping out of the school, higher learner achievement, and better utilization of school facilities.

Invigorating Democracy in Neo-liberal Times

The study also affirms the importance of a more inclusive and participatory mode of school governance as a robust way of reconstructing democracy as a 'lived' experience, one that embodies the possibility of practicing democracy on a continuing basis. As Giroux (1997)espouses that "a radical pedagogy and transformative democratic politics must go hand in hand in evolving a vision of community developed around a shared conception of social justice, rights, and entitlement. By doing this, we can rethink and re-experience democracy as a struggle over values, practices, social relations, and subject positions that enlarge the terrain of human capacities and possibilities as a basis for compassionate social order" (p. 128). The present study signifies that in a socially stratified society, education can act as a potential site to realize democracy as an ongoing struggle by cultivating identities that seek more equitable school experiences and life options, that would eventually construct a more equal social order. Thus, school created a context to develop the unrealized capacities residing in human agency to challenge and transform existing social and political forms, rather than meekly adapting to them. It affirms Sen's (2000, 2006) perspective that as democratization changes embedded institutions, it changes the bases of society: New understandings of social reality emerge, self-definitions are changed, and institutional practices are modified.

CONCLUDING REMARKS

The data collated from disparate rural and urban sources provide a new social imaginary for all education planners and practitioners, a way of progressive transformation of schools along with a realization of social justice in the traditionally unequal Indian society. In an intrinsically participatory framework of school governance, the people experience empowerment by raising concerns, holding the state accountable, setting agendas, building social capital and evolving indigenous solutions. These people-centric efforts further gain significance as they emerged against the backdrop of enduring inequalities and asymmetries embedded in the mainstream educational and social system. However, in the absence of a supporting context, these school renewal practices run a risk of either withering away, or, degenerating into piecemeal measures for crisis intervention, leaving neither a legacy of empowerment nor a hint of systemic change.

For sustaining and scaling-up these micro-level practices in the mainstream framework, a two-pronged strategy is suggested:

- One, to further consolidate and expand the participatory base, so as to have a 'wider ownership' of the school in terms of its functioning; to build the capacity of the local community in terms of knowledge of the rights, roles and responsibilities in the changing scenario; to strengthen the practice of collective decision-making; and to facilitate the emergence of a more inclusive and representative leadership at the grassroots level that supports a culture of accountability and transparency.
- Two, the administrative machinery should be encouraged to engage with the local community and the state should be further influenced to adopt more flexible structures that have an in-built space for community participation, joint planning and accountability in managing schools.

NOTES

1. In terms of social status, the Indian population can be grouped into four categories: Scheduled Castes (SC) or Dalits, Scheduled Tribes (ST) or Adivasis, Other Backward Classes (OBC), and Others. The generic term 'Dalit', originally meaning 'broken, ground down', has been taken as a summary term for those groups otherwise designated as 'Untouchables', 'Harijans' or, more technically 'Scheduled Castes' or 'Depressed Classes'. Traditionally, they were the persons of discreet set of low castes who were excluded from social, cultural, religious and other conventions of an elaborate hierarchical Indian caste system. As of now, its general usage implies a condition of being marginalized and deprived of basic rights on account of their lowly birth (Fuchs & Linkenbach, 2003, p. 1541).
2. This chapter written as part of a larger assessment study of the Programme for Enhancement of School Level Education (PESLE,1999–2007) of the Aga Khan Foundation – India (AKF-I) (2007). I hope it reflects adequately the challenge and struggle of the work undertaken over the years by the social activists, communities, parents, teachers, and practitioners for strengthening people's presence inside the school and around the concerns of education. An earlier version also appeared in *Journal of Research in Rural Education* in 2009.
3. In the Indian context, through the enactment of the 73rd and 74th Constitutional Amendments, the funds and power were devolved to the *Panchayat* institutions, the local bodies elected at the level of the village, the block and the district. Refer to Jayal et al. (2006) for further description.
4. The Sarva Shiksha Abhiyan (SSA) or Universalization of Elementary Education Mission, which is the flagship mission of the Government of India in the education sector, was introduced in 2001 to ensure all eligible children go through eight years of schooling. In the first few years of the program, the focus was on improving access to schools, increasing enrolments and reducing drop-out of children from elementary grades. Increasingly, SSA is now focusing on the quality of education in schools, including teacher presence and activity in classrooms, teacher training and assessment systems.
5. "The implication for local governance is indeed disturbing – a majority of the children in government schools come from poor and disempowered communities while local government institutions (Panchayat, Village Education Committee, School Development and Management Committee, etc.) are essentially in the hands of relatively well-off, whose children do not go to local government schools (be in municipality or Panchayat). Therefore, people in influential positions have little interest in ensuring that government schools function well and provide good quality education" (Ramachandran & Saihjee, 2006, p. ?).[NOTE: Page reference?]
6. The community participation projects as specified in this chapter were realized under the Program for Enhancement of School Level Education (PESLE,1999–2007), an educational initiative of the Aga Khan Foundation – India (AKF-I). Refer to The PESLE Assessment Study (2007) for larger study objectives, methodology and overall findings; additionally, details of PESLE-NGO partners, their ways of supporting school practices and sites of intervention.

DELIBERATIVE DEMOCRACY, PEOPLE'S AGENCY AND EDUCATION

7. A study by Alam and Raju (2007) substantiates that educational backwardness among Muslims is not due so much to religious orthodoxy as it is due to the specific socio-economic stratum in which most of them are located that renders education of little or of no relevance.
8. Walker and Walker (1999) conceptualize 'social exclusion' as a multi-dimensional, inherently "dynamic process of being shut out, fully or partially, from any of the social, economic, political or cultural systems which determine the social integration of a person in society. Social exclusion may, therefore, be seen as the denial (or non-realization) of the civil, political and social rights of citizenship" (p. 8). For Byrne (1999), "exclusion happens in time, in a time of history, and 'determines' the lives of the individuals and collectivities who are excluded and of those individuals and collectivities who are not" (p. 1). Traditionally, the exclusionary tendencies have entered the education system to influence its character. Regulating the access to schooling experiences of the equitable quality is one of the conventionally held ways to maintain the ascribed social order.
9. Bulpitt has defined 'statecraft' as "the art of winning elections and, above all, achieving a necessary degree of governing competence in office" (Bulpitt, as cited in Brown, 1997, p. 401).

REFERENCES

Aga Khan Foundation – India. (2007). *The PESLE assessment study.* New Delhi: Author.

Alam, M. S., & Raju, S. (2007). Contextualizing inter, intra-religious and gendered literacy. *Educational and Political Weekly, 42*(18), 1613–1622.

Apple, M. W., & Au, W. (2009). Politics, theory, and reality in critical pedagogy. In R. Cowen & A. M. Kazamias (Eds.), *International handbook of comparative education* (pp. 991–1007). London: Springer.

Bhattacharya, D. (2001). Civic community and its margins. *Economic and Political Weekly, 36*(8), 673–683.

Brown, P. (1997). The 'third wave': Education and the ideology of parentocracy. In A. H. Halsey, H. Lauder, P. Brown, & A. S. Wells (Eds.), *Education, culture, economy and society* (pp. 393–408). Oxford: Oxford University Press.

Byrne, D. (1999). *Social exclusion.* Buckingham, UK: Open University Press.

Fine, M. (1997). Apparent involvement: Reflections on parents, powers and urban public schools. In A.H. Halsey, H. Lauder, P. Brown, & A. S. Wells (Eds.), *Education, culture, economy and society* (pp. 460–475). Oxford: Oxford University Press.

Flecha, R. (2010). The dialogic sociology of the learning communities. In M. W. Apple, S. J. Ball, & L. A. Gandin (Eds.), *The Routledge international handbook of the sociology of education* (pp. 340–348). New York: Routledge Taylor and Francis.

Fuchs, M., & Linkenbach, A. (2003). Social movements. In V. Das (Ed.), *The Oxford India companion to sociology and social anthropology* (Vol. II). New Delhi: Oxford University Press.

Fukuda-Parr, S. (2006). The human development paradigm: Operationalizing Sen's ideas on capabilities. In B. Agarwal, J. Humphries, & I. Robeyns (Eds.), *Capabilities, freedom and equality: Amartya Sen's work from a gender perspective* (pp. 328–346). New Delhi: Oxford University Press.

Fung, A., & Wright, E. O. (2003). *Deepening democracy: Institutional innovations in empowered participatory governance.* London: Verso.

Fung, A. (2003). Associations and democracy: Between theories, hopes, and realities. *Annual Review of Sociology, 29,* 515–539.

Fung, A. (2004). *Empowered participation: Reinventing urban democracy.* Princeton, NJ: Princeton University Press.

Gandin, L. A. (2010). The democratization of governance in the citizenship school project: Building a new notion of accountability in education. In M. W. Apple, S. J. Ball, & L. A. Gandin (Eds.), *The Routledge international handbook of the sociology of education* (pp. 349–357). New York: Routledge Taylor and Francis.

Gaventa, J. (2006). *Triumph, deficit or contestation? Deepening the 'deepening democracy' debate.* (IDS Working paper 264). Brighton, UK: IDS.

Government of India. (2006). *Select educational statistics 2003–2004*. New Delhi: Department of Education, MHRD.
Govinda, R. (2008). *Education for all by 2015: Will we make it?* (India: Country case study. Country profile commissioned for the EFA global monitoring report, 2008). Paris: UNESCO.
Govinda, R., & Diwan, R. (2003). *Community participation and empowerment in primary education*. New Delhi: Sage Publications.
Jayal, N. G., Prakash, A., & Sharma, P. K. (Eds.). (2006). *Local governance in India: Decentralization and beyond*. New Delhi: Oxford University Press.
Jeffery, P. (2005). Introduction: Hearts, minds and pockets. In R. Chopra & P. Jeffery (Eds.), *Educational regimes in contemporary India*, (pp. 13–38). New Delhi: Sage Publications.
Kabeer, N. (2006). Social exclusion and the MDGs: The challenge of 'durable inequalities' in the Asian context. Retrieved June 24, 2011, from: http://www.eldis.org/vfile/upload/1/document/0708/DOC21178.pdf.
Kumar, K. (2008, January 19–25). Partners in education? *Economic & Political Weekly*, *43*(3), 8–11.
Pinto, M. R. (2006). People-centred development and participatory urban governance: The Mumbai experience. In N. G. Jayal, A. Prakash, & P. K. Sharma (Eds.), *Local governance in India: Decentralization and beyond* (pp. 202–220). New Delhi: Oxford University Press.
Pratham Resource Centre. (2007). *Annual status of education report (ASER: Rural)*. Mumbai: Author.
Putnam, R. D. (2000). *Bowling alone: The collapse and revival of American community*. New York: Simon and Schuster.
Ramachandran, V., & Saihjee, A. (2006). The new segregation in primary education: Implications for local governance. In N. G. Jayal, A. Prakash, & P. K. Sharma (Eds.), *Local governance in India: Decentralization and beyond* (pp. 162–188).. New Delhi: Oxford University Press.
Sen, A. (1999). *Democracy and social justice*. Paper presented at the Seoul Conference on Democracy, Market Economy and Development in February, 1999. Retrieved June 24, 2011, from http://www.devoutreach.com/summer99/SpecialReport/tabid/839/Default.aspx .
Sen, A. (2000). *Social exclusion: Concept, application, and scrutiny*. Social development paper No. 1, Asian Development Bank.
Sen, A. (2005). *The argumentative Indian*. London: Penguin.
Sen, A. (2006). The possibility of social choice. In B. Agarwal, J. Humphries, & I. Robeyns (Eds.), *Capabilities, freedom and equality: Amartya Sen's work from a gender perspective* (pp. xxx–xxx). New Delhi: Oxford University Press.[NOTE: couldn't find page numbers]
Walker, A., & Walker, C. (1997). *Britain divided: The growth of social exclusion in the 1980s and 1990s*. London: Child Poverty Action Group.

Gaysu R. Arvind
Professor in Elementary and Social Education,
Central Institute of Education,
University of Delhi

KEITH HEGGART

SYNTHESIZING PARTICIPATORY HUMAN RIGHTS EDUCATION AND CRITICAL CONSCIOUSNESS IN AUSTRALIAN SCHOOLS

Possibilities and Challenges for Educators Developing a Model of Human Rights Education

ABSTRACT

Human rights education is currently a popular topic amongst educators and academics. The emphasis on education reflects a departure from a strictly legal understanding of human rights and a move towards an emphasis on pedagogy and social justice. However, the history of human rights education in Australia is a limited and fragmentary one; in the past, civics and citizenship educational programs have generally been seen as more important. These programs ostensibly seek to develop informed and active citizens through formal schooling curricula. However despite their lofty aims, these programs are taught in a way that emphasizes didactic teaching, content knowledge and understanding of the history of democracy, all of which maintains the status quo and the attendant oppression on the bases of class, race and gender, rather than equipping students with the knowledge, skills and attitudes to actively seek out and unmask oppression and then challenge that oppression. The problems identified by educators with the current model provide valuable information for the development of a model of human rights education in Australia. It is crucial that such a model not only addresses education about citizenship and human rights, but more precisely education through and for human rights.

This chapter explores the theoretical and practical considerations behind the development of such a model, identifying the problems and challenges for educators. It also identifies the way different models of citizenship education, including those of Dewey, McLaughlin (1992), and Westheimer and Kahne (2004) might be synthesized with Freire's (1970) model of Popular Education to create a more fitting structure of human rights education for schools. In addition, this chapter also seeks to identify the links between civics and citizenship education and human rights education, especially in the context of global citizenship.

This chapter highlights the efforts of a number of human rights education programs in Australian schools, including one such effort to establish a critical citizenship program, whereby students are encouraged to actively take on a role in the democratic leadership of both the school and the community. This program, based in part upon Freire's model of Popular Education, involves school students of all ages in democratic consensus-building and problem solving, where students have had the opportunity to identify the dominant ideology of endemic racism in Western Sydney, and then, through organizing a social movement of their own, and involving the local and global community, challenging this representation of racism and creating a more just community.

INTRODUCTION

The topic of human rights and human rights education is, necessarily, a diverse one. It is often conflated with other issues like education for democracy and civic education, and it resists simple classification. The discussion about human rights has generally moved from focusing on the legal implications of the Universal Declaration of Human Rights and the UN Convention on the Rights of the Child to addressing issues related to education, further confusing the issues at hand. The UDHR and UNCRC have been the main instruments used to analyze and evaluate the success of human rights education on both the global and national level, as they clearly define the expectations of the signatories regarding the rights of a child, how these rights can be implemented, and the reporting requirements of each signatory nation to the United Nations.

Since the United Nations General Assembly adopted the Convention on the Rights of the Child on 20th November, 1989, there has been a burgeoning interest in both the theoretical underpinnings of human rights education, and the particular pedagogical practices that might be implemented in order to deliver such an education. Numerous governments and educational institutions have embraced the convention, and developed specific formal and informal educational programs aimed at promoting social justice and meeting the requirements.

However, more than 20 years after the adoption of the UNCRC by more than 200 countries, it is now appropriate to reconsider this terrain in a critical fashion. Principally, there are specific theoretical concerns relating to the way that human rights and citizenship education have been understood, and the follow-on implications for pedagogy and practice are also worthy of investigation.

Human Rights Education, Civics and Citizenship Education, and Democratic Education

Before one can begin to critique the approaches to human rights education that are present in Australia, it is important to establish the context for the argument. Human rights education is often linked with both education for democracy and civics education. This is because human rights education is an overarching field; within that field, one might find civics and citizenship education, global citizenship education and education for democracy, as well as numerous other schools. Each of these smaller topics addresses one aspect of 'rights' education. For example, civics and citizenship education includes our rights to be an active member of our community. Education for democracy includes our rights to act in a democratic fashion, through voting, community and social movements. Other examples might include environmental justice, which looks at the rights of humans as opposed to the needs of the environment. All of these schools are associated in some way with our rights as humans – our 'human rights' – and there is a great deal of overlapping between the different schools in this field.

This structure becomes even more evident if one examines the various definitions of human rights and civics and citizenship and democratic education. The Australian Commission for Human Rights argues that human rights are "about developing skills, attitudes, dispositions for engagement and understandings about what it means to live with dignity and respect" (Prior, 2009, p. 19). This definition shares striking similarities to the Civic Experts Group's explanation of the Discovering Democracy program, which called upon an "an informed citizenry; without active, knowledgeable citizens, the forms of democratic representation remain empty; without vigilant informed citizens, there is no check on potential tyranny." (Civics Expert Group [CEG], 1994, p. 5). Furthermore, democratic education is generally presupposed to not only include an understanding of the processes and functions of democracy, but also an imperative to take part in that democracy.

There are a number of common themes present in these definitions. Firstly, there is the idea that these kinds of education impart some form of knowledge regarding one's rights and responsibilities within society, whether that society is a local, national or global one. Secondly, there is the emphasis on developing skills in order to take part in that society; one might imagine that these skills might include: consensus-building, social movement organization, literacy and numeracy skills. Finally, as well as knowledge and skills, these kinds of education insist on the development of attitudes and engagement with the community.

It is this final condition that sets human rights education apart from other subjects, and suggests that human rights education needs to be delivered in a different way. Human rights education demands interactivity and engagement; to be a truly successful program, it is necessary to build a culture of human rights that permeates all aspects of the program. It is not simply enough to master the content knowledge and skills.

Of course, this final category also makes the teaching of human rights particularly challenging: Delivered poorly, human rights education can become an exercise in indoctrination, as teachers tell students what to think, rather than developing students' own capacity to draw conclusions. In addition, human rights education is also particularly susceptible to ideological influences, often in the case of government stipulations regarding what can and cannot be taught. Even in democratic countries like Australia, there is a significant level of involvement by the Federal Government in civics and citizenship curriculum, leading to some commentators denouncing it as 'narrow' and 'limited'. It is important, as a human rights educator, to be mindful of these particular issues.

Having established the field of human rights education, attention can now be turned to the instruments used for human rights education. Primarily, these are the UNCRC and the UDHR. When discussing the UNCRC it is usually split into three main divisions. Firstly, there are the rights of provision. These rights deal with access to goods and services, like food, water and shelter. Secondly, there are the rights for protection. These rights detail what children are to be protected from – for example, maltreatment, neglect and exploitation. Finally, there are the rights of participation. There has been confusion about the relative importance of each of these different divisions, as different governments have interpreted the convention in different ways. Thus, governments in developing countries are far more likely to emphasize the provision and protection rights, whereas developed countries, generally having addressed these rights for most children, are more likely to embrace the participation rights. Roose and Bouverne-De Bie (2007) write, "In the west, the added value of the UNCRC compared with former paternalistic international children's rights instruments is mainly viewed from a libertarian perspective, emphasizing the importance of participation rights for children" (p. 432).

The reason for this varying interpretation of the convention is based on the different schools of thought regarding children's rights. These different schools of thought hinge upon the understanding of the autonomy of the child. The libertarian children's rights movement is linked to the wider emancipation movement, and argues that, like women and blacks before them, children are an oppressed group. Although there are divergent factions within this school, their main emphasis is upon the need for the emancipation of children. According to this group, children are understood as a social construct. To be more precise, the oppression of children is a social construct. Thus, there is "an actively negotiated set of social relationships within which the early years of human life are constituted. The immaturity of children is a biological fact of life but the ways in which this immaturity is understood and made meaningful is a fact of culture" (Prout & James, 1990, as cited in Roose & Bouverne-De Bie, 2007, p. 432). According to this school of thought, the current view of children as not yet accountable or rational suggests that they are, to use Verhellen's term, "not yet a human being" (Verhellen, 2000, as cited in Roose & Bouverne-De Bie, 2007, p. 433).

The essential goal of the child liberationist school of thought is for children to have all the rights of adults. According to Roose and Bouverne-De Bie, this is expressed by "preferring to view children as subjects entitled to civil rights and the autonomous exercise of these rights. The underlying assumption is that all people are equal, irrespective of their age" (p. 432).

Another school of thought is that of the reformist trend. Less radical than child liberationists, reformists agree with the traditional view that children are generally incompetent of making their decisions straight away, but argue that children are capable of making rational decisions at an earlier age than commonly thought. This school of thought fits neatly with the paternalistic arguments used about children and other oppressed groups by arguing that they need protecting from themselves for their own good. Purdy (1994) argues that granting rights to children is difficult as it could harm the development of the children, due to an overestimation of their competence. Roose and Bouverne-De Bie (2007) agree with this, stating that the protective rights of the UNCRC outweigh the participative rights, and "the focus is on the duty to protect children, a duty not only for parents but for other actors - in the first place, the state" (p. 433).

The final school of thought is that of the pragmatists. Pragmatists find the middle ground between the reformists and the liberationists by arguing that it may be harmful to children if they were to have access to the same rights as adults, but it is also likely to be harmful to be too overprotective since, according to Hart (1991), it "creates unnecessary dependencies and thus prevents the child from developing competences" (Hart, 1991, as cited in Roose & Bouverne-De Bie, 2007, p. 433). In this school of thought, it is important to maintain a balance between protection and self-determination, and the present and the future; it makes little sense to sacrifice a child's future in the present by granting autonomy they are not yet ready for.

This discussion is important because it strikes to the core of the central purpose of the UNCRC and the way that countries have struggled to implement its articles since its ratification. There is a clash between the different views of children as understood by different societies and as demanded by the UNCRC: Are children citizens, or are they not-yet citizens? One of the core reasons that the UNCRC, despite it being widely ratified throughout the UN, has struggled to gain any traction is that children are often still treated as they were in the past. Children are objects in relationships, rather than subjects; things are 'done' to children, like education, rather than children having any agency of their own. Alderson (1999) suggests the dichotomy between adult and child when she writes, "Often, children are expected to show unquestioning obedience and loyalty, and physical and mental submission to their parents and teachers. Yet in Britain today, these qualities are not only untypical of all other human relationships, they contradict the liberal qualities adults prize and demonstrate in their own lives" (p. 186).

So in what way do the UNCRC and the UDHR recommend that children be treated? This debate generally turns into an argument regarding the legal status of children, which in turn is closely associated with the concept of precisely what a citizen is, and how citizenship might be enacted in a social context. However, it is worth considering there are other ways of looking at the nexus between children and citizenship than the strictly legal sense.

In contrast, one can examine citizenship through a sociological lens: Roose and Bouverne-De Bie (2007) suggest a different kind of citizen, based on collectivist perspectives. They suggest that this collectivist citizen is a person who would be "the politically active citizen who not only stands up for his or her own best interests but for the common good as well. From this point of view, individual rights entail obligations towards other citizens" (p. 434). This idea of 'collectivist citizen' is very important, because it clearly correlates with Westheimer and Kahne's (2004) conception of the 'justice-oriented citizen' which will be discussed later. The emphasis here is upon collective agency, which also links to Freire's (1970) ideas of oppressed groups freeing both themselves and each other.

It is natural to consider what these varying definitions of citizenship mean for the human rights educator. Firstly, it is important to recognize that the UNCRC is predicated upon the fact that children are seen as fellow citizens, and therefore have the rights associated with that, including the most important, the right to self-determination. While this might not be 'legal citizenship' in the sense of attaining the age of majority, it is clear that there is a belief within the UNCRC that children are both capable, and should be entitled to, participate in meaning making within society. This kind of citizenship is 'citizenship as a relationship between people'. According to Roose and Bouverne-De Bie (2007), "it is not so much that people are or are not citizens, but rather that citizenship is 'actualized' in diverse activities and relationships" (p. 439).

As a convention, which is more binding than a declaration, the UNCRC is an agreement between the member states of the obligations each will undertake towards his or her citizens – which in this case, include children. As part of these obligations, there is a clear commitment to achieve those educational goals that were outlined as part of the UNCRC and this commitment necessarily dictates not only what should be taught, but also the process by which it should be taught.

According to Roose and Bouverne-De Bie (2007), "In this interpretation, children's rights and human rights are rights that are to be shaped in a participative way, a process during which parents and children themselves participate in the definition and the content of these rights... It does mean, however, that children must be accepted as co-actors in dialogue about their best interests" (p. 438). Therefore, it would appear that the UNCRC advocates a democratic or participative approach to learning. At the very least, it is expected that children should be able to negotiate with other actors in their lives, be they parents, teachers or other adults, about what they should learn, and what the learning conditions should be like.

However, participative approaches are certainly not common amongst most schools or educational institutions. It is ironic that, in a place of learning charged with teaching students about democracy, a place Ban Ki-Moon says is needed to "contribute to the growth of a culture of peace-building that creates the economic, political and educational institutions to ensure long term peace based on social justice" (as cited in McLeod and Reynolds, 2010, p. 17), children are most likely to experience the precise opposite of democracy: an autocratic existence, subject to oppression and lacking any semblance of autonomy. This point is even clearer when one looks at the articles of the UDHR. According to the UDHR, everyone can assume inviolable human rights to liberty, security, freedom from degrading treatment and freedom from arbitrary detention. However, in many school instances, this is precisely what happens to children. According to Jeffs: "In British schools, pupils are regimented and involuntarily subjected to mass routines to a greater degree than they will be at any other time of life, unless they are sent to prison. As factory regimes disappear from industry, they become more entrenched in schools" (Jeffs, 1995, as cited in Alderson, 1999, p. 188). There is no evidence that the experience of an Australian child is different to that of his or her British counterpart.

In a school environment, students are required to behave in certain ways. They are subject to arbitrary punishment and detention and discipline is rigorously imposed upon them. According to Article 23, people have the right to free choice of employment and to just and favourable conditions of work, yet students are forced to attend school. On this, Alderson (1999) writes, "Democracy is premised on trust in the rational person's informed discretion. Compulsion is based on the assumption, or at least the implication, of mistrust: that children and teenagers are too ignorant, foolish or reckless to attend school voluntarily" (p. 190).

Of course, I have drawn these articles directly from the UDHR, rather than the UNCRC. This, naturally, raises a number of questions regarding to whom, precisely, the UDHR applies. Does it only apply to adults, or do the articles contained therein apply to children, as well? Alderson explored the UNCRC in British schools as well, and the results are even more concerning. According to her research, only 24% of students had heard of the convention, and of those, only 5% felt that they knew a lot about it. Even more concerning is the fact that only 25% of students felt that they were believed by teachers, and only 33% felt that teachers acted in a fair and impartial manner. Alderson summarizes this by saying, "This suggests a general climate of mistrust and of pupils expecting to be mistrusted by their teachers" (p. 194). Finally, Alderson makes mention of the ubiquitous school council – the so-called vehicle for student voice in most schools. More than 50% of students said they had a school council, but less than 20% thought that the council was effective in helping to make their schools a better place. Interestingly, this research is mirrored by the work of John Cogan, who identified a similar feeling regarding the effectiveness of school councils in Australia. Cogan comments that "Activities such as special days are haphazard across schools, students councils are limited to a few students and they have no power, and school parliaments are rare" (Cogan & Morris, 2001, p. 116).

Current Status of Human Rights Education in Australia

Human rights education in Australia has been noticeable for its absence. In many schools and classrooms, the term 'human rights' is non-existent, or only mentioned vaguely. The reason for this absence is easily identified; human rights is not valued by the policy-makers in Australian educational systems. A study of the important curriculum guidance documents issued in Australia since 1996 reveals that human rights are barely mentioned at all.

The Melbourne Declaration on the Educational Goals for Young Australians, released in 2008, outlines the direction of Australian schooling, as agreed by all state and federal governments in Australia. However, at no point in the document does it mention the importance of human rights, although it does state that one of the goals is for young people to become 'active and informed citizens' who are committed to justice and equity. The document suggests that this might be realized through the study of civics and citizenship. Upon consulting the Statement of Learning for Civics and Citizenship, it is not surprising that there is, again, no mention of human rights or the UDHR or UNCRC.

Although it would appear that human rights are not central to the policy-maker's agenda, there are elements of human rights present in the documents outlined above. For example, both documents mention the importance of social justice, equality and the common good. In addition, the documents also mention the three key features of human rights education discussed earlier: knowledge, skills and attitudes. According to Warren Prior, the reason for this absence is because, "yet again, educational policy is driven by economic imperatives and that curriculum is a social construction representing the prevailing political ideology" (Prior, 2009, p. 19).

To understand why there is such a reluctance to address human rights or the UNCRC through school curriculum, it is necessary to be familiar with the history of civics and citizenship education in Australia. Civics and Citizenship education has had a long history in Australia – classes existed in civil and moral education in New South Wales as early as 1904. Traditionally, these classes reflected the governmental dominance; during World Wars One and Two, there was an emphasis on patriotism and duty to the Commonwealth. Following World War Two, the increased number of refugees and migrants meant that social studies emphasized the benefits of multiculturalism and assimilation. During the early 1990s, a number of senate reports about this issue led to the establishment of the Civics Experts Group (CEG) in 1994, who released, later that year, a report entitled, 'Whereas the people...'

This report identified what became known as the 'civics deficit' amongst young Australians. It argued that "significant social and economic change had occurred that made it more important that Australians understood how their civic and political freedoms and wellbeing were maintained" (Macintyre & Simpson, 2009, p. 124). It identified a "widespread ignorance and misconception about the structure and the function of Australia's system of government, about its origins and the ways it can serve the needs of its citizens" (CEG, 1994, p. 5).

In order to remedy this, the federal government at the time ordered the development of a civics and citizenship education program known as Discovering Democracy, which was to be delivered to all students between Year 3 and Year 10. Originally conceived as a participatory curriculum, Discovering Democracy was significantly altered after the Howard Government came to power in late 1996. Whereas under the Keating Government, there was an emphasis on active participation, this was changed, apparently at the urging of the Prime Minister, to reflect a historical approach rather than a participatory democratic approach. Academics identified this issue immediately, stating there was "a shift from what we desired here in Western Australia, which was an active citizenship focus to one that tended to be... about the schools of citizenship in a fairly formal sense" (Criddle, Vidovich, & O'Neill, 2004, p. 31). David Kemp, the education minister at the time, said, "the emphasis on developing active citizenship skills to participate in current civics issues was lessened in order that greater emphasis be placed on knowledge of the historical development of Australian democracy" (Kemp, 1997, p. 1). What was intended to be an active program, aimed at encouraging student participation in civic life, became a dry effort intended to hammer home the facts of Australian democratic history.

The Discovering Democracy program is best summed up by the report of the Ministerial Council for Education, Early Childhood Development and Youth Affairs [MCEECDYA] (2007), who wrote, "By 2007, civics and citizenship education had a more prominent place and an agreed focus in curriculum policies in Australian states and territories than was the case in 2004, but not in such a way as to impact at the school or classroom level" (p. xix).

The failure of this attempt at civics and citizenship education is a salient point for any educator contemplating human rights education. There are some vital lessons that need to be considered when developing human rights education programs. Firstly, human rights education needs to be placed at the heart of a school's mission and ethos; in the case of Discovering Democracy, it was seen very much as an add-on, which meant that teachers sought ways to avoid teaching it, and the fact that Discovering Democracy was meant to be delivered across the whole curriculum ultimately meant that no one department had responsibility for the delivery of the program, which led to a haphazard and ultimately unsuccessful approach. "Thus, respondents at macro, meso and micro levels of the policy trajectory had different views of the intentions of the curriculum package" (Criddle et al., 2004, p. 33). This was further complicated because, despite being a federal program, it was left to the states to implement. For example, "in the state of Western Australia, no formal approval for the use of Discovering Democracy in schools was given and it was not officially incorporated into the curriculum" (Criddle et al., 2004, p. 28). Rather, human rights education programs need to be grounded, firstly, in the education system's policy, and then, secondly, in individual schools' mission statements.

In addition to this lack of clarity regarding the goals of this program, another consideration that is vital is the requirement for both pre-service professional development and ongoing professional development regarding human rights education. This lack of training and education was another contributing factor to the failure of Discovering Democracy. Suzanne Mellor (2003), attempted to resolve some of the issues facing schools who were implementing civics and citizenship education. Mellor advised the teaching of CCE should always be linked to the idea of the problematic; that is, based on understanding and solving issues of relevance. She suggested that it should be linked to many different subjects, and quite airily, leaves the question of how best to deliver these problematics up to the school.

Mellor did raise the issue of teacher professional development; that is the capability of teachers to actually engage in teaching civics and citizenship education. She cites statistics stating that only 1% of teachers took a citizenship course at the undergraduate level, and only 3% had any form of postgraduate citizenship qualifications. In fact, 33% of teachers said that they were 'not at all confident' teaching civics.

Thirdly, the implementation of civics and citizenship programs was unclear regarding time allocated and where it fit within the curriculum. The original intention was for Discovering Democracy to be taught across the whole curriculum, but this led to its own problems. Cogan was critical of the various whole school approaches to civics and citizenship education that he observed. He wrote, "Difficulties arise from integration of civics as a theme within other school subjects" (Cogan & Morris, 2001, p. 116). Whether it was a whole school approach or not, there were still issues with fitting the extra material into a curriculum that teachers already felt was far too crowded with content.

Finally, the actual content of the civics and citizenship program was not relevant to the children who were studying it. The program covered four major topics: Who

Rules, Laws and Rights, The Australian Nation, and Citizens and Public Life. Most of this content was addressed to adults, people who had attained the legal age of majority, and therefore was not relevant to the students who were studying it. In addition, the materials that dealt with the history of democracy in Australia, like the Eureka Stockade, were from events that were at least 100 years ago and therefore distant from the students' interests or experiences.

Clearly, this evidence demands a re-evaluation of governmental policy regarding the importance and place of human rights education in Australia. Any program that was delivered in a similar manner to the Discovering Democracy program would surely face the same level of failure; rather, it is appropriate to reconsider the methods and also the aims of human rights education in Australian schools. One of the pleasing aspects of human rights education in Australia is the seriousness with which it is being treated recently. In 2010, there was a conference held in Sydney specifically for the purpose of initiating a dialogue regarding human rights education in Australia. Both the Prime Minister and the Leader of the Opposition sent messages outlining their support for the conference and affirming their commitment to the development of human rights in Australia.

However, the Shadow Minister for Education, Christopher Pyne, spoke about human rights education in Australia at the same conference; after congratulating the Howard government for the 'success' of the Discovering Democracy program, which was questionable, Pyne then outlined his vision of the way human rights education should be delivered in Australian schools. According to Pyne, "The Coalition has advocated that human rights education is best served by being placed in the history curriculum where it can highlight the common challenges, rights and responsibilities that all Australians share and have shared over time, as well as those unfortunate instances where not all Australians have been accorded the same rights" (Pyne, 2010). To drive this approach, Pyne recommends a number of policies, including a nationwide essay competition, a debating competition and human rights courses being compulsory for students studying law.

This understanding of human rights is precisely the issue that is impeding the development of human rights within the Australian education system. Just like the Discovering Democracy program outlined above, there is far too much emphasis on education 'about' human rights, in an abstract or isolated sense, and for too little emphasis on learning for the practice of human rights or learning to enact human rights in personal, professional and societal relations. The content of Discovering Democracy didn't have any relevance to students and therefore inspired no engagement or interest with the material. While governmental policy continues along these lines, there is no reason to expect that student engagement and teacher understanding will be any more successful than similar, previous efforts.

Critical Consciousness and Human Rights Education

The answer to this dilemma lies in a clearer understanding of the purpose of human rights education. Essentially, in a very similar way to citizenship education, the goal of human rights education is to develop citizens who are, in the first instance, capable of recognizing injustice and breaches of human rights, and then are also capable of working collectively to address this injustice in the form of positive social change. Although simply stated, this is a complex process; it requires a combination of knowledge regarding their world and society, an ability to work collaboratively through social movements, and a willingness to engage in such a challenging process. Paulo Freire (1970) suggests that "man's ontological vocation (as he calls it) is to be a subject who acts upon and transforms his world, and in so doing move towards ever new possibilities of fuller and richer life individually and collectively" (p. 32).

The process of developing such a program of education is not an easy one. Many schools still adopt what Freire would call a 'banking model' of education, where students are relegated to the role of passive receivers of knowledge. Freire writes, "education thus becomes an act of depositing in which the students are the depositories and the teacher is the depositor... the scope of action allowed to the students extends only as far as receiving, filing and storing the deposits... In the banking concept of education, knowledge is a gift bestowed by those who consider themselves knowledgeable upon those whom they consider to know nothing..." (Freire, 1970, p. 72).

The banking model of education is not a tool for creating positive social change; rather, it is the means used to socialize students to the status quo, and thus ensure the dominant hegemony remains in place. The emphasis on the history of democracy in Australia in the Discovering Democracy program is one such example of this; rather than empowering students to enact positive social change through the use of contextually based and student negotiated curricula, the material was distant from the students, and often taught in such a way as to make it nothing more than the rote memorization of facts, despite the original intentions of the program. Therefore, if human rights education is going to be meaningful in Australian schools, it needs to adopt a different pedagogical method. Problem-posing education (Freire, 1970) emphasizes a number of important features, including teachers and students working together, a relevant, student-negotiated curriculum, and the importance of dialogue as the process by which we come to understand the world.

The ultimate goal of this form of education is the development of critical consciousness. This, according to Mustokova-Possardt (2003), is achieving a deep understanding of the world, and the political and social contradictions and injustices inherent within it, and then taking action against these oppressive injustices, through individual and collective action, in order to make the world a fairer place. Critical consciousness is at the heart of human rights education; the UDHR and UNCRC are documents that require intelligent, critical interpretation rather than a lifeless, rigid application and thus it is necessary for human rights educators to seek to develop in students an understanding of the social complexities of the world.

This kind of education is closely related to the principles of maximal citizenship education (McLaughlin, 1992). McLaughlin argued that most citizenship education programs could be placed on a continuum between maximal and minimal citizenship education. Minimal citizenship education programs are those where "there is nothing in interpretations of this kind which require the development in students of a broad critical reflection and understanding..." and "nor is there concern to ameliorate the social disadvantages that may inhibit the students from developing into citizens in the significant sense" (McLaughlin, 1992, p. 236). Maximal citizenship education is much more egalitarian and focused on challenging oppression and removing disadvantage. There is an emphasis in maximal citizenship upon critical thought, inclusiveness, participatory processes and activism – all of which are important in Freire's problem-posing education.

The ultimate goal of human rights education is predicated upon the idea of positive social change. The actors within such social change are often termed 'active citizens'. Within the literature, there is a lot of discussion regarding the precise nature of 'active citizenship'. Rather than 'active citizen', I propose using Westheimer and Kahne's term 'Justice-Oriented Citizens' because I think that it is much clearer precisely what is meant by this term, and it also makes the connection between action and justice more obvious. According to Westheimer and Kahne (2004), a justice-oriented citizen is a citizen who can critically assess social, political and economic structures and who seeks out and addresses injustice, armed with a knowledge and understanding of social movements. These citizens have learnt to question and change established systems where those systems produce injustice.

It is important to note the commonalities between all of these concepts: firstly, critically conscious citizens and justice-oriented citizens emphasize the need to critically assess the world around them – this is the deep understanding of the world that is the first step in the process. However, both also suggest that assessment is the beginning – next there must be action to remedy these injustices. Finally, both also identify the need for collective action, rather than individual action.

It is possible to synthesize these ideas together to create a model of human rights education for the Australian context. The goal of such a model is to develop people who might be termed justice-oriented citizens. In order to develop the qualities that make people justice-oriented, it is necessary to encourage amongst them critical consciousness – an ability to perceive the world critically. Finally, the teaching methodology required to develop this critical consciousness is a maximal one: a pedagogy that embraces participatory, process-driven and student-led learning activities. McLeod and Reynolds (2010) put thisanother way: "But content transmission is not enough. Classroom pedagogy must also reflect human rights, so the classroom experience models the ideal of the convention" (p. 18).

Possibilities for the Future of Human Rights Education in Australia

However, it is important to realize that there are significant challenges involved in changing the context of Freire's work. Kathryn Choules, an Australian scholar, writes "A wholesale adoption of popular education's instructional approach can cause significant problems for social change education in the west" (Choules, 2007, p. 161). According to Choules, the main point of difference lies in the question: Who does the social change education benefit? In the context of Freire's work in South America, clearly the marginalized groups that Freire worked with had much to gain from increasing their freedom and alleviating their social oppression. On the other hand, in a different context, such as within the Australian schooling system, a teacher might very well be working with members of the dominant social group. In this context, Choules cautions, "When working with the dominant social group, or those who benefit from existing inequitable systems, the social change vision may well not be shared. Realization of the vision may well threaten the students' status, power and wealth" (Choules, 2007, p. 161).

There are a number of other concerns that are related to the problem of context. Whereas in Brazil there are very obvious examples of inequality and oppression, perceiving injustice is more challenging in prosperous countries like Australia or the United States. One of the key principles of popular education is the idea of learning to perceive the reality of the world – to become fully, critically conscious; this, necessarily, requires the skills to identify and deconstruct the dominant ideologies present in particular contexts, which is a difficult challenge for adults in marginalized environments, much less children in contentious ones.

In addition, one must be aware that, rather than dealing with exclusively marginalized groups, as is the case with many Popular Education projects, this is problematic in Australia, where a popular educator might have to work with mixed groups of the marginalized and the elite, or groups comprised entirely of members of the elite. Choules (2007) warns that "the rational process of ideology critique will rarely have the same positive affective component for a person from the dominant group" (p. 166).

Furthermore, the relationship between the teacher and students, as espoused in popular education, is difficult in and of itself; when students begin discussing their experiences, it is possible that the more dominant groups within the class can hijack the discussion. Choules warns that, "When such students assert experiences of individual discrimination against themselves, this can result in an individualized discourse around discrimination and a denial of structural oppression and discrimination. It also allows the dominant group to (mis)position itself as the victim in relation to a particular social justice issue" (p. 169).

In this example, it is important to remember the critical element of Popular Education. Every point raised in discussion should be analysed critically for assumptions; this critical evaluation of discussion will ensure that individual discourses do not overpower the structural discourse that is important in gaining critical consciousness. Choules also advises adopting a kind of ideology critique, which she terms 'privilege critique': "A useful equivalent of 'understanding reality' is to work to expose privilege with those who have it and gain awareness of what is happening behind the hegemonic facade" (p. 167).

Finally, the methodology of Popular Education is challenging for educators, too. One of the central tenets of Popular Education is that of dialogics. According to Freire and Macado, "Dialogue is the central learning process in popular education. It is a dialogue of equals, and through this social process, knowledge and learning are generated" (as cited in Choules, 2007, p. 177). The links to citizenship education are made even more explicit by Choules, who writes, "Dialogue puts into practice in the educational setting the political outcome sought: radical democracy" (p. 171).

Fortunately, there are a number of successful examples of this kind of education taking place in Australia. Kerry Ang (2010) has been working with schools in the field of human rights education for a number of years, and has developed his own theoretical model of human rights education. Building on the work of Tibbitts (2002), who identified models such as transformational, accountability and awareness, Ang suggests a fourth model: that of participatory human rights education. Ang suggests that "critical pedagogy and transformative learning are found to be suited to the teaching of human rights to secondary students, and the characteristics of the adolescent student are ... seen to be appropriate for engagement in the challenging field of human rights education" (Ang, 2010, p. 1).

Ang uses Tibbitts' (2002) clarification of the purpose of human rights education: "human rights education encourages teachers to involve learners in what can be termed an 'empowerment process' a belief in the power of learning to improve the human condition With this in mind, Ang developed numerous examples of human rights education at Australian high schools based around this participatory model of human rights education. This participatory model took the form of a week long, intensive case study of a human rights violation. The emphasis during this study was on transmitting technical, practical and what Welbourne (1995, as cited in Ang, 2010, p. 11) calls emancipatory knowledge, so that the students who took part felt empowered to take action.

There are, I believe, some omissions in Ang's participatory model. Firstly, there seems to be little effort to begin with examples of injustices that are truly at the heart of a student's experiences. The in-depth case studies that Ang suggests, like ethnic cleansing and religious persecution, are, of course, very serious, but there are other human rights violations, especially those from the participatory articles of the UNCRC, that are completely ignored. Ang, by overlooking these violations, misses an opportunity to truly engage with his audience in the terms of a context that has direct relevance to their lives. Freire emphasized the importance of beginning with the concerns of the people, rather than a top-down, teacher directed approach to the content.

Furthermore, there seems little emphasis on student leadership within these programs. Admittedly, this is more of a popular education perspective than one of critical pedagogy, but it is important to realize that, as part of developing the skills required to challenge injustice within the community, it is necessary for students to develop leadership skills, in order to effectively manage social movements.

Although still in its very early, stages, the e-Citizens project is another example of a more critical approach to human rights education. It is an attempt at a Sydney school to develop a model of human rights education that is based upon the concept of justice-oriented citizens exhibiting critical consciousness. This project, which began late in 2010, has taken the form of a youth participatory action research project. Currently, there are two phases within the project; the first phase requires an exploration of human rights practices within the school, and then the development, through a collaborative process, of a film documenting their findings. The students have, during phase one, had the opportunity to critically interrogate their schooling context using the UDHR and the UNCRC as instruments for this interrogation. This interrogation took the form of observation of schooling practices, interviews with students and other stakeholders and reflections, via students' journals, of their own experiences.

This program is having a significant impact upon the way that students view the world. The students meet once a week, for an hour, and these meetings are tools for sharing, through a dialogical model, the findings that students have identified throughout the week, as well as opportunities for facilitating the next steps in the project. For example, students might consider whether the makeup of the student council is unjust due to the fact that some groups are not represented on the council.

This project has raised a number of crucial pedagogical ideas related to the idea of developing justice-oriented citizens. Whereas previously projects of a similar nature had focused on charity, for example, raising money for Caritas Australia, the e-citizens project is aimed at positive social change. This is important because, by focusing on this idea of change, students are forced to confront the root causes of the problem, and therefore have to explore the idea of injustice, and the way their lives are linked to this concept, before they can consider how best to address these issues in order to affect their goal: positive social change. This ensures that students begin to develop the deep understanding about the world that is the first step in critical consciousness. Or, as Ang (2010) suggests, "If we can give young people some understanding of the causes of inequalities and injustices in our society, we may be more successful in taking action in response to these issues" (p. 2).

In addition, the e-Citizens project allowed the students to identify issues that were important to them. Again, programs of this nature often only have a fleeting link to the lives of the students who are part of the program. In the previous example of Caritas, Australia, students raised money for child labourers in the Philippines, an activity, though no doubt important, that had no relevance to their own lives.

Within phase one, these issues were related to the school environment, and the injustices that were present there, but it is envisioned that when phase two begins, students will be able to explore issues related to the local community, including, but not limited to, the ideas of racism and refugees in Western Sydney, or the environmental degradation of the Nepean River. This two-phase process is vital, because the development of justice-oriented citizens requires not just the development of attitudes, but also skills and knowledge. Therefore, the first in-school phase allows students the opportunity to develop these skills in a safer environment, before they can then utilize those skills in a wider context. In addition, part of being a justice-oriented citizen requires individuals to work for the betterment of everyone in society, and not just themselves. Therefore, after having worked to enact positive social change on their own behalf, they have an opportunity to work with the wider community to collaboratively enact positive change.

At all times, it is important to note, students have had the opportunity to lead the process. In this way, it has been a truly collaborative and participatory program. For example, in phase one, students could lead both the exploration of human rights in their school but also the nature of the film that they produce and, indeed, who they present their final product to. In phase two, there will be even more opportunities for student leadership: Having developed their skills and knowledge in phase one, they will then be able to employ them in phase two, as well as having a wider range of issues to choose from. This is similar to McLeod and Reynold's (2010) ideas regarding the peaceful pedagogy: "Critical to this model of curriculum is the opportunities for students to enact their knowledge, values and skills of human rights and their classroom experience of modelled peace-building to effect more equitable conditions and opportunities in their own environment with the aim of long-term development of attitudes, beliefs and values of social justice and equity" (p. 20).

CONCLUSION

As stated earlier, human rights education, and especially the parts related to citizenship education, has unique challenges and possibilities. However, in the Australian context, there is much for educators to learn from the previous programs that have undertaken the aim of developing active and justice-oriented citizens. In one such example, Discovering Democracy, the program failed for a number of reasons, primarily the fact that the program itself was not supported enough by the government, nor was there enough consideration given to the development of the curriculum or the provision of professional development.

Therefore, for human rights education to be successful, there are a number of important considerations. Firstly, and most importantly, the purpose of the human rights education must be matched by the practice and the pedagogy. In other words, there is no point teaching about human rights unless the teaching environment exhibits a respect for human rights – that is, a human rights culture. In addition to teaching about human rights, there is a need to teach for human rights, and to teach to enact human rights. This form of teaching requires a different approach precisely because the aim is different: Rather than an attempt to submerge the consciousness of students, the aim is to raise the consciousness to a critical level. This is best done through programs of education that are maximal in nature; that is, they are student-led, relevant to the students, and based in their own experiences and understandings. This kind of program allows students to develop into justice-oriented citizens, with the knowledge, skills and attitude required to effect positive social change.

In conclusion, then, it is clear that there are examples of such programs in Australia, and, although this kind of education is still a recent development, the evidence suggests that these programs have been successful in creating critical citizens. Therefore, it is imperative that the educators responsible for these programs disseminate this knowledge as widely as possible, in order to generate a critical mass of human rights practitioners.

REFERENCES

Alderson, P. (1999). Human rights and democracy in schools: Do they mean more than "picking up litter and not killing whales"? *The International Journal of Children's Rights*, 7(2), 185–205.

Ang, K. (2010, November). *Human rights education: A best practice model for secondary schools*. Human Rights Education Conference, University of Western Sydney, Parramatta Campus, Sydney, Australia.

Choules, K. (2007). Social change education: Context matters. *Adult Education Quarterly*, 57(2), 159–176.

Civics Expert Group (CEG). (1994). *Whereas the people... civics and citizenship education* (Report of the Civics Expert Group [CEG]). Canberra: Australian Government Publishing Service.

Cogan, J. J., & Morris, P. (2001). The development of civics values: An overview. International *Journal of Education Research*, 35(1), 1–9.

Criddle, E., Vidovich, L., & O'Neill, M. (2004). Discovering democracy: An analysis of curriculum policy for citizenship education. *Westminster Studies in Education*, 27(1), 27–41.

Freire, P. (1970). *Pedagogy of the oppressed*. New York: Continuum.

Hart, S. N. (1991). From property to person status. Historical perspectives on children's rights. *American Psychologist*, 46(1), 53–59.

Jeffs, T. (1995). Schooling, education and children's rights. In B. Franklin (Ed.), *The handbook of children's rights: Comparative policy and practice* (pp. 45–59). London: Routledge.

Kemp, D. (1997, May). *Discovering democracy*. Ministerial speech presented at the Curriculum Corporation Conference, Sydney, Australia.

Macintyre, S. & N. Simpson (2009). Consensus and division in Australian citizenship education. *Citizenship Studies*, 13(2), 121–134.

McLaughlin, T. H. (1992). Citizenship, diversity and education: A philosophical perspective. *Journal of Moral Education*, 21(3), 235–246.

McLeod, J., & Reynolds, R. (2010). Teaching human rights across the curriculum. *Ethos*, 18(3), 17–21.

Ministerial Council for Education, Early Childhood Development and Youth Affairs. (2007). *Report into the teaching of civics and citizenship education*. Canberra: Australian Government Publishing Service.

Mellor, S. (2003). *Solving some civics and citizenship education conundrums*. Department of Education, Employment and Workplace Relations, Australian Government. Retrieved from http://www.curriculum.edu.au/cce/default.asp?id=9318.

Mustakova-Possardt, E. (2003). *Critical consciousness: A study of morality in global historical context*. London: Praeger. Retrieved from www.elenamustakova.net.

Prior, W. (2009). Teaching about human rights. *Ethos*, 17(2), 18–21.

Prout, A., & James, A. (1990). A new paradigm for the sociology of childhood? Provenance, promise and problems. In A. Prout & A. James (Eds.), *Constructing and reconstructing childhood: Contemporary issues in the sociological study of childhood* (pp. 7–34). London: Falmer Press.

Purdy, L. (1994). Why children shouldn't have equal rights. *The International Journal of Children's Rights*, 2(3), 223–241.

Pyne, C. (2010, November). *Keynote speech*. Human Rights Education Conference, University of Western Sydney, Parramatta Campus, Sydney, Australia.

Roose, R., & Bouverne-De Bie, M. (2007). Do children have rights or do their rights have to be realised? The United Nations Convention on the Rights of the Child as a frame of reference for pedagogical action. *Journal of Philosophy of Education*, 41(3), 431–443.

Tibbitts, F. (2002). Understanding what we do: Emerging models for human rights education. *International Review of Education*, 48(3–4), 159–171.

Verhellen, E. (2000). *Convention on the rights of the child. Background, motivation, strategies, main themes*. Leuven, Belgium: Acco.

Westheimer, J., & Kahne, J. (2004). Educating the "good" citizen: Political choices and pedagogical goals. *Political Science and Politics, 38*(2), 1–7. Retrieved from PSOnline www.apsanet.org

Keith Heggart
Faculty of Arts and Social Sciences,
University of Technology, Sydney

LEE JEROME

CHILDREN'S RIGHTS AND TEACHERS' RESPONSIBILITIES

A Case Study of Developing a Rights Respecting Initial Teacher Education Programme

INTRODUCTION

As a teacher educator in England it feels like we have simultaneously lived through the best of times and the worst of times in the past decade. We have seen schools recording year on year progress, with rising examination outcomes and more young people staying on at university. In a parallel development, teachers have become professionalised like never before, with higher pay, better codified professional expectations, and a clearly defined career path with rewards for *advanced* and *excellent* teachers. In the worst of times government has become more closely involved in directing the work of teachers and teacher educators, issuing guidance on how to teach lessons for school teachers and publishing annual course priorities for teacher educators. In schools the unprecedented success has been achieved partly through a narrowing of the curriculum and a restrictive 'teaching to the test', which has left significant numbers of young people apparently disconnected from the education system, leaving school with almost no qualifications and subsequently remaining outside education, training or employment. In teacher education there has been a bureaucratisation centred on the Standards for Qualified Teacher Status and across education these processes are monitored closely for the government by a powerful inspectorate, whose decisions affect funding and institutional viability. This case study tells the stories of teacher educators and student teachers at London Metropolitan University as the course team has attempted to orientate their programmes in this polarising context. In preparing teachers for their place in what appear to be the best and worst of schools, children's rights has been identified as the foundation stone.

Teaching as a political activity and the challenge for professional training

In our struggle to articulate a model for professionalism within our programme, we have drawn on the notion of the teacher as *change agent*. Michael Fullan argued that in order to undertake the complex role of the teacher within systems of education which all too often lead to a 'sense of inconsequentiality' (Fullan 1993) one must remain aware that teaching is at its core a moral profession, and that to enact one's moral commitment one must also prepare to become an agent of change. Fullan's model requires teachers to pay attention to four sets of competencies. First, teachers must develop mastery, or a technical competence in their work. Second, teachers should be prepared and able to inquire into practice and to generate new understandings to inform their subsequent development. Third, teachers must be able to collaborate, in order to build alliances and to develop through professional relationships with colleagues and others. Finally, and echoing his initial commitment to the moral dimension to education, Fullan argues it is essential that teachers remain conscious of their vision for education, as this will provide them with the stability and certainty to judge the changing context and policy agendas and continue to pursue their own role in providing meaningful educational experiences for young people.

Children's Rights and Education

Reflecting as a group of teacher educators on Fullan's model, it seemed reasonable to ask ourselves what vision we could articulate that would both enable us to commit morally to the Post Graduate Certificate in Education (PGCE) programme and provide a sufficiently robust and inclusive moral vision for the students who attend the university. Narrow and partisan political agendas are clearly unsuitable for such a task and yet it is important, as Fullan reminds us, not to deny the essential moral dimension to our work in education. Our starting point in this project is the UN Convention on the Rights of the Child (UNCRC) and the vision of education that flows from a commitment to this document. This provides us with a normative framework which both resonates with government policy and provides a critical perspective from which to critique that policy (Osler & Starkey, 2005; Alderson, 2008; Department for Children, Schools and Families [DCSF], 2009). As teacher educators we felt we needed to engage with the UNCRC afresh, rather than rely solely on the previous or current administration's interpretations of it. What follows is an account of our intellectual re-engagement with children's rights as we sought to orientate our courses to the shifting policy landscape of teaching in secondary schools in England.

The rights embodied in the UNCRC are partly aspirational and conditional on contextual circumstances. They are therefore limited and one of the important limiting factors is the necessity to balance rights between people. On this reading rights are social, i.e. an individual claiming his or her rights simultaneously accepts and acknowledges the equivalent rights of others, which leads logically both to a sense of how one's rights are limited and to an associated sense of obligation to others (Alderson, 2008, p.18). This acknowledgement that rights are not simple commodities to be given or taken indicates what fertile ground the UNCRC provides for adults who are employed by the state to work with children. Rather than provide a prescription for action, the UNCRC provides an ethical framework (Osler & Starkey, 2005, pp. 35–37), the principles of which provide a challenge to deep and critical reflection on the nature of one's professional work.

There are three partly overlapping kinds of rights all of which have implications for education (Alderson, 2008, p. 17). Firstly, provision rights relate to necessary services to which children are entitled, and clearly education is one of these areas of provision. On this view schools provide the institutional means for achieving this right (at least for most children), and teachers are employed as agents of such institutions to provide the front line services. This much is simply to re-state an already existing institutional arrangement in rights-friendly language, but the challenge comes from appreciating that these institutional arrangements have to meet the educational rights of *all* children, and this links to a more challenging agenda for inclusive education (Stubbs, 1998). Once one has grasped the significance of this entitlement, the practical day-to-day task of differentiating classroom activities effectively moves beyond a simple question of technical teaching strategies and is powerfully linked to broader issues about school structure, the roles of schools in reproducing existing inequalities and the potential role of the teacher in mitigating against the worst excesses of these tendencies. By engaging with the fundamental question of whether schools and classrooms operate in ways which meet all children's entitlement to an education, or maintain inequalities in provision which are predictable, one is led to the political question of whether such practices can be interpreted as 'coincidence or conspiracy' (Gillborn, 2008).

The second kind of right embodied in the UNCRC is protection rights, and these relate to the need to protect children from neglect, abuse or discrimination. Schools have named members of staff responsible for child protection and clearly entrants to the profession need to understand how the system works and what role they may play within such a system, for example passing on a concern if they have spotted signs of possible neglect. As well as being prepared to deal with these issues there are day-to-day problems relating to bullying, hidden bullying (such as cyber-bullying), and deeper examples of prejudice, such as homophobia. In this regard protection from harm becomes a more expansive and complex issue than simply the archetype of protection from physical harm. One moves towards a more subtle and critical requirement to establish a psychologically safe environment, which requires a high level of alertness in the classroom and a willingness to reflect critically on one's own stance. Professional education should therefore support teachers to explore their own position in relation to these issues, and to develop a more conscious appreciation of their role (Epstein, O'Flynn, & Telford, 2003; Pearce, 2005). In his critical discussion of Freirean pedagogy, Au (2009) illustrates that one of the most significant principles established by Freire's view of the world is that we can come to know about the experiences of others (i.e., people who are 'Othered' through processes of oppression) and we can therefore tackle this in our teaching.

The third category of rights in the UNCRC relates to participation rights and in relation to education the most significant of these relates to article 12, which requires young people to be given the opportunity to express their views, and to have those views taken into account. In reality this desire to promote participation has wide implications for teachers and article 12 has influenced a range of initiatives in English schools to promote school councils (Whitty & Wisby, 2007), student voice and consultation (Flutter & Rudduck, 2004; DCSF, 2008), student researchers

(Fielding & Bragg, 2003; Kellett, 2005a, 2005b) and student observers, who provide feedback and advice to their teachers (Davies & Yamashita, 2007). This commitment to participation rights raises interesting issues for student teachers about how they can explore student voice in their own teaching, without subverting these into mere extensions of managerialist approaches, i.e. how can they retain the emancipatory dimension to such practices within often restrictive hierarchical institutions. More practically from the student teacher perspective, we have to tackle how they can manage the dual imperative of promoting student autonomy whilst rising to the challenge of behaviour management, which is a perennial problem in many English classrooms (National Union of Teachers [NUT], 2010).

So far then, taking the UNCRC as a starting point we have arrived at three principles, which we have sought to incorporate into our teacher education programme:

1. Teachers need to be prepared to understand the processes that include and exclude learners, from the classroom to the system level.
2. Teachers must be prepared to critically reflect on their own values and beliefs in order to engage fully with the need to create positive and inclusive learning environments.
3. Teachers should recognise the potential in young people to develop greater control over their education and to develop appropriate methods to enable them to form and express their opinions about it.

Case study methodology

The case study combines an element of evaluation (Yin, 1994) with Bassey's (1999) story-telling approach to educational case study. Through focusing on the experiences of university tutors and student teachers it captures some of the perceptions of participants, rather than setting out to tell any objective single account. Through allowing a variety of stories to be told the case study demonstrates the complexity of achieving change and illustrates the various ways in which change impacts on participants (Ball, 1993/2006).

Data about the student experience

This case study draws on a range of data sources. First, in order to gain an overview of the student teachers' experiences on the course we included three relevant questions in the general end of a course evaluation survey. These optional questions were answered by 110 students in 2009–10 and by 72 students in 2008–9 (approximately 160 students were eligible to participate in each year). The three questions were:

> What did you find most useful about our attempt to promote a *Rights Respecting PGCE*?
> What advice would you give the course team about promoting a *Rights Respecting PGCE* more effectively in the future?
> Do you think your teaching promotes and respects children's rights?

A focus group was also held with five volunteers during the final week of the 2009–10 course. This group was also joined by an education officer from UNICEF UK, who had been working on the programme. The group was run in a relatively unstructured way for 50 minutes, with occasional questions or prompts from the facilitator. Further examples of students' engagement with children's rights were also drawn from course assignments.

Data about the tutor experience

For this case study the Modern Languages tutor and the Citizenship tutor were interviewed, and data were also drawn from several conference papers in which colleagues have reflected on Rights Respecting projects within their subject teaching on the PGCE (Jerome & Bhargava, 2009; Jerome & Brook, 2009; McCallum & Jerome, 2009; Bhargava & Smith, 2010; McCallum, 2010; McCallum & Brook, 2010).

Case study context

The Secondary PGCE programme at London Metropolitan recruits approximately 180 student teachers a year, across seven subjects. The course is 36 weeks long and two-thirds of the time is spent in school, teaching classes, whilst the remaining twelve weeks are spent in university and preparing assignments. Those twelve weeks are divided into Professional Studies, where student teachers work across subjects, and Curriculum Studies, where they work in subject specialist groups. At the end of the course students gain Qualified Teacher Status (QTS), which qualifies them to teach in the state sector, and they also gain the academic award of PGCE. Each course is run by one member of staff and so the course team consists of only eight people (seven tutors plus the programme director). This makes it relatively easy to discuss and resolve issues and implement change. In the spring and summer terms of 2008 the course team met with representatives from several human rights organisations to discuss the possibility of incorporating a Rights Respecting approach into our programme. This was implemented in 2008–09, reviewed informally by the team at the end of that year and slightly revised for 2009–10. The first year's experience enabled the tutors to identify a simple model to describe the ways in which we were seeking to use a rights focus to extend our practice and lend coherence to the programme. The model includes the following three dimensions:

1. Knowledge about rights,
2. Rights as pedagogy,
3. Rights as a values framework for the children's workforce.

This model was shared with the student teachers during the second year of the programme as one way in which we could provide a clear explanation about how the Rights Respecting theme could be linked to the course overall.

There are several practical strategies we have adopted across the course to embed the rights theme and promote the model of teacher as change agent. Here we note some of the key features, to provide a snapshot of the experiences student teachers encounter during their training.

- *Portfolio Assessment* This assignment explicitly promotes the model of the teacher as change agent. The portfolio is described as a 'patchwork text' and embodies the four characteristics of the teacher as change agent: (1) it includes reflections on the technical dimensions of teaching, (2) inquiries into practice, (3) collaboration on reflection and reflection on collaboration, and (4) the articulation of a personal vision.
- *Inclusion theme in Professional Studies.* All students are introduced to historically established and currently reproduced patterns of inequality in education. A series of lectures, experiential workshops and discussion groups examine equality issues relating to ethnicity, class, gender, English as an Additional Language, Special Educational Needs, refugees, and sexual minorities. This strand is discussed in relation to children's rights.
- *Rights Respecting Pedagogy.* Our lectures on learning include both theory / research informed answers to the question, 'how do children learn?' and ethical answers to the question, 'how should we teach?', drawing on a series of pedagogical principles directly derived from the UNCRC (Osler & Starkey, 2005).
- *Student Voice.* All student teachers attend workshops which are run by school students. This gives them an experience of being taught by the people they are preparing to teach and helps to illustrate, through experiential learning, that children are capable of independence and formulating and expressing views on learning and teaching.
- *Cross-curricular initiatives.* All students use the rights theme as the basis of cross-curricular collaboration, to help them to think about the broader applications of the rights framework outside of their own curriculum area.
- *Rights in Professional Studies.* Our lecture programme starts with a keynote lecture from the head teacher of a rights-respecting school, who outlines the principles which guide her management of the school. This is followed by an interactive workshop introducing all students to the UNCRC. Links are made to the UNCRC in other lectures, wherever possible, including: personalisation, classroom behaviour, assessment, and policy.
- *Curriculum Studies.* In addition to the whole PGCE programme outlined above, each course leader runs workshops relating their subject focus to children's rights.

DISCUSSION OF FINDINGS

The student evaluations reflect a broadly positive response to the rights theme. In 2010 79% of comments about the rights theme were supportive and 89% of respondents talked positively about how rights related to their classroom practice. By contrast only one student teacher directly questioned the value of children's rights, asserting that, "there is far too much emphasis on children's rights and far too little on their corresponding responsibilities" (Student 105, 09–10 evaluation). This is a frequently heard refrain in schools (Howe & Covell, 2010) and it is significant that only one student raised this as an issue. Far more were able to conceptualise rights with a positive connection to responsibilities and respect, which Howe and Covell refer to as one of the defining features of schools which are able to fully integrate rights education. The following section identifies three broad themes emerging from the student responses.

Theme 1: Classroom behaviour

Classroom behaviour is a key concern for teachers (NUT, 2010) and for student teachers in particular this is often *the* major concern at the start of their training. These responses indicate that two important developments are happening during the course, at least for some student teachers. First, they are able to develop positive rather than punitive approaches to regulating pupil behaviour in the classroom. The second point, which is linked to the first, is that the student teachers are able to expand their understanding of behaviour to incorporate the broader notion of establishing productive relationships in the class and devising activities that build such positive relationships.

> In my relationship with the pupils I taught I tried to involve them in decision making and it wasn't based on me holding all the power and not them. Respect was one of the class principles my year 7 class [11 year olds] came up with and behaviour management focused around respect: we respect others and don't talk when they are; I respect you, you respect me. When I did use sanctions I used a restorative justice approach and spoke to pupils about how we could sort out the problem together. (Student 30, 09–10 evaluation)

This reflects the good practice identified by Howe and Covell in their evaluation of the large-scale introduction of rights education in Hampshire schools. They argue that some schools try to make *responsibilities* a priority in their teaching because of the perceived need to establish effective behaviour management, whereas in practice the most powerful learning is *rights*-driven. Once rights are understood, children are able to make the connections to their own and others responsibilities, as they conclude, "a focus on responsibilities does not promote responsibility in children. A focus on rights does" (Howe & Covell, 2010, p. 101). This was echoed by a student teacher in the end of year focus group who, when asked to comment on the accusation that children know too much about their rights, said they should be given an opportunity to think about other's rights as well as their own, and that the answer lies in this expanded understanding of rights.

Other students go further than using rights to formulate a classroom charter, and are able to articulate how rights inform their broader approach to relationships in the class:

> The revised National Curriculum further enables us to ensure students' rights are respected - particularly with its emphasis on giving students the

opportunity to have more say over HOW they learn as well as WHAT they learn. This is something I tried to focus on in my lessons - giving students ownership over the work and endeavouring to make them independent learners. (Student 44, 08–09 evaluation)

This overcomes the dichotomy one often finds in the way behaviour is discussed, which can be separated from decisions about teaching and learning.

A maths student in the focus group at the end of the year illustrated how he had taken into consideration his knowledge of how frequently a difficult child was excluded from lessons when teachers followed behaviour management guidelines. He argued that his own approach to dealing with the boy was influenced by the overarching priority he accorded to his right to education. Therefore he pursued short term 'time-out' from class followed up with individual conversations and a focus on relationship building, rather than the use of the 'on-call teacher' to remove the boy from the class. In this example the student teacher was clearly able to use the notion of children's rights to reconsider strategies he was observing and to come up with alternatives. The Citizenship tutor thought that some of his students were still struggling to find the right balance between their conscious attempts to be a 'rights respecting teacher' and the need to address behaviour problems as they arose. As a consequence he felt that some of them had still to find a way to combine this broad approach with the kind of teacher interventions that were sometimes necessary in fraught moments, in other words they held back from using sanctions but did not always have alternative strategies ready to implement. For him this represented a teaching challenge for the forthcoming year and he planned to be more explicit about how to manage this balance and how to use (and explain) sanctions when they are necessary. He also discussed the need to encourage student teachers to use their commitment to a rights respecting framework in the class as a starting point for their own (self-critical) evaluations of their practice, and thus avoid the danger of "lip-service" to the rights agenda.

The Modern Languages tutor also drew attention to behaviour in her discussion of rights in the PGCE. She recounted a lesson where she felt a student teacher failed to respect his children's rights and created an environment in which children were intimidated and felt psychologically unsafe. She contrasted this with another lesson where the student teacher had taken the time to get to know the pupils and had incorporated this knowledge in the lesson, thus leading to an inclusive lesson in which pupils were engaged and enjoyed their learning. Reflecting on the comparison she concluded:

That's the bit we need to say to the trainees...It's not about being soft, it's not about not daring to tell anybody off... it's about making them enjoy learning and enjoy coming to your lesson and feeling comfortable in it. (Modern Languages tutor interview)

The role of the rights respecting classroom in planning to teach comes to the fore when tutors think about how to prepare student teachers for tackling controversial issues, for example in McCallum and Brook (2010). In this context the Citizenship tutor discussed the role of teaching responsibilities, taking as an example the responsibility to be respectful of other's opinions. He was clear that whilst this should be explicitly taught as the general rule, one has to be prepared for a successful discussion of controversial issues to present more complex issues.

> In real political life people get emotional and don't think about their responsibilities to listen calmly... the House of Commons is an example of that... but I think it's naive to think (and that's why in reality it never happens) that you can... have the rights respecting framework for managing classroom discussion and all class discussion will naturally, if you teach children enough... they'll get into that approach to listen carefully. (Citizenship tutor interview)

Here there is a sense that the rights and responsibilities framework that might normally be promoted has itself become the focus of critical analysis. As he says, in a Citizenship classroom, with serious political engagement, and an honest exchange of diverging political opinions, one must acknowledge that simply abiding by rules is not possible, nor ultimately desirable.

> Some contributions might be extremely inflammatory and I'm not really sure I'd like to see children sitting there, you know, quite politely listening to someone who might come out with that. I would like children to get quite angry and passionate about that and that might actually lead to a behaviour issue, if someone stands up and says... 'what you're saying is abhorrent... and I don't want to hear it'... I'd be happier... for a child to stand up...(Citizenship tutor interview)

It is evident from the university tutors and some of the student teachers' reflections that the rights respecting framework is far from providing a straightforward list of things to do and things to avoid. Instead of providing a clear and categorical way to approach classroom relationships, it is seen as a set of principles which provide the backdrop to more nuanced decisions which can only be judged in the context of that classroom, on that day, with those children. The alternative, which is to use rights in a more simplistic and formulaic way, is more likely to lead to superficiality.

Theme 2: Inclusion

Some of the student teachers' responses, especially in relation to the question about their own teaching, referred to aspects of inclusion. This often focused on equality of access in general:

> All students had the right to a decent education, I tried to promote conditions under which that could occur and I endeavoured to deliver the curriculum to the best of my ability. (Student 82, 09–10 evaluation)

Sometimes students mentioned specific dimensions:

> ...teaching science inclusively with regards to religious beliefs, safe working environment... (Student 67, 09–10 evaluation)

> Working with refugees and asylum seekers - making the extra effort to meet the needs of pupils with EAL [English as an Additional Language], they want to learn, but need that extra support. (Student 28, 08–09 evaluation)

Given that so much of the professional studies programme on the PGCE is concerned with aspects of equality (and inequality) the emergence of this theme is not surprising. Some students are able to go further though and start to relate inclusion to notions of student voice.

In these more developed responses, and building on the positive approach to behaviour noted above, students discussed how creating opportunities for pupils to express their views and beliefs created a more genuinely inclusive learning environment. Some respondents made general assertions about this aspect of their practice but others made specific connections to classroom approaches:

> I use children's beliefs, backgrounds and cultures as an asset in the classroom. For example, during form time I had students prepare and deliver short presentations on religious festivals that were important to them. As a matter of course I always ensure that my students are clear that their voice will be clearly heard in my classroom, within the bounds of good behaviour. I try to create a collaborative classroom where all can contribute, be heard and be valued. (Student 57, 09–10 evaluation)

These responses only form a minority of the data but they do indicate that some student teachers are able to expand their notion of inclusion to incorporate a view of the learner as more likely to achieve valuable learning through their active participation.

Theme 3: Teacher identity

Clearly, a small minority of the students were largely unengaged with the rights dimension and sceptical about how it could relate to them. One student felt that that the dimension said nothing to his actual experiences of teaching:

> I found this to be the most problematic course, one which looked more like government propaganda than any realistic look at what happens in education. (Student 52, 08–09 evaluation)

This response was from an older male student who also defined inclusion as, "a lot of hard work, especially for badly behaved pupils who had no interest in learning." Taken together, these comments indicate that he was still going through a process of creating a positive self-identity as a teacher that incorporated the real demands of the role. Linking inclusion to "bad" pupils, rather than to notions of need or entitlement implies a deficit view of learners, which is unlikely to foster further reflection on his own development needs and professional identity.

Whilst this student dismissed this element of the course as being unrealistic, the next student found it to be redundant for another reason:

I did not find these lectures and workshops particularly enlightening, I think everything that has been said during these was mostly common-sense knowledge that should be crystal clear to every 'wanna-be' teacher. (Student 85, 09–10 evaluation)

This was echoed any another student, who also asserted that this approach was simply part of who he was:

...it is embedded instinctively into both my social and professional behaviour. (Student 75, 09–10 evaluation)

Other students had been able to incorporate the rights dimension into their developing sense of professional identity. One student in her portfolio at the end of the first year of our Rights Respecting programme outlined how this dimension to the course had prompted her to think about this broader dimension. She said that the preparation for the course (the application, interview, admissions paperwork, responding to interview targets, general reading and moving house) had become a list of practical obstacles to overcome to start the course, but the introduction of the rights theme had prompted her to think again about the enormous responsibility she was about to undertake, and the ethical implications. In the limited space available in the on-line evaluations, such responses were echoed in the following answer:

As Teachers, we are role models for groups of young people, who at times are quite impressionable. Through the lectures and workshops we were able to learn about and put into practice methods of integrating Rights into our lessons and teaching practice. If we act as responsible role models, this will help our students in being better citizens and... hopefully make better judgments in the future. (Student 49, 09–10 evaluation)

Some of those for whom the rights dimension had become a critical dimension to the way they viewed their role also used it as a critical tool for reflecting on the ways in which schools operated in practice, to include and exclude. One of these students in his evaluation noted:

As much as my teaching is developing in the way of a true dialogue between teacher and learner, I think it reflects a healthy respect for children's rights. Unfortunately, some of the structures of secondary education, especially with regard to curriculum and exam board requirements do not adequately support a focus on children's rights. For example, much of the time in KS4 [14–16 year olds] is spent on getting through material, and teaching to exam specifications, rather than allowing enough time for exploratory talk. (Student 78, 09–10 evaluation)

For his assignment he observed the experiences of students assigned to one of three groups in their final year of secondary school – those who had already passed their Maths exam at A-C level, those who had a very good chance of gaining a grade C at the end of the year; and those deemed to have little chance of achieving grade C, either through poor behaviour and lack of engagement or low achievement to date. Through taking a simple focus on access to a suitable education, the student described how the first group had been sent to the library to effectively self-tutor in Advanced maths, the third group had been reorganised into large classes and assigned to temporary teachers and the middle group received intensive lessons by experienced specialist staff. This project clearly had a profound impact on how the student viewed his subject, himself and the role he might undertake in any future teaching job. It also reflected earlier academic research on streaming, maths and access to education (Gillborn & Youdell, 2000). What is significant in relation to teacher identity is that he has started to think about how he will engage with the ethical dilemmas posed by school systems which appear to be at odds with his understanding of inclusion. In this one might say he is preparing to see himself as a 'change agent'.

This issue of teacher identity has also emerged in the reflections of university tutors. In the Modern Languages tutor's interview, she discussed a collaborative project she had undertaken with the Citizenship tutor (Bhargava & Smith, 2010). Their joint evaluation of the project focused more on the issues it had thrown up in relation to teacher identity than about rights. In particular they drew on Bernstein's analysis of subject identity in schools to clarify the challenges this cross-curricular project had posed. In her own engagement with this, the tutor reflected:

> I identified myself as a languages teacher and I had to work really hard to really understand where my subject fitted into that [rights project]... I could do it on a really superficial level, I know I could talk about child poverty in wherever... but it's still something that I'm working on really about how to make it run through the course and part of being a teacher. (Modern Languages tutor interview)

This led her to think about how the role and purpose of languages may be taken for granted, especially given the high number of native speakers she recruits to the course, and the implications of this for teacher identity. She was also starting to explore how languages, culture and identity come together for her student teachers, and plans to explore the possibility of connecting these issues through discussion of rights.

This tutor also sounded a note of caution about using rights as an ethical framework:

> It's too easy to take things for granted and I think it's too easy to make presumptions about what people's views are and I don't know I can make a presumption that the people who are starting in September are necessarily going to agree... There are some people who would say 'I'm in a classroom and I don't...' [sentence not completed]... So what we need to do is to say, 'well this is what we represent'... I kind of think well you haven't got a place in teaching if you don't believe that... But I think we need to be more explicit about what we mean... The trainees are from such a range of backgrounds I don't think we can make presumptions... People become teachers for so many different reasons. (Modern Languages tutor)

CHILDREN'S RIGHTS AND TEACHERS' RESPONSIBILITIES

Although in the end she comes down on the side of the argument that it is justifiable for us as teacher educators to espouse a set of values which go beyond mere compliance with the Standards for Qualified Teacher Status, she is clearly somewhat uneasy about the overt ethical stance this requires, and the implications for our relationship with student teachers. This echoes the concerns of the minority of students who said in the questionnaires that they were uneasy with this development, and indeed she also discusses the realistic possibility of an additional group who simply go along with this framework, because they lack the confidence or motivation to rock the boat.

Does a rights perspective make any difference?

Given that many of the student teachers' responses identified specific issues which were always taught in a PGCE, such as positive behaviour management techniques or aspects of inclusion, the question emerged, 'what difference does our use of rights language make to the way these issues are experienced?' In other words, was there any tangible value added by the use of rights language as an additional layer beyond the individual issues? It may simply be that as a course team we effectively used the rights agenda as a mechanism for refreshing our approaches to inclusion and other issues, and so what we were measuring was a broad level of satisfaction with these elements of the course. In terms of developing a conceptual model for the development of professional knowledge, we seem to have imposed the following, and the question was essentially whether the top layer was helping in any way, or simply adding a patina.

Figure 1. Articulating the role of rights in the teacher education programme.

Increasing levels of generalisation		Rights as a framework
		Generalisable mini-theories about: Inclusion, Behaviour, Progression etc.
	Evidence about what works based on experimentation, reflection and guidance on school experience and in training workshops.	

This question was reinforced by one or two comments in evaluations which were in no way representative, but which nevertheless seemed to raise potentially significant issues. One student in particular, who was very thoughtfully engaged with these issues and who might have been expected to embrace this dimension made the following comment in his evaluation:

> What I actually feel about it now is that it is an issue for government policy and I'm not sure that it is necessarily in the interest of a training programme to put it at the centre of its agenda.... Anyone who does not respect the rights of children has no business being a teacher, and I wouldn't quite understand why they would want to be. (Student 82, 09–10 evaluation).

When asked what, if any, difference the Rights Respecting PGCE context made to his teaching of controversial issues, the Citizenship tutor thought it was useful:

> rights clarifies it... it provides an overarching framework that... gives them a way of thinking when you're analysing the strengths and weaknesses and issues... it does provide you with a way of standing back and thinking both more broadly and deeply... (Citizenship tutor interview)

When asked how (if) our rights agenda changed the way traditional course content was covered, the Modern Languages tutor felt that we needed to be much more specific about the implications of the rights agenda. She thought,

> there is a benefit to sending out trained teachers who have a strong idea and a strong identity about what their position is in the classroom and in the school. If you give people a strong identity which includes their responsibility to promote a rights respecting classroom it's an advantage for them because it's an added layer of what you are as a teacher. (Modern Languages tutor interview)

Here then the justification of the rights perspective is more conditional and pragmatic, and this creates another possible route for discussions with student teachers – the comparative advantage one might gain in school by being familiar with children's rights and able to draw links between them and one's professional role as a teacher. This pragmatic dimension is also evident in evaluations of rights respecting schools in Hampshire, where Covell and Howe (2005) discussed how this agenda contributed to higher teacher morale. This connects to the previous discussion of teacher identity, to the extent that it affects teachers' sense of what they are doing in schools – getting children through tests or engaging in a more holistic education.

The Citizenship tutor was also asked about whether the rights dimension had made any appreciable difference to the way he engaged with issues like differentiation, which would feature in any teacher education programme. He returned to the theme of criticality and referred to the maths student (student 78, 09–10 evaluation, discussed above in Theme 3), who was in his professional studies group. He felt that for this student, his project on unequal treatment for year 11 maths students based on their previous attainment had led to powerful learning.

> Understanding the issue, and also understanding it from a rights perspective, [potentially] enables him to have a dialogue with people who make that kind of decision and if you can couch it in those terms (and all too often it's not couched in those terms, it's an issue of expediency)... if you bring it back to rights... their rights to have an education, and they're clearly not getting an

appropriate maths education at this point... it makes it pretty powerful... it's difficult to argue against rights. (Citizenship tutor interview)

Here we can see the rights agenda merging with the model of teacher as change agent, as the tutor is explicitly reflecting about the lessons this student may have taken away from this experience for his future employment. As he put it, the evidence of the learning impact may not be seen for a while, but will ultimately manifest itself in this teacher either participating in departmental or whole school discussions about ability setting, deployment of resources etc, or at the least making personal professional decisions designed to mitigate the worst effects of such iniquitous school systems. In this the teacher is characterised as a change agent, and teaching is seen as a political activity.

CONCLUSION

Two years into our Rights Respecting PGCE project it appears that the implementation is showing some successes. At the very least the evidence discussed above indicates that the majority of student teachers value this dimension to the course and can relate it to their classroom practice. There is evidence that some students are engaging with the theme to deepen their understanding of two previously significant elements of the course – behaviour and inclusion. The reflections discussed above indicate that some students are able to articulate a relatively sophisticated understanding of the inter-relationship between these two issues.

Furthermore, in the assignments referred to, and in the tutors' reflections on them, it appears that for some students the rights dimension is providing a framework to promote criticality. In some cases this criticality is directed at the school and the unintended consequences of policies; in other cases students use the rights perspective to critically assess their own actions.

Members of university staff have responded to the rights agenda in different ways and at different paces, yet the papers by course tutors (referred to above) and the interviews conducted for this case study illustrate another, less anticipated, benefit to our programme review. The nature and quality of tutor collaboration has changed and the rights dimension is providing tutors with a framework for discussing pedagogy. Of course, this could be developed on the back of any theme we had chosen to pursue across the programme, but the discussions that have taken place within the team indicate that the rights agenda certainly has the scope for developing a shared language about teacher education as a whole and also provides sufficient flexibility for subject specialists to develop their own subject contribution.

These glimpses of our programme illustrate the ways in which we have attempted to support new teachers to appreciate the political nature of education and to see themselves as moral agents within the system. The main point to emerge from student evaluations is that we should maintain this dimension and embed it even more thoroughly in the different elements of the programme. Through staying true to our vision, through collaboration and through critical inquiry we aim to continue to develop our rights respecting course, and in doing so to act in some small way as change agents – to promote the kinds of education that serve the best interests of children while respecting and promoting their rights. In this way our ultimate aspiration as teacher educators is to see ourselves as change agents and as facilitators of change agentry in others.

REFERENCES

Alderson, P. (2008). Young children's rights: Exploring beliefs, principles and practice. London: Jessica Kingsley.
Au, W. (2009). Fighting with the text: Contextualizing and recontextualizing Freire's critical pedagogy. In M. W. Apple, W. Au, & L. A. Gandin (Eds.), The Routledge international handbook of critical education (pp. 221–231). Abingdon, UK: Routledge.
Ball, S. J. (1993). What is policy? Texts, trajectories and toolboxes. Reproduced in S. Ball (Ed.). (2006). Education policy and social class. The selected works of Stephen J. Ball (pp. 43–53). London: Routledge.
Bassey, M. (1999). Case study research in educational settings. Buckingham, UK: Open University Press.
Bhargava, M., & Smith, R. (2010). Language, culture and identity: Using rights as a theme for cross-curricular collaboration between citizenship and modern languages trainee teachers (Paper presented at the 12th annual Children's Identity and Citizenship in Europe [CiCe] Conference: Lifelong Learning and Active Citizenship, Universitat Autonoma, Barcelona, Spain). In P. Cunningham & N. Fretwell (Eds.), Lifelong learning and active citizenship (pp. 140–148). London: CiCe.
Covell, K., & Howe, R. B. (2005). Summary of RRR research by Covell and Howe. Retrieved from www3.hants.gov.uk/education/childrensrights/.
Davies, L., & Yamashita, H. (2007). School councils, school improvement: The London secondary school councils action research project. London: School Councils UK & Centre for International Education and Research.
Department for Children, Schools and Families (DCSF). (2008). Working together: Listening to the voices of children and young people. London: Author.
Department for Children, Schools and Families (DCSF). (2009). The children's plan: Two years on (DCSF-01162-2009). London: Author.
Epstein, D., O'Flynn, S., & Telford, D. (2003). Silenced sexualities in schools and universities. Stoke on Trent, UK: Trentham.
Fielding, M., & Bragg, S. (2003). Students as researchers: Making a difference. Cambridge, UK: Pearson.
Flutter, J., & Rudduck, J. (2004). Consulting pupils: What's in it for schools? London: Routledge Falmer.
Fullan, M. G. (1993). Why teachers must become change agents. Educational Leadership, 50(6) (The Professional Teacher), 12–17.
Gillborn, D. (2008). Racism and education: Coincidence or conspiracy? London: Routledge.
Gillborn, D., & Youdell, D. (2000). Rationing education: Policy, practice, reform and equity. Buckingham, UK: Open University Press.
Howe, R. B., & Covell, K. (2010). Miseducating children about their rights. Education, Citizenship and Social Justice, 5(2), 91–102.
Jerome, L., & Bhargava, M. (2009, June). A rights respecting PGCE – The case of citizenship. Paper presented at the Human Rights and Citizenship Education Conference organised by Children's Identity and Citizenship in Europe (CiCe), Malmo University, Sweden.
Jerome, L., & Brook, V. (2009, July). A rights respecting PGCE – The case of science. Paper presented at the Human Rights and Citizenship Education Conference organised by the International Centre for Education for Democratic Citizenship, Birkbeck, London.
Kellett, M. (2005a). How to develop children as researchers. London: Paul Chapman.
Kellett, M. (2005b). Children as active researchers: A new paradigm for the 21st century?

Published online by ESRC National Centre for Research Methods, Review Paper (NCM/003) www.ncrm.ac.uk/publications.

McCallum, A. (2010, May). From article 12 to student voice - making children's rights real in the English classroom (Paper presented at the 12th annual Children's Identity and Citizenship in Europe [CiCe] Conference: Lifelong Learning and Active Citizenship, Universitat Autonoma, Barcelona, Spain). In P. Cunningham & N. Fretwell (Eds.), Lifelong learning and active citizenship (pp. 163–171). London: CiCe. McCallum, A., & Brook, V. (2010, July). 'Making a difference': Inclusion, classroom talk and voice on a rights-respecting PGCE course. Paper presented at the UK Teacher Education Network on Education for Sustainable Development and Global Citizenship 3rd annual conference: Education of Hope: the impact of ESD / GC on the wellbeing of teachers and young people, London South Bank University.

McCallum, A., & Jerome, L. (2009, October). Children's rights as a path to social cohesion? Exploring the experiences of promoting a rights-based perspective in initial teacher education. Paper presented at The Centre for Lebanese Studies Annual Conference, Education for Social Cohesion. American University of Beirut, Lebanon.

National Union of Teachers (NUT). (2010). Pupil behaviour: Advice, guidance and protection from the National Union of Teachers. London: Author.

Osler, A., & Starkey, H. (2005). Changing citizenship: Democracy and inclusion in education. Maidenhead, UK: Open University Press.

Pearce, S. (2005). You wouldn't understand: White teachers in multi-ethnic classrooms. Stoke on Trent, UK: Trentham.

Stubbs, S. (1998). Avoiding issue overload: Core principles and diverse discrimination. Retrieved from www.eenet.org.uk/theory_practice/avoiding.shtml.

Whitty, G., & Wisby, E. (2007). Real decision making? School councils in action (Research Report DCSF-RR001). London, DCSF.

Yin, R. (1994). Case study research: Design and methods (2nd ed.). Newbury Park, CA, Sage.

Lee Jerome
Secondary PGCE Programme Director
Faculty of Humanities, Arts, Languages and Education
London Metropolitan University

SAM MEJIAS AND HUGH STARKEY

CRITICAL CITIZENS OR NEO-LIBERAL CONSUMERS? UTOPIAN VISIONS AND PRAGMATIC USES OF HUMAN RIGHTS EDUCATION IN A SECONDARY SCHOOL IN ENGLAND

ABSTRACT

This chapter presents the findings from a research project that explored a partnership between human rights non-governmental organisation (NGO), Amnesty International, and a comprehensive state secondary school in London to implement whole-school human rights education (HRE). We explore the types of opportunities, challenges and understandings of both the NGO and school in partnering to deliver whole-school projects, in the context of a neo-liberal educational climate based on what Apple (2004) calls conservative modernization. This climate encourages schools to use the voluntary sector to give students enhanced choice in the curriculum. However, there is potential conflict between neoliberal objectives and the aims and purposes of more critical and progressive forms of education promoted by NGOs. Amnesty International promotes a perspective informed by concern to protect human dignity and oppose abuses of state power. Its concern with solidarity and critical politics contests the premises of a neoliberal, personalized concept of education. This chapter explores the forms of pragmatic uses of school partnerships envisaged and enacted by schools. It investigates ways in which NGO-school partnerships affect and are affected by ongoing school development processes within traditional school structures. The chapter provides evidence of the varied understandings of human rights by school community members. It highlights key challenges of implementing whole-school projects with external agencies, particularly the tension between the operational and political transformation envisioned by NGO stakeholders and the neoliberal results-driven imperatives placed on schools by official policy.

INTRODUCTION

Development, human rights, and environmental NGOs have been supporting citizenship and global education in state schools in England for decades and have played a critical role in offering teacher training, extracurricular projects, original resources and curriculum development (Hicks, 2003; Marshall, 2007; Starkey, 1994). However, in recent years, some NGOs have recognized the limitations of previous small-scale projects often driven by enthusiastic individual teachers and have begun to propose holistic approaches that recognize that educational innovation requires a whole- school approach.

At the same time, there has been an increase in the factors driving state schools to work with NGOs. Many NGOs provide extra resources, often at low or no cost, providing a free good to schools during a time of budget constraints. The Education and Inspections Act 2006 mandated state schools in England to promote 'community cohesion' and compliance was inspected by the educational inspectorate, the Office for Standards in Education (Ofsted). Schools turned to NGOs as evidence of the establishment of community links and to demonstrate their engagement with civic groups in the community. Such partnerships were also officially encouraged from 2002 with the introduction of statutory citizenship education. The areas in which NGOs offer schools their expertise, particularly human rights, development, and environmental sustainability require up-to-date knowledge, a grasp of global issues and a willingness to engage with conflict and controversy. These have been identified by inspectors and researchers as areas where teachers have the least confidence (Kerr et al., 2007; Ofsted, 2006, 2010).

Yet despite the now household-name status of the many NGOs that operate in schools (such as UNICEF, Oxfam, Care, Plan, Save the Children and Amnesty International to name a few), and the current recognition in government policy of the importance of both global understanding and citizenship in education and of NGO input into that policy, there is virtually no empirical research exploring the impact of such projects or the ways in which NGO-school partnerships are carried out by stakeholders on both sides.

The chapter investigates a specific dimension of citizenship education, human rights education, and a particular strategy for its implementation in schools, the whole-school approach. The case study presented here, of a whole-school human rights education (HRE) project initiated by Amnesty International and offered in one London school, can help us to better understand how the perspectives and actions of stakeholders in NGO-school partnerships influence the development of school-wide learning on human rights and democratic values.

We found that the school stakeholders approached this external partnership aimed at increasing understandings of human rights with optimism. School leaders and the teaching staff expressed a sense of the potential of the approach to positively influence the work of the school. They nonetheless concurrently conceptualized the project as part of a larger effort to address issues of school performance, and to a lesser extent, to meet the needs of students as consumers by offering increased choice. Whilst contributing to wider moral aspirations linked to human rights discourses, the partnership appeared pragmatically useful in a neoliberal educational context. The school side of the partnership was also concerned to improve behaviour; create increased choice for students as educational consumers; improve overall academic performance; and enhance the school's status on performance measurement targets. In other words the school aimed to position itself as a progressive 21st century learning environment in response to government accountability and performance protocols (Ball & Maroy, 2009; Maguire, Ball, & Braun, 2010).

This article begins by reviewing initiatives in global education as the longest standing NGO-supported area of curriculum development (Osler, 1994). It then explores the current educational context for NGO-school partnerships in England and introduces the case study. It reports on the views and perspectives of key project stakeholders (including students, teachers, school leaders and administrators, and NGO administrators and project leaders) as expressed in interviews and focus groups. Analysis focuses on the ways the whole-school project was understood by the different partners. We hope to contribute to understandings of the capacity of whole-school HRE projects to promote critical citizenship and facilitate transformations in schools.

NGO-SUPPORTED GLOBAL EDUCATION IN ENGLAND

Global education has been used as an umbrella term for educational approaches that advocate values connected to human rights and social justice, that include a democratic or participatory component, and that imply global interdependence, or a sense of global solidarity (Marshall, 2007). Teaching about sustainable development, global social justice, and human rights as part of a wider global education agenda is a response to the need to prepare national citizens for participation in an increasingly interconnected and globalised world. The introduction of formal citizenship education opened a contested discursive space where the tensions between an emphasis on patriotic or national citizenship and cosmopolitan citizenship are in play. Globalization encourages transnational perspectives, but national education systems inevitably prioritize the nation-state (Osler & Starkey, 2005).

NGO-supported global education projects have been a feature of education in England since the 1970s (Hicks, 2003). UK-based NGOs such as UNICEF UK, Amnesty International, Plan International, Oxfam, CARE, ActionAid and Save the Children aim to build a supporter base for their development programs overseas by providing education programs in the UK. These organisations share rights-based missions and clear principled agendas to promote human rights, issues often marginalized or absent from schools where neoliberal economics obliges them to push to achieve standards and higher rankings in examination league tables at the expense of a broader curriculum. However, with the advent of formal citizenship education, NGOs have occupied a role as experts on these issues and have developed educational materials, trainings and projects. They have also forged relationships with government departments that have placed them in a role of service provision of sensitive and politically powerful values agendas. UK government departments, such as the Department for International Development (DFID) and the Department for Education (DfE) in particular, have funded NGOs to develop teaching resources and training, and work independently with schools to promote elements of the national curriculum that support department goals. As issues regarding global development and human rights are often viewed as politically sensitive or contentious, NGOs working in state schools have faced the challenge of promoting their agendas in a way that supports national learning objectives. Consequently, learning about human rights has been framed by NGOs in terms of contributions to national citizenship education goals. One example is the British Institute of Human Rights' (2008) *Right Here Right Now: Teaching Citizenship through Human Rights* resource for teachers, developed in partnership with the UK Ministry of Justice. Within this context, NGO-led education projects in primary and secondary schools based on universal frameworks such as human rights are contributing to the development and delivery of global education in England's formal education curriculum.

NGOS, HUMAN RIGHTS AND CITIZENSHIP EDUCATION IN ENGLAND

Since its introduction in 1988, the national curriculum in England has prioritized a number of social education subjects within the overall framework of what schools should teach learners. This created opportunities for consideration of environmental and sustainable development, citizenship and human rights within the formal school curriculum. With the formalization of the citizenship programs of study in the first decade of the 21st century, the UK government emphasized understanding of global social responsibility, using environmental, development and citizenship frames. England's citizenship curriculum for Key Stage 4 encourages learners to develop competencies so that they can play a "role in the life of their schools, neighbourhoods, communities and wider society as active and global citizens" (Qualifications and Curriculum A, 2007, p. 41). Most primary and secondary state schools in England now teach in some form about sustainable development, global inequalities, intercultural understanding and human rights.

In England, there is a clear intersection between state education policies on global education and NGO participation in the implementation of those policies. This is particularly true of the citizenship curriculum. For example, in its 2008 document "Standards for the Certification of the Teaching of Citizenship," the ministry specified that teachers should "use voluntary and statutory organisations to plan and resource relevant aspects of the citizenship curriculum across and beyond the school," (Department for Children Schools and Families, 2008), effectively mandating teacher usage of external organisations for implementing the citizenship curriculum.

NGOS AND SCHOOLS IN THE NEO-LIBERAL AGE

Although many parents, headteachers and staff support a broad curriculum with global perspectives, the educational climate in which NGOs operate in schools can affect the way in which their initiatives are conceptualized and implemented. Schools face external pressures to meet standardized state targets for attainment, which are predominantly based on a neoliberal script of market-based performance and enhanced choice as the solution for problems. Critical scholarship from progressive and democratic education advocates has noted the ability of market-based educational discourse and practice to have a significant influence on how schools operate. Michael Apple identifies four elements underpinning many of the current discourses of school performance in both England and the United States that together comprise what he terms *conservative modernization*: market solutions for educational problems, neo-conservative emphasis on raising standards, religious conservatism clinging to narrowly defined traditions, and organisational philosophies of accountability, measurement and management (Apple, 2004) Whilst acknowledging the conflict and tension among these notions, Apple maintains that they all cohere to provide educational conditions for increasing international competitiveness as well as private sector profit, and discipline. This is often driven by myths of a romanticized past where idealised families strove to better the chances of their children through application to schooling. Apple (2004) argues that educational objectives have thus begun to take on the same shape as those driving national economic and social welfare policies:

> They include the dramatic expansion of that eloquent fiction, the free market; the drastic reduction of government responsibility for social needs; the reinforcement of intensely competitive structures of mobility both inside and outside the school; the lowering of people's expectations for economic security; the "disciplining" of culture and the body; and the popularization of what is clearly a form of social-Darwinist thinking. (p. 15)

Consequently, attempts by NGOs and schools to promote global education are unfolding in an educational climate dominated by an unceasing neoliberal orthodoxy, which comes into conflict with the aims and purposes of more progressive forms of education, particular those that stress community cohesion and solidarity over a neoliberal concept of education (Fielding, 2006).

NGOS AND WHOLE-SCHOOL HUMAN RIGHTS EDUCATION

Since 2000, five major UK NGOs (Amnesty International, Oxfam, Plan International, the British Institute of Human Rights and UNICEF UK) have implemented whole-school citizenship education and/or human rights education projects to extend human rights and democratic practices beyond the classroom and into the daily policies and practices of school life at all levels. What is also called the *holistic* approach to HRE is rooted in the notion that human rights must be simultaneously learned and practised throughout the school in order to be successful, and that a rights-based philosophy can lead to improved outcomes. This view has support not only in theoretical and practical literature on HRE approaches (Amnesty International USA, 2008; British Institute of Human Rights, 2008; Nieuwenhuis, 2007; O Cuanachain, 2005; Osler & Starkey, 2005; Oxfam, 2007) but also in official policies and initiatives of international and regional government organisations, notably the United Nations (UNESCO, 2006) and the Council of Europe (Backman & Trafford, 2007; Council of Europe, 1985). The approach is consistent with international discourses on HRE since the mid-1980s that have advocated holistic approaches to teaching human rights (Council of Europe, 1985; Cunningham, 1991; Osler & Starkey, 2005; Verhellen, 2000).

The most recent and relevant example of international support for the whole-school approach is the ongoing UN World Program for Human Rights Education (WPHRE), which in its Plan of Action for the First Phase calls for a "holistic, rights-based approach" that includes human rights *in* education and human rights *through* education, a distinction that refers to the promotion of human rights "in" curricula, materials, methods and training, and "through" the daily, rights-respecting practices of the school and its community members (UNESCO, 2006, p. 3).

Because it requires full organisational participation, the institutionalizing nature of whole-school HRE suggests that NGOs who implement such projects are in a position to contribute positively to school development policies and that their projects may be sustained over the long term. All of the projects conducted by the NGOs mentioned above have involved some form of collaboration with state schools and with specific government departments in support of national curricular goals. This raises questions about the nature and potential of such interventions in state schools. How are the divergent agendas of schools and NGOs negotiated in the pursuit of common educational objectives? How do school leaders conceptualize the usages of NGO projects focused on promoting universal values, and how do NGOs advance their work through educational collaboration? How can schools and NGOs possibly speak the same language of educational development if they come from profoundly different perspectives and with different forces acting on their organisational work?

By focusing on Amnesty International, this case study offers insight into some of the dynamics and tensions of NGO education work, whilst also providing a window into the ways in which schools in England engage in politically sensitive and potentially ethos-transforming initiatives as a part of their wider mission to improve educational outcomes.

AMNESTY INTERNATIONAL AND WHOLE-SCHOOL HRE

Amnesty International is perhaps the best-known human rights organisation in the world, with global name recognition and a history of pioneering human rights advocacy and development efforts in the UK and abroad. Amnesty International started in 1961 as a network of campaigns to free prisoners of conscience around the world, and transformed itself into a global human rights watchdog with an established currency of moral authority (Hopgood, 2006). Over many decades, Amnesty International has cultivated a strong reputation for protecting and defending human rights, advocating on behalf of human rights victims and causes, and raising awareness of the importance of human rights in all societies. In the 21st century the organisation continues to use education as a key tool for promoting its mission in the UK and abroad. Amnesty International has a strong historical commitment to HRE and to working with schools. It started to develop whole-school HRE in both the Ireland and Northern Ireland jurisdictions to support the Good Friday Agreement of 1998 to promote a human rights culture on the Island. Amnesty International's most recent efforts to promote increased HRE within formal education in the UK are aimed at creating entire school communities where human rights are respected, promoted and defended.

AMNESTY INTERNATIONAL'S *HUMAN RIGHTS FRIENDLY SCHOOLS* PROJECT IN A LONDON SECONDARY SCHOOL

Amnesty International's first coordinated global education project for secondary schools, *Human Rights Friendly Schools,* was launched as a pilot phase from 2009 to 2011 in 14 countries around the world by the organization's International Secretariat (IS), with the support of national Amnesty sections. The IS HRE team (consisting of three full-time staff and 10 volunteers) determined on this approach to support its overall mission to promote a global culture of human rights (Amnesty International, 2009a). Amnesty also maintains that the project is the organisation's contribution to the UN World Program for HRE. The project sets an ambitious agenda for participating schools to incorporate ten core principles, developed from key international human rights instruments into four areas of school life: governance, community relations, curriculum (including extracurricular activities), and school environment.

In each participating country, a national Amnesty International section partnered with one secondary school to develop and implement a one-year action plan to begin working with the school to become a human rights friendly community. In London, the Amnesty UK section partnered with Buckingham School to pilot the project in the 2009–2010 and 2010–2011 academic years.

Amnesty International (2009a) defines a human rights friendly school as embracing human rights as core operating and organising principles.

> It is a school that fosters an environment and a community in which human rights are learned, taught, practiced, respected, defended and promoted. It is a place in which all are included and encouraged to take part, regardless of status or role, where cultural diversity is celebrated. In short, a human rights friendly school ensures that equality, dignity, respect, non-discrimination and participation are at the heart of the learning experience and present in all major areas of school life; it is a school that is friendly to human rights. (p. 12)

This vision of a school embracing transformative education challenges many of the premises on which schools operate. Fundamental changes in school operations (and thus school culture) may be required in order for the realization of human rights for school community members, including students, teachers and staff (Carter & Osler, 2000; Covell, 2010; Osler & Starkey, 2010).

Amnesty International offers a unique case study within a crowded NGO educational field in the UK. It is not a registered charity but rather a recognised political organisation, not dependent on government funding for its educational projects. Many other charities are either directly funded by or work in close collaboration with UK government departments. Amnesty's aim is to encourage the promotion of human rights activist values. Despite this, in order to have credibility with schools, Amnesty has to develop materials that can be used to support the government's curricular objectives for citizenship education. For example, Amnesty published a resource for teachers delivering the program of study for ages 14 to 16 known as Key Stage 4 (Amnesty International, 2009b) The *Human Rights Friendly Schools* project has also been offered to the London school in which it is being implemented as an initiative that will support larger national curriculum goals such as student participation and student voice within the larger framework of citizenship.

This chapter draws on data from fieldwork visits to the school to analyse three key areas of the *Human Rights Friendly Schools* project, namely the respective aspirations of Amnesty International and Buckingham School and the ways in which Buckingham School used the project to achieve its mission and objectives. In focusing on these three areas we intend to shed light on the nature of the relationship between schools and NGOs in jointly developing whole-school approaches to human rights education and how the relationship influences the implementation process. The research employs a case study approach, focusing specifically on planning meetings at the school, at Amnesty International offices, and at other locations. Ethnographic data were collected through participant-observation of the partnership in practice; semi-structured interviews with key stakeholders (including students, teachers, other school personnel, and Amnesty staff); focus groups; and document analysis.

The following sections discuss the aspirations of project partners and the instrumental uses of *Human Rights Friendly Schools* one year into its pilot phase. We employ the notions of *utopianism* and *pragmatism* to draw a distinction between, on the one hand, the ways in which Amnesty and the school conceptualize *Human Rights Friendly Schools* as contributing to a better world through developing awareness of human rights, and, on the other hand, the more instrumental uses of NGO-school partnerships and of human rights frameworks for achieving internal and external educational goals as defined by the state.

Utopia is, amongst other things, a sociological concept developed by Mannheim in the 1930s (Mannheim, 1929/1936/1991) as characterising a motivating force for a better world. It has been theorised by Giddens as 'utopian realism' and Rawls as 'realistic utopia'. Pragmatism is a concept in the educational philosophy of John Dewey that recognises the importance of action as well as reflection and the importance of trying out ideas as well as generating them theoretically (Biesta & Burbules, 2003). It is used in political and social theory to emphasise that "practice, rather than theory, is at the heart of all knowledge" (Festenstein, 2004, p. 292).

AMNESTY INTERNATIONAL'S RATIONALE FOR THE PARTNERSHIP

Drawing initial conclusions from a research study on NGOs working in the field of citizenship education and their partnerships with universities, Gearon (2006) characterizes the work of NGOs in schools as an "emancipatory educational framework," arguing that the "raison d'être" of NGOs working in education is to advocate for radical social structural changes that challenge the government status quo (Gearon, 2006, p. 17). In other words, NGOs, particularly those with rights-based agendas, could be said to seek to apply a utopian framework to their education projects. Amnesty International's vision of a school as "a community in which human rights are learned, taught, practiced, respected, defended and promoted", cited above, is certainly utopian given the hierarchical structures and disciplining processes that 21st century schools have inherited.

Simultaneously Amnesty's *Human Rights Friendly Schools* (HRFS) project is a pragmatic response to the practical difficulties of justifying an education program with costly staffing implications. HRFS was intended to contribute to Amnesty's wider organisational goals of expanding its activity and membership in England and abroad. It also provided an opportunity to develop its educational work and integrate it with the global organisation's wider work on human rights education. The project team envisaged HRFS as a framework for some of the existing teacher training and curricular resource development Amnesty had been doing. The investment of resources was considerable since the process leading up to the implementation of HRFS in 14 countries lasted three years, and generated over 20 internal and external strategy, vision and curriculum documents in the period leading up to the pilot implementation. This was supported by intensive meetings and consultations.

BUCKINGHAM SCHOOL'S RATIONALE

Key stakeholders at Buckingham School, well aware of the moral purpose of Amnesty's wider work in the UK and abroad and also of the moral force of human rights language and discourses, recognised advantages to reinforcing the school's mission and vision statement through engagement with the partnership as well as the potential competitive advantage that could be gained by identifying with Amnesty's hugely respected brand and uncompromisingly principled world view.

From a utopian perspective the school recognized that the realization of the project involved changing the school's ethos, or its core values, to be more in line with human rights. All stakeholders interviewed apart from students (who did not use the word ethos in any interviews or focus groups) cited orienting school ethos towards a rights-based framework as the project's key purpose. The school's current ethos, as explained by school leaders, was connected to its motto, displayed prominently on its website, in the school's literature and letterhead and around the school itself in hallways and classrooms. The motto is the acronym STARS standing for Smart; Talented; Adventurous; Respectful; Students. STARS plays on the idea of students as individual 'stars', and the school's explanation of the motto on its website confirms that "students are at the centre of all our work: they are STARS."

During interviews, school leaders expressed confidence that HRFS could potentially become a framework under which other efforts to improve the school could be linked. The assistant head commented that using HRFS to impact the school ethos was about tapping into "the core of what people believe in," by changing the culture of the school to "bring up citizens who will go with that feeling of what is right and wrong into society and into communities, and take on [leadership] roles in society that therefore have this knock on effect." In a separate interview, Buckingham's headteacher similarly described a goal of HRFS to "become built into the ethos of the school, and into many dimensions of the school work so that again everything is framed through the idea of human rights." Both comments underscore a conception of HRFS and HRE as transformative in its ability to empower and spread human rights within the school as a set of values that permeate the school's work and are accepted by individual school community members.

The assistant head further described HRFS as potentially capable of bringing together many existing elements within the school that are already embedded and effective in order to make the project something tangible for the entire student body. He stated:

> Not just students and teachers but all people within the school community, whether it's cleaners, dinner ladies, or secretaries or police officers or parents, everybody is given the opportunity to buy into a shared ethos about what education should be for young people. The project could provide a sort of shared language that hasn't always existed before that everybody can feel as a result of that.

This demonstrates a utopian vision of the school as a single, shared community and shows that school leaders see the potential for the school to be transformed to achieve the HRFS goals through the development of a shared language of human rights.

Whilst Buckingham School is in many ways typical of a state school operating within the British education system, it is notably atypical by virtue of its demography, particularly its disproportionately high percentage (99%) of ethnic minority students. One of the ways in which school stakeholders conceptualized the potential of HRFS related to the demographics of the school, the surrounding community, and its impact on school community cohesion. According to the headteacher, the school is over 50% Asian Indian background, with the rest of the students from other Asian countries, Africa, Eastern Europe, and post-conflict countries such as Somalia and Afghanistan. One teacher expressed that HRFS could help students with different backgrounds to have a "multicultural view of the world, and to be tolerant and understanding of where others come from," while the assistant headteacher noted that "there is a huge cross-section of society within our school that reflects the local community" and identified cultural diversity as both a challenge and opportunity for the project's implementation.

Speaking about students from post-conflict countries, the headteacher expressed concern that many of the students come from "traumatic" areas and events and could thus benefit from being able to reflect on their past experiences and current education within a human rights context. The headteacher revealed a deep concern for students from "war torn parts of the world," particularly Somalia and Afghanistan, when discussing how HRFS could impact the school community:

> These children come having not been to school before, not speaking English, and in some cases they have themselves experienced extreme trauma. Or

members of their family have been killed, for example their parents are dead...some of these people are effectively all alone in the world.

The headteacher's remarks show an understanding of and concern for the need to assist students with culturally sensitive and traumatic backgrounds in adjusting to British life and its education system, and a belief in the ability of HRE to address these issues. Tensions between cultural groups in the school are also at the forefront of concerns for school leaders in promoting HRFS, and while a desire to use human rights principles to mediate and celebrate cultural differences is utopian, there is also a pragmatic desire to address and head off potential sources of conflict amongst differing groups within the school community.

RIGHTS AND RESPONSIBILITIES

When elaborating the potential for HRFS to inform the school's ethos, the headteacher drew parallels between the embedding of a school ethos inclined towards human rights and the achievement of behavioural improvement amongst students:

There are obviously clear rules that students have to follow, they have to behave in lessons and interact politely towards each other. If we could kind of frame the whole of our ethos in terms of human rights, so whenever we're following up issues with students we'd do so in that framework of human rights. We're going to do some work with the students in September on behaviour as part of the curriculum and [it would be good] if that work had a very strong human rights focus to it, so that it was always in the consciousness of [students].

The link between improved behaviour and increased human rights education was commonly expressed amongst school leaders. This was not surprising given the commonly held perception in UK rights education discourse about the need to balance rights with responsibilities. The constant expression of this concern by school leaders and teachers shows a de-emphasising of the importance of expanding rights knowledge and a greater emphasis on the ability of HRE to facilitate good behavioural outcomes.

The emergence of a strong discourse of responsibilities was a key finding of school leaders' and teachers' understandings of the potential of HRE and HRFS for Buckingham School. Citing research conducted in the UK on citizenship and human rights education, Osler and Starkey (2005) note "a tendency in discussions on citizenship education to emphasize the responsibilities of young people rather than their rights" (p. 154) and point to an established 'responsibilities' rhetoric in contemporary UK political discourse. Osler and Starkey suggest that "the word 'responsibilities' can be used as a bland and de-politicized device" which can serve to undermine the political dimension inherent in HRE and orient it towards controlling students (p. 154).

In separate interviews, both the headteacher and the assistant headteacher drew on the concept of, and repeatedly used the phrase "rights and responsibilities" to discuss the potential of the project and the development of students' understanding of human rights. They hoped HRFS would help students to better understand their responsibilities as well as their rights in the context of interactions with other people in the school community. The headteacher commented that HRFS should "explore the whole area of, what are our rights as an individual but what are our responsibilities towards other people, so [that we have] a much greater consciousness of that in the school." She also linked student satisfaction and a positive working environment to good behaviour when explaining school goals, asserting that "it is very important for students to be safe, happy and proud of their school, so we insist on the highest standards of behaviour to ensure that all students can feel comfortable and able to learn."

Further discussion revealed that HRFS was conceptualized instrumentally as a way in which behavioural issues at the school could be addressed. The headteacher considered that the development of empathy for others was strongly linked to human rights:

> When one child calls another child a name, [or] when one child starts spreading malicious gossip about another child, or when one child interferes with another child's learning in a lesson, it's deeply hurtful to that child. It's those sorts of things I think are important to help the young people take responsibility for their behaviour towards others. I'm expecting students to be much more conscious of their actions as individuals and to be much more considerate of others.

The notion of responsibilities and good behaviour are linked by the headteacher in a moral dialectic, as the headteacher is essentially equating the responsibilities that go along with rights to a sense of empathy and self-regulation about moral actions by students towards each other. The data generally found that in conversations with school leaders the importance of responsibilities was emphasised at the expense of discussion on the importance of students' authentic understanding of rights.

A teacher at the school who is also the school's citizenship coordinator echoed the potential of HRFS to give both students and staff a greater awareness of their rights and responsibilities, offering an example:

> Everyone has the right to education, but also they have the responsibility to make sure that they don't take that right away from somebody else by disrupting a lesson, for example. And also from a teacher perspective, like, you know, being able to talk to students in an appropriate manner, I think it's gonna impact behaviour massively, hopefully.

Just as both the headteacher and assistant head reported, discussion of rights and responsibilities was immediately linked to behaviour. However, this teacher's perspective on "appropriate" behaviour extends beyond a conception of what HRFS can do to improve students' behaviour and actually applies it to teachers, who through HRFS may themselves learn to "behave" by talking to students in an appropriate manner. This was a unique response among school leaders and teachers interviewed.

Teachers interviewed at Buckingham offered wry comments about their students' clever invocation of their rights as a means for evading some of their normal classroom responsibilities, and one teacher, claiming that students in the school were actually *too* exposed to human rights, offered an example which elicited laughter amongst the other teachers present during a focus group conversation: "I asked Abdul to sit in his chair this morning, [and] he said 'miss, that's against my human rights' so they know all about their human rights." When presented with this type of logic from students about rights in the classroom (even if said in jest), it is clear that the issue is not simply a misunderstanding amongst school leaders and teachers about HRE being used to balance rights and responsibilities; it is also about the way in which students may be understanding rights education as a form of sanction-free, general empowerment to behave as they want. This suggests that projects such as HRFS must contend with and address established perceptions of rights education in schools, and that the 'rights and responsibilities' paradigm is one area where pragmatic visions of school community members to use HRE as a form of behavioural control outstrip visions of using HRE to empower students to struggle for their rights.

Another area of pragmatic conceptualization of the partnership was found in the notion that external partnerships add value to the school's work and profile. The headteacher explained that the benefits of external partnership include "skills and expertise that partners will bring to the school that are very different from those of teachers." The headteacher continued:

> I also think that for young people to meet other people who are not teachers and to interact with those other people is quite powerful and it can be very inspiring to people and it can give them an insight into the sort of career they might want to have in the future. And I think in terms of staff CPD [continuing professional development], it's very powerful.

In the section below on pragmatic uses by Buckingham School of HRFS, we provide an illustration of how HRFS was used to add value to the partnership for external school inspectors.

BUCKINGHAM SCHOOL AND THE INSTRUMENTALIZATION OF HRE

After exploring the aspirations of the school for HRFS in the previous section, we now turn to a consideration of the ways in which the project was actually implemented in the school by its leaders. Analysis above on the conceptualizations of HRFS by both Amnesty and Buckingham School focused on how each partner envisioned the project's use for its organisational purposes. However, there is a marked contrast between Buckingham's conception of HRFS and the ways in which they enacted the pilot in its first year.

Like many of the school's other external partnerships and initiatives, Buckingham's school leaders say that HRFS is used as part of an agenda to improve the school's performance. School leaders interviewed about their involvement in the project used results-driven, neoliberal language when talking about how the project could contribute to wider school goals. Specifically, the notion of providing choice to students, which framed the students as consumers of the school's services, was a strong theme emerging from interviews with school leaders. The headteacher commented:

> We're looking at how we can create a curriculum that is more suited to the 21st century and to the particular needs of our students. It focuses on choice, on students making informed choices. So it's about students taking responsibility for their own learning and the choices they make in relation to their own learning and their own future.

The school's progressive work on curriculum is encapsulated by its 'personal development curriculum,' which is meant to give students the skills for succeeding in a 21st century globalised world. Part of the changes for the second year of the pilot involved an additional five hours of citizenship teaching every fortnight, which the school planned to use in order to integrate more HRE work related to HRFS. When discussing a new change in school curricular policy for the 2010–2011 academic year that would give students an option to select from a number of innovative curricular options (including the increased citizenship lessons that would contribute to HRFS implementation), the assistant head commented:

We're trying to give kids as much choice in the curriculum as possible...that kind of trend of trying to introduce choice, kind of a structured form of choice. And a sort of realization that actually as a curriculum, is it meeting the needs of our students? Possibly not. What are the needs of our students?

Buckingham's website offers students and parents a downloadable "course options booklet" which explains the way in which courses can be selected at the school. The introductory note from the headteacher immediately frames the document in terms consistent with a neoliberal discourse of individualised consumer choice specifically for Key Stage 4/GCSE learners, offering a "curriculum that tries to achieve a balance between a core curriculum for all and a variety of options to meet the individual needs and interests of students." Although the school's materials stop short of referring to students as customers, they explain that students are given an option to choose some subjects because:

> The choices students make are important because they influence their success at school and they can affect career choices and future studies. It is important that students choose subjects that they enjoy as well considering what is relevant for future career options.

This reminds students that, while they might want to choose subjects that they enjoy, it is important to think about the effect the choice has on their career. Whilst use of the word "choice" repeatedly emphasised in school literature and by key school leaders driving the HRFS project would suggest that the school's leaders believe their students should be empowered to select parts of their own education, they are still nonetheless careful to remind students that making choices should not be done just for personal enjoyment but in order to provide future career options.

Perhaps the most salient example of how the school sees value being added to its work through partnership is evident through the ways in which the school used their partnership with Amnesty International during an unannounced school inspection by the national inspection service, Ofsted, in May 2010. One of the authors was asked by the assistant headteacher to speak to an inspector on behalf of the school about what Amnesty was doing in the school to improve outcomes. His experience of the meeting was compelling but brief. He was interviewed together with another external school partner, a physicist from Imperial College, London, who had been working with the school to increase student participation in sciences. The inspector interviewed the physicist first, and made it clear that she thought very highly of the potential of physics for benefiting the school. Turning to the co-author, the inspector appeared less engaged about the work of HRFS at Buckingham, focused mainly on why he was not present in the school more regularly as a partner, and ended the interview after about five minutes with little positive affirmation and some apparent suspicion.

The assistant head and headteacher were both concerned at this interlude, particularly since the overall result of the inspection was a disappointing grade. The school managers were convinced that the positive benefits of HRFS and partnership with Amnesty should have been seen as evidence of the ambitions and efforts of the school to improve outcomes. However, the episode illustrates the limitations of a utopian vision, since, in the view of the inspectors, the importance of the prestigious subject of physics clearly outweighed any benefits from expanding the curriculum to include human rights. The inspectors' judgments are made public and influence parents when they choose a school for their children. Thus the very survival of the school in a quasi market-driven system depends on positive grades from inspection, leaving little scope for idealism.

DISCUSSION

Our research explored how the HRFS project partnership was constructed and its effect on implementation. We observed that two members of the management team, namely, the headteacher and the assistant headteacher responsible for student voice, together with the citizenship coordinator, drove the school's participation in the project. However, Buckingham School already had a tradition of international whole-school events that raised awareness both of international issues and democracy. The school's annual international conference in 2009 was used to great effect to raise the profile of Amnesty and HRFS at the school. Three groups of students from Amnesty HRFS schools in Denmark, Israel and Mongolia attended the conference and participated with Buckingham School students in international and human rights activities.

One of the major contributions to the school from Amnesty was a full day teacher training workshop for all of the school's teachers to introduce the concept of HRE and the HRFS project through interactive workshops that explained human rights principles and their relevance to education. Apart from this, although Amnesty International staff set up the project, they had limited contact with the school during the first pilot year. Thus although Amnesty project staff have a strong awareness of the aims and purposes of HRE in schools, their impact in raising awareness among the school populace in general of HRE, or even of Amnesty and HRFS, was limited.

From the findings, a picture emerges of the participating school as slowly adopting certain elements of HRFS that fit easily with existing objectives and practices. Buckingham School conceptualizes and uses HRFS in a number of ways that are both utopian and pragmatic. The language of "rights and responsibilities" has been easily adopted by many of the teachers and administrators in the school, but this conservative discourse simply covers the granting of privileges to children in accordance with improved behaviour now defined as being responsible. Neo-liberal educational policies and popular conceptions of educational effectiveness have made their way into the everyday language of school leaders, who use free-market logic (of school choice and performance standards, for example) to describe the benefits of NGO-supported HRE. However, this strategy came to grief when tested by a crucial inspection. What is left is a policy that instrumentalises HRFS simply as a project contributing to improved behaviour in the school.

The utopian vision inherent in human rights and the transformative potential of HRE are aspirations that are severely tested by the realities of school life in an age of conservative modernisation. Factors such as pressure on the curriculum, high stakes inspections and lack of teacher buy-in challenge the idealism of NGO partnerships. Struggles for equity, justice and cosmopolitan perspectives require partnerships certainly, but also long-term commitment and perseverance. Education is crucial to the achievement of human rights and justice, and this includes not only the education of young people but the education of ministers, officials, headteachers and teachers, parents and the wider community.

REFERENCES

Apple, M. W. (2004). Creating Difference: Neo-Liberalism, Neo-Conservatism and the Politics of Educational Reform. *Educational Policy, 18*(12), 12–44.

Amnesty International. (2009a). *Guidelines for human rights friendly schools*. London: Amnesty International - International Secretariat.

Amnesty International. (2009b). *Making human rights real: Teaching citizenship through Human Rights*. London: Amnesty International.

Amnesty International USA. (2008). *Integrating human rights education into the school environment*. New York: Author.

Backman, E., & Trafford, B. (2007). *Democratic governance of schools*. Strasbourg: Council of Europe.

Ball, S. J., & Maroy, C. (2009). School's logics of action as mediation and compromise between internal dynamics and external constraints and pressures. *Compare: A Journal of Comparative and International Education, 39*(1), 99–112.

Biesta, G., & Burbules, N. (2003). *Pragmatism and educational research*. Oxford: Rowman & Littlefield.

British Institute of Human Rights. (2008). *Right here, right now: Teaching citizenship through human rights - A resource for key stage 3 citizenship teachers in England*. London: Author.

Carter, C., & Osler, A. (2000). Human rights, identities and conflict management: A study of school culture as experienced through classroom relationships. *Cambridge Journal of Education, 30*(3), 335–356.

Council of Europe. (1985). *Recommendation No. R(85)7 of the committee of ministers to members states on teaching and learning about human rights in schools.* Strasbourg: Author.

Covell, K. (2010). School engagement and rights-respecting schools. *Cambridge Journal of Education, 40*(1), 39–51.

Cunningham, J. (1991). The Human Rights Secondary School. In H. Starkey (Ed.), *The Challenge of Human Rights Education* (pp. 90–104). London: Cassell.

Department for Children, Schools and Families. (2008). *DCSF Standards for the Certification of the Teaching of Citizenship.* London: Author.

Festenstein, M. (2004). Deliberative Democracy and Two Models of Pragmatism. *European Journal of Social Theory, 7*(3), 291–306.

Fielding, M. (2006). Leadership, personalization and high performance schooling: naming the new totalitarianism. *School Leadership and Management, 26*(4), 347–369.

Gearon, L. (2006). NGOs and Education: Some Tentative Considerations. *Reflecting Education, 2*(2), 8–22.

Hicks, D. (2003). Thirty Years of Global Education: A reminder of key principles and precedents. *Educational Review, 55*(3), 265–275.

Hopgood, S. (2006). *Keepers of the flame: Understanding Amnesty International.* Ithaca, NY, and London: Cornell University Press.

Kerr, D., Lopes, J., Nelson, J., White, K., Cleaver, E., & Benton, T. (2007). *Vision versus Pragmatism: Citizenship in the Secondary School Curriculum in England* (Citizenship Education Longitudinal Study: Fifth Annual Report). London: DfES.

Maguire, M., Ball, S., & Braun, A. (2010). Behaviour, classroom management and student 'control': Enacting policy in the English secondary school. *International Studies in Sociology of Education, 20*(2), 153–170.

Mannheim, K. (1991). *Ideology and Utopia: An Introduction to the Sociology of Knowledge.* London: Routledge. (Original work published 1929, 1936)

Marshall, H. (2007). Global education in perspective: fostering a global dimension in an English secondary school. *Cambridge Journal of Education, 37*(3), 355–374.

Nieuwenhuis, J. (2007). *Growing Human Rights and Values in Education.* Pretoria: Van Schaik Publishers.

O Cuanachain, C. (2005). Human rights education: the process towards understanding and action on global and development issues. *Development Education Journal, 11*(2), 21–24.

Office for Standards in Education (Ofsted). (2006). *Towards consensus? Citizenship in secondary schools.* London: Author.

Office for Standards in Education (Ofsted). (2010). *Citizenship established? Citizenship in schools 2006/09.* Manchester: Office for Standards in Education Children's Services and Skills.

Osler, A. (Ed.). (1994). *Development Education: Global Perspectives in the Curriculum.* London: Cassell.

Osler, A., & Starkey, H. (2005). *Changing Citizenship: Democracy and Inclusion in Education.* Maidenhead, UK: Open University Press.

Osler, A., & Starkey, H. (2010). *Teachers and Human Rights Education.* Stoke-on-Trent, UK: Trentham.

Oxfam. (2007). *Oxfam Education Resources Index: Global Citizenship in the Whole School.* Oxford: Oxfam GB.

Qualifications and Curriculum Authority (QCA). (2007). *Citizenship: Programme of study for key stage 4.* London: Author.

Starkey, H. (1994). Development Education and Human Rights Education. In A. Osler (Ed.), *Development Education: Global Perspectives in the Curriculum* (pp. 11–31). London: Cassell.

UNESCO. (2006). *Plan of Action: World Programme for Human Rights Education, First Phase*. Paris: Author.
Verhellen, E. (2000). Children's Rights and Education. In A. Osler (Ed.), *Citizenship and Democracy in Schools: Diversity, Identity, Equality* (pp. 33–43). Stoke on Trent, UK: Trentham Books.

Sam Mejias and Hugh Starkey
Institute of Education, London

HELEN TRIVERS AND HUGH STARKEY

THE POLITICS OF CRITICAL CITIZENSHIP EDUCATION

Human Rights for Conformity or Emancipation?

ABSTRACT

Claims that whole-school human rights education (HRE) projects have been particularly successful have been made in the UK Parliament and in research studies focusing on the Rights, Respect, Responsibility initiative in Hampshire and the UNICEF UK Rights Respecting Schools Award. Such claims have encouraged schools to join these programmes, attracted by expectations of positive impact on behaviour and general school improvement. However, a close examination of the literature and the evaluative studies suggests that whereas relationships between children and their relationships with teachers may well be perceived as improving, what is actually happening may not be HRE as it is defined and recognised in authoritative international agreements. HRE must include learning about human rights, and also learning in an environment where the principles underpinning human rights, such as equality, participation and respect, are practiced and lived. However, HRE is also intended to help pupils to explore power relationships in society through supporting them to identify and take action on real human rights issues. Evidence from the evaluations of these approaches suggests that some schools implement the programmes as behaviour management projects, focusing on responsibilities over rights, and equating human rights with good behaviour and obeying rules. In these cases a lack of political content and analysis, coupled with token participation, fails to provide children with their right under the Convention on the Rights of the Child to learn about their rights. The article concludes with suggestions for ensuring a more critical edge to implementation.

INTRODUCTION

Education either functions as an instrument which is used to facilitate integration of the younger generation into the logic of the present system and bring about conformity or it becomes the practice of freedom, the means by which men and women deal critically and creatively with reality and discover how to participate in the transformation of their world. (Freire, 1970, p. 16)

Human rights are the core element of an international endeavour aimed at promoting human dignity in order to achieve freedom, justice and peace in the world. The principles expressed in human rights instruments provide the standards by which governments at national or local levels and their institutions, including schools, may be judged. The articles of human rights charters provide a language for naming injustice, oppression and unfair discrimination. Human rights education (HRE) introduces and explores the implications of these normative standards and one of its purposes is to enable learners to struggle for their rights as members of the human family and to evaluate the extent to which governments and institutions promote a democratic agenda of equity and inclusion. Given that human social systems are inevitably imperfect and given the significant inequalities in any society, HRE is necessarily transformative. It aims to support the progressive realisation of a world where the human rights of all are respected, protected and promoted. It aims to enable people to understand what rights people have and who has responsibility for upholding those rights. It encourages active engagement in struggles to effect change.

The Convention on the Rights of the Child (UNICEF, 1989) defines participation rights for young people. It challenges the historical development of schools as places where children are treated as citizens-in-waiting rather than as citizens with agency here and now. Recognising children as citizens with rights to expression and participation is the basis for whole-school human rights education projects. Such projects aim not simply to teach children about rights, but to integrate human rights into the school system, enabling children to learn about human rights and develop skills for acting on rights in an environment where human rights are practised and lived.

Two projects in the UK have attracted particular attention, namely the *Rights, Respect, Responsibility* (RRR) initiative of Hampshire County Local Authority (school district) in the South of England and the *Rights Respecting Schools Award* (RRSA) of UNICEF UK, which has been piloted in five local authorities across England. Initial evaluations of these programmes have been very positive and findings from the research have been used to support claims that these projects contribute to general school improvement. Particularly notable was a parliamentary report endorsing these projects as contributing to citizenship education, improving behaviour and reducing bullying and school violence (House of Commons Education and Skills Committee, 2007). There is even a suggestion that such initiatives may counter social disadvantage (Covell, Howe, & Polegato, 2011).

However there have been concerns that some schools are implementing the programmes for the purposes of behaviour management rather than as transformative projects. If schools focus on responsibilities over rights and equate human rights with good behaviour and obeying rules they lose the connection to struggles for justice (Osler & Starkey, 2010). This chapter reports on an examination of the evaluative studies of these HRE programmes and argues that whereas relationships between children and their relationships with teachers and other adults may well be perceived as improving, what is actually happening may not be HRE as it is defined in authoritative international agreements (Council of Europe, 1985, 2010; United Nations Human Rights Council, 2011). We suggest that lack of political content and analysis, coupled with token participation, fails to provide children with their right under the Convention on the Rights of the Child to learn about their rights.

WHAT IS HRE?

The importance of educating people about human rights is articulated in the preamble to the Universal Declaration of Human Rights (UDHR):

> Every individual and every organ of society, keeping this Declaration constantly in mind, shall strive by teaching and education to promote respect for these rights and freedoms. (United Nations General Assembly, 1948)

The right to learn about human rights is inextricably linked with the right to education, a key human right outlined in Article 26 of the UDHR which states not only that everyone should be able to access education, but defines the content and purposes of education, namely to: "Strengthen respect for human rights and fundamental freedoms", "promote tolerance and friendship", and "further the activities of the United Nations for the maintenance of peace" (United Nations General Assembly, 1948). Given the universal assent by governments to the UDHR, reinforced by subsequent commitments, including the legally binding Convention on the Rights of the Child (CRC), there is a strong case in international law that there is a right to human rights education.

As with other rights, the right to education has been codified through a number of international treaties and conventions including the International Covenant on Economic, Social and Cultural Rights (ICESCR) and the Convention on the Rights of the Child (CRC). The CRC, arguably the most important human rights treaty for children and young people, contains two articles addressing the right to education. Article 28 outlines the responsibility of states for the progressive realisation of the right to education, whilst Article 29 focuses on the aims and content of education. United Nations experts, in a formal General Comment, affirm that the effective implementation of Article 29 requires significant changes to the way education is delivered including, "the fundamental reworking of curricula to include the various aims of education and the systematic revision of textbooks and other teaching materials and technologies, as well as school policies" (United Nations High Commissioner for Human Rights 2001, p. 18). In other words schools need to review their programmes of study, their teaching materials and the regulatory and policy frameworks they develop.

The last decade of the 20th century saw the development of a global movement to promote human rights education following the global Vienna Conference on Human Rights (United Nations General Assembly, 1993; United Nations High Commissioner for Refugees [UNHCR], 1994). The United Nations launched a Decade for Human Rights Education (1995 to 2005) and the subsequent World Programme for Human Rights Education, beginning in 2005 and ongoing (United Nations High Commissioner for Human Rights, 2004, 2010). Regional initiatives in Europe have also encouraged strategic thinking about how to ensure sustainable programmes of HRE (Council of Europe, 2010).

The World Programme of Human Rights Education offered the very general definition that HRE is activities designed to "convey fundamental human rights principles, such as equality and non-discrimination, while affirming their interdependence, indivisibility and universality" (United Nations High Commissioner for Human Rights [OHCHR] & UNESCO, 2006, p. 1). Experts subsequently worked on more detailed guidance and a United Nations Declaration on Human Rights Education and Training was adopted by the United Nations Human Rights Council in March 2011. This emphasises a more political and active approach including "combating and eradication of all forms of discrimination, racism, stereotyping and incitement to hatred, and the harmful attitudes and prejudices that underlie them". It also insists explicitly on gender equality and on the benefits of diversity (United Nations Human Rights Council, 2011). We should therefore expect any evaluation of an HRE programme to keep these dimensions in mind.

THE EMERGENCE OF WHOLE-SCHOOL APPROACHES TO HRE

Whilst articles 28 and 29 of the CRC address education and schooling directly, other rights in the CRC are also highly relevant to education since the CRC requires governments not only to recognise education as a key human right for all children and to provide education for human rights, but also to, "respect the human rights of children within the education system" (Lansdown, 2007, p. 37). This is sometimes expressed as the right *to* education, rights *in* education and rights *through* education (Verhellen, 2000) or education *about*, *for* and *through* human rights (Lister, 1984). Through education *about* human rights, people develop knowledge and understanding about human rights, through education *for* human rights people develop skills for recognising and taking action on human rights issues and education *through* human rights involves experiencing a school climate where the respect of rights is the basis for all activities. This conception of HRE is also taken up in the UN declaration where the aim is "empowering persons to enjoy and exercise their rights and to respect and uphold the rights of others" (United Nations Human Rights Council, 2011). Upholding the rights of others is certainly a responsibility and in this sense education for rights and responsibilities is complementary and reciprocal.

Attempting to develop school structures and education systems that embody the concepts of respect, justice and democracy is not a recent phenomenon. John Dewey founded a laboratory school at the University of Chicago at the end of the 19th century and built on this experience to theorise, in his book *Democracy and Education* (1916/2002), education based on democratic dialogue and shared values. His principles promote both individual freedom and collective well-being and he was concerned to encourage young people (and their teachers) to look outward to the world beyond their school and their national borders. He also placed considerable importance on the quality of interpersonal relationships within the institution of the school.

Pioneering work on human rights education developed by the Council of Europe in the 1980s was based on the principle that HRE requires a whole-school approach. A recommendation of the ministers of education (Council of Europe, 1985) asserted that, "schools are communities which can, and should, be an example of respect for the dignity of the individual and for difference, for tolerance and for equality of opportunity"'. It went on to highlight the importance of a climate of human rights.

> Democracy is best learnt in a democratic setting where participation is encouraged, where views can be expressed openly and discussed, where there is freedom of expression for pupils and teachers, and where there is fairness and justice.

In the UK, two substantial projects have promoted a whole school approach to HRE. The first is Hampshire County Council's *Rights, Respect, Responsibility (RRR)* initiative which has been running since 2004 and which has been taken up by some 200 schools including 45 secondary schools (Covell & Howe, 2008). The initiative developed following a study trip to observe innovative work on children's rights being developed at the Children's Rights Centre at Cape Breton University in Canada (Covell & Howe, 2005). The aim is to integrate the values of the CRC into the daily life of the school. It encourages and supports schools to provide an education consistent with Article 29 of the Convention on the Rights of the Child (CRC). The project is based on the premise that when children learn about their own rights and the concept of universality of rights, this can lead to more respectful behaviour. The initiative is open to all schools in Hampshire Local Authority in the South of England and involves the training of headteachers and staff on human rights, and the encouragement and support of schools, both directly by the local authority, and through a peer-to-peer approach.

Many Hampshire schools implementing RRR were also involved in the development and piloting of a linked initiative. The *Rights Respecting School Award* (RRSA) is a national award scheme taken up by some 600 schools developed by UNICEF UK, an NGO supporting the work of UNICEF. The aim of the Rights Respecting Schools Award is to embed the principles and values of the CRC in the ethos and curriculum of schools (UNICEF UK, 2008). Schools receive the award when they can demonstrate that the CRC is known and understood by their leadership and integrated into management, curriculum, and classroom climate. Pupil participation in decision-making is also a criterion for the award. Schools can work towards either a Level One or a Level Two award depending on how well integrated rights are within the school. Level One is awarded when they can demonstrate that they have shown good progress in four dimensions. Level Two is achieved when they can demonstrate that they have 'fully embedded' the principles and values of the CRC.

EVALUATING THE WHOLE-SCHOOL INITIATIVES

Canadian academics Covell and Howe, whose work at Cape Breton University had attracted the attention of elected members and staff of the Conservative-controlled Hampshire local authority, were contracted to assess the initial implementation of the initiative in 2005. This was followed by a three-year research project funded by a Social Sciences and Humanities Standard Research Grant from the Government of Canada which aimed to assess factors that facilitated and challenged the implementation of the RRR project in schools, as well as to track the impact of the project on teachers and pupils (Covell & Howe, 2007, 2008).

Covell and Howe's initial research (2005) was based on interviews with headteachers and teachers from 15 schools in Hampshire and a subsequent online questionnaire completed by 75 teachers and headteachers. In the three-year research project (2006 to 2009) they initially examined 18 infant, primary and junior schools, though this had fallen to 13 by year three. They used a mixed approach of observation, questionnaires, interviews and focus groups involving headteachers, teachers and pupils.

The evaluation was based on a comparison of schools where RRR was 'fully implemented' (FI) and schools where RRR was 'partially implemented' (PI). Teachers were asked to rate how fully their school had implemented RRR on a scale of 1–8, and RRR was deemed to be 'fully implemented' when at least two-thirds of teacher respondents and the headteacher rated the implementation of children's rights at the maximum level of 8 (Covell & Howe, 2007). At the start of the study about a quarter of the schools involved had 'fully implemented' RRR. It is unclear what guidance schools were given about how to base their judgement of where a school has fully or partially implemented RRR, or whether judgements by teachers about the level of implementation were comparable across the sample of schools. However, the evaluators feel sufficiently confident to conclude that, "RRR has been demonstrated to be a very effective means not only of children's rights education, but also of education" (Covell & Howe, 2008, p. 2). They propose that this model be replicated in all education systems.

Academics from the University of Sussex were contracted by UNICEF UK in 2007 to carry out an evaluation of a three-year pilot of the Rights Respecting School Award (RRSA), which had been funded by the UK government's Department for Children, Schools and Families (Sebba & Robinson, 2009, 2010). The research aimed to assess the impact of the RRSA specifically on the *well-being* and *progress* of children in participating schools. Well-being of children was of particular concern for the UK government since a 2007 UNICEF study on child well-being in rich countries placed the UK last out of 21 countries overall and 17 out of 21 for educational well-being (UNICEF, 2007). Sebba and Robinson's research involved a wider age-range than Covell and Howe, who restricted their study to the primary schools (up to age 11). The UNICEF evaluation covered 12 primary, middle and secondary schools at varying stages of engagement with RRSA. A mixed method approach was used, including the collation of background information on the population of pupils in each school; the collection of descriptive quantitative data on pupil attainment in national tests, attendance levels and number of fixed term and permanent exclusions; individual interviews conducted with headteachers, teachers, teaching assistants, midday supervisors, parents and governors, and small group interviews with pupils; documentary analysis of policies, staff development materials, teaching resources and pupil work in order to triangulate findings. In the second year of their research, Sebba and Robinson also interviewed pupils who had moved from a junior or primary school involved in the RRSA initiative to a high school or secondary school not participating in the initiative.

The research focuses on schools participating in the project some of which had not yet achieved the RRSA, and others that had achieved the award at both Level 1 and Level 2. The authors report that all schools involved in the study claim that the RRSA has provided coherence for other policies; increased pupils, staff and parents sense of well-being and belonging; improved engagement; improved behaviour and relationships and supported children to make a positive contribution locally, nationally and globally. They also report increased attainment in five schools (41% of those involved), and increased pupil participation in nine of eleven schools (Sebba & Robinson, 2009).

Similar findings from the Hampshire RRR programme have been interpreted as contributing to overcoming social disadvantage. The reasoning is that socially disadvantaged children are at risk of school failure, characterised by low levels of school engagement and achievement. If, as the researchers suggest, the RRR programme provides real opportunities for participation, pupils are "more likely to feel empowered, develop a sense of their own inherent value and see school as a positive welcoming place" (Covell, Howe & Polegato, 2011, p. 194). Consequently, it is argued that the socially disadvantaged students stand to gain more from the programme than students from wealthier backgrounds who are likely to be well-motivated in the first place. The authors supply strong empirical evidence of the effect of the programme, and there is a logical case to support their interpretation. The deprivation in Hampshire is, however, relative since of the 149 local authorities in England it is in the 10th least deprived (Henry, 2008). Further investigation would be required to identify why the HRE initiatives evaluated were situated in prosperous and culturally relatively homogeneous areas and whether this context in any way challenges the validity of the conclusions drawn.

DO THESE PROJECTS CONSTITUTE HRE?

Human rights education aims at empowering young people to contribute towards a utopian vision of a universal culture of human rights. For young people to contribute to the development of such a culture, they need to have knowledge about rights, skills for recognising and acting on human rights issues, and must be disposed to contribute to this culture of rights. Human rights education in schools therefore necessarily contains a number of elements; learning *about, for* and *through* human rights. Learning through human rights implies a school where the rights of all are respected and a human rights-based approach to education is embodied.

Both RRR and RRSA projects report an increase in an understanding of human rights by teachers and students in the programmes. Sebba and Robinson (2009) report increased awareness of the CRC, claiming that there is evidence of it being referred to by adults and children both inside and outside of the classroom. Covell and Howe (2008) too claim that children in schools where RRR is fully implemented demonstrated a greater understanding of rights than children in schools where the approach is only partially implemented. There is little evidence in research reports on either of the two projects, or a wider scan of documentation[1], of children learning about the wider concept of human rights or developing understandings of human rights and struggle locally or globally.

Covell and Howe (2008) reported that in some schools which had only partially implemented the RRR initiative, rights had not yet been taught as they were focusing on responsibilities first or that, "It had been decided that it was no longer necessary to teach the specific rights in the Convention because they had been absorbed into the school ethos" (p. 11). This suggests that some schools involved in the project did not understand the importance of children developing knowledge and understanding about human rights. In fact it can be argued that such approaches are not human rights education because whilst they promote a moral perspective they do not promote a critical awareness. This would require some exploration of the underlying principles on which human rights theory is based and contextualising local struggles within the global human rights movement (Jennings, 2006). There is no longer a shortage of resources to support teachers adopting such approaches even with young children.

However, rather than adopt a critical approach, the evidence from Hampshire suggests that pupils associate rights with good behaviour and obeying rules rather than struggle. A resource consisting of a PowerPoint presentation developed by pupils from three primary schools in the RRR project and posted on the Hampshire website to disseminate perceived good practice asks its audience to determine which features of schools described are and are not rights respecting (Hampshire County Council, 2007). Aspects of a school which the pupils deem not to be rights respecting include a library where children are throwing books around and being loud and a lunch hall which is messy, where children are having food fights and trading food. On the other hand, in a rights respecting school the pupils suggest that that children in the library would be choosing books in a sensible manner, being quiet and calm and doing what they are told. In the dining hall the pupils would have table manners, not push in the line and not shout along tables. In their dining room example, the right which they claim is not being respected is CRC Article 24 which outlines children's right to the highest attainable standards of health, including access to adequate nutritious food. It perhaps trivialises this right to suggest that it is denied when children shout in the canteen. In fact, it appears that children are being encouraged to consider rights as an element of a self-disciplining process rather than as something to be won through struggle.

In the evaluation visits they conducted in 2008, Sebba and Robinson noted confusion regarding the relationship between rights and responsibilities. They observed that staff and students "sometimes presented rights and responsibilities as though they corresponded one-to-one" (Sebba & Robinson, 2009, p. 6). This confusion about the link between rights and responsibilities was also raised by Covell and Howe (2008). As a result of this finding UNICEF introduced clearer guidance for schools on the relationship between unconditional rights and learned

THE POLITICS OF CRITICAL CITIZENSHIP EDUCATION

responsibilities. A globally disseminated UNICEF publication asserts that "there is no requirement on the part of a child, for example, that she or he demonstrate a responsible attitude in order to 'earn' an entitlement to education" (Landsdown, 2007, p. 22). The RRSA guidance was adapted to include a clear statement that "the rights of the child are not conditional on responsibilities. Rights do imply responsibilities but are independent of responsibilities" (UNICEF UK, 2010c, p. 3). UNICEF UK concludes that rights may not therefore be withdrawn or withheld. However it may be legitimate to prevent pupils infringing the rights of others.

A whole-school human rights education project requires support for teachers to ensure that they themselves accept and agree with the concept and value of HRE, and that they have the necessary knowledge, skills and confidence to deliver effective HRE. It is reported that, in a number of countries, educators, like the general public, lack familiarity with human rights instruments (Osler & Starkey, 2010). The RRSA project seems to have overcome this to a certain extent since in a majority of the schools visited, all staff knew about the RRSA project and staff development opportunities were provided (Sebba & Robinson, 2009). Whilst this addresses awareness of the project itself, there is no clear evidence about the level of knowledge and understanding amongst teachers about human rights content and processes. The tendency noted above to make rights conditional on responsibilities indicates that there may be further need for professional development opportunities for staff on human rights.

EDUCATION *FOR* HUMAN RIGHTS

Headteachers interviewed for the RRR research reported an improvement in students' critical thinking, persuasive-argument, decision-making and collaborative learning skills (Covell & Howe, 2007). These are certainly important skills for recognising and acting on human rights issues. The RRSA project helped pupils gain more confidence to talk out in class, resolve conflict and work together and express their own views (Sebba & Robinson, 2009). These are certainly key elements of learning *for* human rights. However it is unclear whether the pupils necessarily had the opportunity to practice these skills in relation to human rights issues.

Both evaluations found an increase in pupil participation in school decision-making as a result of the RRR/RRSA initiatives. One example of pupil participation noted by Covell and Howe (2008) is "input into school spending" (p. 10). However, this seems a slightly exaggerated claim since it did not refer to influencing the overall school budget but concerned the purchase of an aquarium. In RRSA schools there are examples of pupil participation which include school councils, involvement in teacher recruitment and selection, and evaluating lessons. It is unclear from the reports whether schools had found mechanisms to enable all children to participate through these activities. Indeed, pupils raised the issue of the lack of inclusivity in school councils. They were concerned that only the most popular or academic pupils were involved. This suggests that pupil participation may still often be teacher-led and tokenistic (Hart, 1992). However the evaluators also reported that schools claimed to be taking measures to increase inclusivity in these areas (Sebba & Robinson, 2009).

The RRSA is said to result in pupils becoming actively involved in upholding or defending the rights of others, however the evidence for this claim is weak. There are references in the reports to school projects on global issues, but these tend to adopt approaches which are traditional and apolitical such as school linking and fundraising. It is not clear to what extent students are actually involved in considering or taking action on these issues from a human rights perspective and the extent to which such work is largely teacher-led. Staff in three schools involved in the evaluation suggested that their work supporting pupils to fundraise for issues may simply be tokenistic, providing "a strong feel-good factor by those involved, but no greater understanding of the effect of their actions" (Sebba & Robinson, 2009, p. 10).

EDUCATION *THROUGH* HUMAN RIGHTS

The intention of both the RRR and RRSA projects is that rights are integrated into the ethos, culture and practices of the participating schools. The evaluation of the RRR initiative concludes that the objective of having a rights-based school ethos was met, whilst the RRSA has provided the "underlying values" for schools (Sebba & Robinson, 2009, p. 1). There is evidence that the language of rights is explicitly used not just in teaching and learning, but also in peer interaction and conflict resolution inside and outside of the classroom. However, much of the focus of the evaluations relates to improvements in behaviour. Both reports claim that when rights are integrated into schools and used as a framework for pupil codes of conduct, behaviour improves, as pupils learn to respect the rights of others.

In RRR schools where the approach is only partially implemented, the focus was in fact more on responsibilities than rights. In these schools Covell and Howe (2008) report it is recognised that RRR "was used only as a tool for behaviour management" and that children "understood their rights to be nothing more than the rules of their classrooms" (p. 11). Consequently "pupils appear to have more understanding of responsibilities than rights" (p. 16). Illustrative of this, one child reportedly claimed that a friend was "very badly behaved before we learned about rights, respect and responsibilities, but now he behaves" (Covell & Howe, 2008, pp. 17–18). As schools where the approach was only partially implemented accounted for eight out of the 13 schools involved in the evaluation, this issue may be not untypical of the project. It would appear that even in some schools involved in RRR, the ethos is less 'rights respecting' and more 'responsibility respecting.'

This focus on responsibility may respond to legitimate concerns often raised by parents and teachers about teaching children about their human rights, as it is claimed that children already know too much about their rights (Howe & Covell, 2005; Alderson, 2008). However, other research has demonstrated that knowledge and understanding of rights leads to more awareness of responsibilities (Hudson, 2005). Indeed, when the focus shifts from individual responsibilities to the responsibilities of authorities and governments for upholding rights, then the element of struggle and transformation returns (Osler & Starkey, 2005; Kuper, 2005; Pogge, 2005).

Some students in a Rights Respecting School claimed that they "found it difficult to continue behaving in a rights-respecting way outside of school, saying that it was stressful to behave in a rights-respecting way all of the time" (UNICEF UK, 2008, p. 8). The danger in focusing on responsibilities to the detriment of rights, therefore, is that children fail to see human rights as a mechanism for the advancement of a society based on equality and justice for all and instead associate them simply with compliance. Indeed, the RRR evaluators have come to recognise this as a weakness in the programme as implemented and argue that when teachers unduly focus on responsibilities, this is miseducation about children's rights (Howe & Covell, 2010).

RIGHTS *IN* EDUCATION

Despite the aims of both projects focusing on the integration of the CRC into the ethos and practice of schools, neither evaluation considered the extent to which schools integrated rights into school policies, whether teaching methodology is rights respecting, or whether the project is having a positive impact on children whose rights are traditionally less well respected, such as refugee children, children who speak English as an Additional Language or children on the register of Special Educational Needs. In Covell and Howe's (2005) initial research on RRR, they asked participants to report on impact on pupils' behaviour and understanding and the effect on themselves rather than the extent to which children's rights were being upheld. Teachers and heads were asked to rate the extent to which they had seen changes in pupils in a number of areas including being less confrontational with peers and teachers; use of rights language; more mature debate; more interest in learning; more empowered; more engaged in school; less fighting, bullying, and disruption in class; greater acceptance of personal responsibility (Covell & Howe, 2005). Heads in schools where RRR was fully implemented asserted that there was a "central place for the rights of the child in policy statements" (Covell & Howe, 2008, p. 10).

This focus on the knowledge and understanding of rights and behaviour of pupils is also reflected in the evaluation of the RRSA. In one of the primary schools, the RRS lead teacher had matched CRC articles to a school policy "as a means of reviewing the policies to ensure their consistency with the RRSA" (Sebba & Robinson, 2009, p. 14). The fact that this was singled out as good practice in one school indicates that this is not systematically being done across all schools involved, even though this is advised in UNICEF UK's Action Plan guidance (UNICEF UK, 2010a, 2010b).

In both research reports, improvements in aspects such as increased participation and improved behaviour are attributed to the RRR/RRSA approaches. However, during the period of the evaluation there were a number of other initiatives such as Every Child Matters and Social and Emotional Aspects of Learning (SEAL) that make it problematic to attribute changes to one factor.

Indeed some headteachers were "uncomfortable attributing positive changes [uniquely] to RRR" (Covell & Howe, 2007, p. 5). Sebba and Robinson also acknowledge that it is difficult to attribute findings to one initiative and consequently attempt to draw evidence from a range of sources to support their conclusions.

CONCLUSIONS

It is important that all organisations implementing whole-school human rights education projects, including UNICEF and Hampshire, ensure that they reflect on the broader conception of human rights education and that all elements of HRE are built into their programmes. There is a particular need for the further development of elements of education *for* human rights, encouraging schools to support children to develop skills for identifying and acting on human rights concerns, and human rights *in* education, especially the systematic integration of specific rights into policies and procedures. It appears that whole-school projects such as RRR and RRSA would benefit from emphasising the human rights content so that learning about the CRC is situated within a wider human rights framework and a global or cosmopolitan as well as local perspective.

Internationally it is agreed that there is a need to support and further develop existing work through the delivery of effective teacher training, since this is key to the development of effective human rights education practices in schools (United Nations High Commissioner for Human Rights & UNESCO, 2006). There are a number of useful frameworks outlining teacher competencies for HRE which could be adapted for teachers participating in such initiatives. These originate in the work of the Council of Europe (Brett, Mompoint-Gaillard, & Salema, 2009) and in the USA (Jennings, 2006). These frameworks reinforce the idea that teachers must themselves develop a good understanding of human rights concepts and laws and develop teaching methodologies and classroom practices that embody rights principles and encourage critical reflection and action.

The very valuable evidence provided by the evaluations about how schools engage with human rights is summarised for sponsors in terms that are politically positive such as impact on behaviour, attendance and achievement. When this message is also communicated to schools, the expectations of the instrumental benefits of the projects may lead to a focus on behaviour management rather than the transformation of schools as institutions and of society. Instead of embarking on the projects because children have a right to learn in an environment where their rights are respected, to learn about human rights and to become empowered to defend the rights of those and others around them, schools may sign up because they think that it will improve children's behaviour and make them more compliant.

We believe that projects such as RRR and RRSA are highly significant examples from the UK that can stimulate emulation elsewhere and provide models of educational reform at the school level that can transform the experience of education for children and their teachers (Council of Europe, OSCE/ODIHR, UNESCO, OHCHR, 2009). Since there is now evidence that in these project schools teachers treat their students "as persons with rights rather than as objects to be moulded" (Covell et al., 2011, p. 203), it is not surprising that the climate of the schools is positive and that disaffection is less pronounced than in traditional authoritarian and strongly hierarchical schools. Perhaps this initial step of transforming teacher/student relationships will open up a space for emancipation rather than conformity and the acceptance of conflicts as a potentially creative opportunity for exploring different ways of reconciling difference without resorting to violence. The struggle for the dignity of students in schools may lead to engagement in wider struggles for recognition and for democracy in the wider society. The tension between the requirements for behaviour management and the transformative potential of human rights education is itself a site of struggle for educators and researchers.

NOTES

[1] Including the Hampshire RRR webpage http://www3.hants.gov.uk/education/childrensrights/ and participating school webpages

REFERENCES

Alderson, P. (2008). *Young Children's Rights: Exploring Beliefs, Principles and Practice* (2nd ed.). London & Philadelphia: Jessica Kingsley Publishers.

Brett, P., Mompoint-Gaillard, P., & Salema, M. H. (2009). *How all teachers can support citizenship and human rights education: A framework for the development of competencies*. Strasbourg: Council of Europe.

Council of Europe. (1985). *Recommendation No. R(85)7 of the Committee of Ministers to Member States on Teaching and Learning about Human Rights in Schools*. Strasbourg: Author.

Council of Europe, OSCE/ODIHR, UNESCO, OHCHR. (2009). *Human Rights Education in the School Systems of Europe, Central Asia and North America: A Compendium of Good Practice*. Warsaw: OSCE Office for Democratic Institutions and Human Rights (ODIHR). Retrieved June 6, 2011, from http://www.ohchr.org/Documents/Publications/CompendiumHRE.pdf

Council of Europe. (2010). *Charter on Education for Democratic Citizenship and Human Rights Education*. Recommendation CM/Rec(2010)7 and explanatory memorandum. Strasbourg: Author. Retrieved June 10, 2011, from http://www.coe.int/t/dg4/education/edc/Source/Pdf/Downloads/6898-6-ID10009-Recommendation%20on%20Charter%20EDC-HRE%20-%20assembl%C3%A9.pdf

Covell, K., & Howe, B. (2005). *Rights, Respect and Responsibility - Report on the RRR Initiative to Hampshire County Education Authority*. Sydney, NS: Cape Breton University.

Covell, K., & Howe, R. B. (2007). *Report on the Hampshire County Initiative*. Sydney, NS: Cape Breton University.

Covell, K., & Howe, R. B (2008). *Rights, Respect and Responsibility: Final Report on the County of Hampshire Rights Education*. Sydney, NS: Cape Breton University.

Covell, K., Howe, R. B., & Polegato, J. L. (2011). Children's human rights education as a counter to social disadvantage: A case study from England. *Educational Research, 53*(2), 193–206.

Dewey, J. (2002). Democracy and education: An introduction to the philosophy of education. In S. J. Maxcy (Ed.), *John Dewey and American Education Vol. 3*. Bristol, UK: Thoemmes. (Original work published 1916)

Freire, P. (1970). *Pedagogy of the Oppressed*. London: Penguin Books.

Hampshire County Council. (2007). *RRR Primary Conference Presentation*. Winchester, UK: Hampshire County Council. Retrieved June 6, 2011, from http://www3.hants.gov.uk/rrrpriconf2007-pupilspresentation.pdf

Hart, R. A. (1992). *Children's participation: From tokenism to citizenship*. Florence, Italy: UNICEF.

Henry, G. (2008). *A Study of the 2007 English Index of Multiple Deprivation for the Hampshire County Council Area*. Winchester, UK: Hampshire County Council. Retrieved June 6, 2011, from http://www.basingstoke.gov.uk/NR/rdonlyres/6175A8B3-EA14-4B77-8D69-07DDB3D71245/0/IndicesofDeprivation2007Hampshireanalysis.pdf

House of Commons Education and Skills Committee. (2007). *Citizenship Education Second Report of Session 2006–07*. London: The Stationery Office Limited. Retrieved August 12, 2010, from http://www.publications.parliament.uk/pa/cm200607/cmselect/cmeduski/147/147.pdf

Howe, R. B., & Covell, K. (2005). *Empowering Children: Children's Rights Education as a Pathway to Citizenship*. Toronto: University of Toronto Press.

Howe, R. B., & Covell, K. (2010). Miseducating children about their rights. *Education, Citizenship and Social Justice, 5*(2), 91–102.

Hudson, A. (2005). Citizenship Education and Students' Identities: A school-based action research project. In A. Osler (Ed.), *Teachers, Human Rights and Diversity: Educating citizens in multicultural societies* (pp. 115–132). Stoke on Trent, UK: Trentham.

Kuper, A. (Ed.). (2005). *Global Responsibilities: Who must deliver on human rights?* Abingdon, UK: Routledge.

Jennings, T. (2006). Human rights education standards for teachers and teacher education. *Teaching Education, 17*(4), 287–298.

Lansdown, G. (2007). *A Human Rights-Based Approach to Education for All*. New York & Paris: UNICEF & UNESCO.

Lister, I. (1984). *Teaching and Learning about Human Rights*. Strasbourg: Council of Europe.

Osler, A., & Starkey, H. (2005). *Changing Citizenship: Democracy and Inclusion in Education*. Maidenhead, UK: Open University Press.

Osler, A., & Starkey, H. (2010). *Teachers and Human Rights Education*. Stoke on Trent, UK: Trentham.

Pogge, T. (2005). Human Rights and Human Responsibilities. In A. Kuper (Ed.), *Global Responsibilities: Who must deliver on human rights?* (pp. 3–36). Abingdon, UK: Routledge.

Sebba, J., & Robinson, C. (2009). *Evaluation of UNICEF UK's Rights Respecting Schools Award: Interim Report at the End of Year Two*. London: UNICEF.

Sebba, J., & Robinson, C. (2010). *Evaluation of UNICEF UK's Rights Respecting Schools Award: Final Report*. London: UNICEF UK.

UNICEF. (1989). *Convention on the Rights of the Child*. New York: Author. Retrieved June 10, 2011, from http://www.unicef.org/crc/

UNICEF. (2007). *Child poverty in perspective: An overview of child well-being in rich countries* (Innocenti Report Card 7). Florence, Italy: UNICEF Innocenti Research Centre.

UNICEF UK. (2008). *UNICEF UK Rights Respecting Schools in England* (Briefing paper 2008). London: UNICEF. Retrieved June 10, 2011, from http://www.renecassin.org/downloads/rrs-briefing.pdf

UNICEF UK. (2010a). *Level 1 Action Plan for the Rights Respecting Schools Award*, London, UNICEF. Retrieved August 22, 2010, from http://www.rrsa.org.uk/file.php/1/rrsa_documents/Level_1_Action_Plan.doc

UNICEF UK. (2010b). *Level 2 Action Plan for the Rights Respecting Schools Award*. London: UNICEF. Retrieved August 22, 2010, from http://www.rrsa.org.uk/file.php/1/rrsa_documents/Level_2_Action_Plan.doc

UNICEF UK. (2010c). *Rights Respecting School Award Charters*. London: UNICEF. Retrieved June 10, 2011, from http://www.rrsa.org.uk/file.php/1/rrsa_documents/Charters.pdf

United Nations. (1999). *The Right to Human Rights Education: A Compilation of Provisions of International and Regional Instruments Dealing with Human Rights Education*. New York &

Geneva: Author. Retrieved June 10, 2011, from http://www.ohchr.org/Documents/Publications/RightHReducationen.pdf

United Nations General Assembly. (1948). *Universal Declaration of Human Rights*. New York: United Nations. Retrieved June 10, 2011, from http://www.un.org/en/documents/udhr/index.shtml

United Nations General Assembly. (1993). *Vienna Declaration and Programme of Action* (A/CONF.157/23). Retrieved August 19, 2010, from http://www.unhchr.ch/huridocda/huridoca.nsf/(symbol)/a.conf.157.23.en

United Nations High Commissioner for Human Rights. (2001). *General Comment No. 1 on Article 29 of the UNCRC* Geneva: Author. Retrieved June 10, 2011, from http://www.unhchr.ch/tbs/doc.nsf/(symbol)/CRC.GC.2001.1.En?OpenDocument

United Nations High Commissioner for Human Rights. (2004). *United Nations Decade for Human Rights Education (1995-2004): Report on achievements and shortcomings of the Decade and on future United Nations activities in this area* (E/CN.4/2004/93). Geneva: Author. Retrieved June 10, 2011, from http://www2.ohchr.org/english/issues/education/training/decade.htm

United Nations High Commissioner for Human Rights (OHCHR) and UNESCO. (2006). *Plan of Action for the First Phase of the World Programme for Human Rights Education*. New York & Geneva: Authors. Retrieved June 10, 2011, from http://www2.ohchr.org/english/issues/education/training/planaction.htm

United Nations High Commissioner for Human Rights. (2010). *Plan of Action for the second phase (2010-2014) of the World Programme for Human Rights Education* (A/HRC/15/28). Geneva: Author. Retrieved June 10, 2011, from http://www2.ohchr.org/english/issues/education/training/secondphase.htm

United Nations High Commissioner for Refugees (UNHCR). (1994). *Human Rights: the new consensus*. London: Regency Press.

United Nations Human Rights Council. (2011). *Draft United Nations declaration on human rights education and training as adopted by the Open-ended Working Group on the draft United Nations declaration on human rights education and training* (A/HRC/WG.9/1/2). Geneva: UN General Assembly. Retrieved June 10, 2011, from http://www2.ohchr.org/english/bodies/hrcouncil/advisorycommittee/HR_education_training.htm

Verhellen, E. (2000). Children's rights and education. In A. Osler (Ed.), *Citizenship and democracy in schools: Diversity, identity, equality* (pp. 33–43). Stoke on Trent, UK: Trentham Books.

Helen Trivers and Hugh Starkey
Institute of Education
University of London

PAUL. L. THOMAS

WRITING COMMUNITY

Composing as Transformation and Realization

"If education cannot do everything," Freire (1998) argues, "there is something fundamental that it can do. In other words, if education is not the key to social transformation, neither is it simply meant to reproduce the dominant ideology" (p. 110). These words are at the core of my calling as an educator primarily concerned with literacy and the impact of poverty on children, their lives, and their learning as well as the tension I feel as a critical educator coming to terms with a transition in my own beliefs about public education.

Throughout this chapter, I will examine the need for critical classrooms to establish an environment that fosters empowering literacy, specifically the writing curriculum, in order to reinforce critical citizenship. Teaching, education, empowerment, and literacy are all intertwined for critical educators as elements of praxis, of radical change in the lives of individuals and in the realities of society.

I was born, grew up, and began my teaching career all in the Upstate of rural South Carolina—a place of conflicting messages about affluence, race, education, and language. It is in this place that I unconsciously embodied many beliefs (about race, class, and gender) against which I later rebelled, but the rural South of my youth and my entire teaching career has been essential for me to move away from the social reconstructionist stance that brought me to teaching—I initially did believe education could "do everything," including changing the world—and toward a recognition that language and education matter immeasurably at the personal level but that language and education are often powerless against larger social forces that must be acknowledged and addressed so that education can fulfill its role supporting the empowerment of free people.

This recognition rests on rejecting the fatalism that Freire (1998, pp. 92–93) warns against while embracing the power for critical pedagogy (Freire, 1993, 2005; Greene, 1995; Kincheloe, 2005; hooks, 1994, 1999) to speak against the "myths that deform" (Freire, 2005). My own journey parallels what I envision for all free people—a powerful connection between literacy (reading and rereading the world, writing and rewriting the world) and awareness, leading to social consciousness and social praxis.

Idealistic and naïve, I embraced college and teaching with faith in literature and my longing to be a writer and teacher—but I was unaware at any conscious level of my class-based and race-based advantages *not of my doing*. In other words, I was a winner who was certain the rules of the game were fair—I had earned everything by working hard, by doing what I was expected to do, including writing that was grammatically correct and restating for anyone who asked exactly what I was told to say (and think). The mechanistic and positivistic assumptions of traditional schooling had worked for me, and I intended like a self-righteous missionary to return to the school from which I graduated and help those others who were like me. The dehumanizing results of paternalism and behaviourism were lost in the cloud of my self-righteousness.

My paternalism and uncritical view of education were sincere and genuine, but hidden to me until I entered a doctoral program at the University of South Carolina in the mid-1990s after just more than a decade of teaching; during that decade, the cracks in my idealism were significant as the humanity of my students began to raise their voices against the tyranny of my teacher-centred crusade. Steeped in Dewey's progressivism and dedicated to the history of the field of education, my doctoral program offered me a journey that led to my own empowerment as a writer, a thinker, a scholar, and an educator.

First, I discovered constructivism as an alternative to behaviourism; then, I came to understand more fully the inherent deception in statistics, experimental/quasi-experimental research, and positivistic views of the world. This door opened in my doctoral program is captured well in one incident—a professor's response to my writing.

I was in my mid-30s and had been a practicing writer and teacher for many years, all the while praised since high school as not only a good writer, but also an excellent writer. During a doctoral course on qualitative research, I had received similar praise for my informal journal pieces submitted early in the course. But when I submitted my first draft of the required inquiry essay, the professor changed his message; in fact, he became confrontational, asking me, "Where did you go?"

At first, his displeasure in my work caught me off guard—it didn't match my winner status I had enjoyed for more than three decades—and then I was completely lost in his question, *Where had I gone?*

As we talked, I came to realise that my journal writing and my academic writing displayed two different voices—I was front and centre in my journal writing, but my academic work was posing behind the objective authority I had been trained to adopt. My professor, Dr. Jim Sears, was the first person to confront me with this essential dishonesty, this loss of self, trapped within traditional and oppressive views of scholarship.

Today, as I draft this piece, I am committed to an education for all people at all moments of their lives that confronts them in ways that honour their voices, but for this to happen, the ways in which we view and teach writing must change, must reject the accountability/standards/testing dynamic that embraces reduced views of expression that must conform to prompts, timed writing, and multiple-choice tests labelled "writing" tests.

And more broadly, the writing experiences offered in our schools must step away from demanding work in isolation to acknowledging community, collaboration, and cooperation. And that is my message here.

CRITICAL LITERACY IN A POSITIVIST WORLD

A great paradox of U. S. public education involves the fact of how we "do school" as it conflicts with the cultural narrative about schools. This paradox is captured well by Kohn (2008):

> Despite the fact that all schools can be located on a continuum stretching between the poles of totally progressive and totally traditional—or, actually, on a series of continuums reflecting the various components of those models—it's usually possible to visit a school and come away with a pretty clear sense of whether it can be classified as predominantly progressive. It's also possible to reach a conclusion about how many schools—or even individual classrooms—in America merit that label: damned few. The higher the grade level, the rarer such teaching tends to be, and it's not even all that prevalent at the lower grades.

While the general public, politicians, and the media persist in portraying public schools as failures in the 21st century, that claim of "failure" includes direct and indirect implications that a large component of blame lies with progressive education and progressive educators.

It is debatable that public education is a colossal failure, but if we accept that premise, the truth is that *traditional* public education has failed. Now if we take a step further and consider how often public schools or even individual teachers are critical, we can add emphasis to Kohn's conclusion about how many classrooms are anything other than traditional—*damned fewer*.

The reality of public education is that it is conservative, primarily focused on maintaining the status quo, passing on cultural norms, and preparing young people to be compliant in order to reinforce a stable workforce. Few people in the broader public or within the education establishment itself, including politicians, pause to consider how these traditional commitments of public education in fact clash with our stated ideals, our claimed concern for the individual, for critical thinking, and for freedom.

While popular discourse often pits traditional ideology and progressive ideology—and both directly and indirectly laying the blame for failing schools at the feet of progressives, such as John Dewey—traditionalists and progressives are little different in their bureaucratic and corporate commitments to the structures of schooling—authoritarian administration (discipline), authoritarian teachers, scripted curriculum, objective and standardised testing, labelling and stratifying students (grades, class rank), and fragmented and highly structured course designations and daily class schedules. Public schools are not now, nor have they ever been, truly progressive and clearly not critical. Thus, the work of critical educators faces many roadblocks in the vast majority of classrooms across the U.S.—positivist assumptions, behavioural assumptions, cultural myths (rugged individualism, for example).

For critical educators, literacy is central to empowerment. When we persist in prescribing and restricting language and voices of students (and their teachers), we are indirectly denying students (and their teachers) self-determination and self-realization. Here, briefly, I want to examine how the critical classroom establishes the environment necessary for empowering literacy, specifically the writing curriculum, in order to reinforce critical citizenship. Using selected passages from arguments made by Freire (1998), I outline below the distinctions between traditional/progressive approaches to schools and the critical possibilities that I will examine later through reframing writing instruction in classrooms dedicated to critical citizenship.

> To educate is essentially to form. To deify or demonise technology or science is an extremely negative way of thinking incorrectly. To act in front of students as if the truth belongs only to the teacher is not only preposterous but also false. To think correctly. . .presupposes an openness that allows for the revision of conclusions; it recognises not only the possibility of making a new choice or a new evaluation but also the *right* [emphasis in original] to do so. (Freire, 1998, p. 39)

A profound contradiction of traditional, and even progressive, education is the status of the student and the role of the teacher. While we have claimed for decades that public education is essential to support the ideals of a free people, a thriving democracy, we have created schools that honour teachers as the sole locus of power (as agents of institutional mandates, not their own professionalism) and that deny children of all ages the "*right*," as Freire emphasises, to explore and discover their own empowerment.

U. S. public education functions fully under the banking concept of education Freire (1993) rejected because of its premium placed on decision-making *by* the teacher and *for* the students. The pervasive atmosphere of schools is one of authority and prescription—leaving little room for confrontation, experimentation, debate, or discovery.

For students, school is a place where teachers tell them what texts matter, what texts reveal; for students, school is a place where teachers tell them what form writing should take, what ideas their writing should convey.

And weaved throughout those facts of public schools is the exact deifying of science and technology about which Freire warns. We constantly call for more technology in the schools for students (with little mention of books), just as we repeatedly call for an *idealised* scientific model of what constitutes good teaching.

The critical classroom that honours the teacher/student and student/teacher, along with valuing the art and craft or teaching, then, fights against a powerful tradition of authority and mechanization that pervades most public school classrooms.

> [T]o know how to teach is to create possibilities for the construction and production of knowledge rather than to be engaged simply in a game of transferring knowledge. (Freire, 1998, p. 49)

Instead of endorsing a codified body of knowledge, the critical classroom seeks to provide opportunities for student discovery; the teacher seeks to *invite* students instead of command. One of the most technical and reductive aspects of teaching is lesson and unit planning. In the past 30 years during the rise of the accountability movement, lesson planning has placed on top of the traditional behavioural objective and linear lesson plan the mandates of complying with standards and preparing students for high-stakes assessment.

While the critical teacher moves to the classroom with the student in mind, the traditional teacher is required to teach with the end in mind. The backward design that now dominates lesson and unit planning has been championed as bringing transparency to the classroom, suggesting that making students aware of what is expected of them is being humane.

Of course, this argument ignores that the students themselves are being entirely omitted from deciding what knowledge matters. As with backward design, standards, and high-stakes tests, students and teachers are now bound to rubrics as well. The detailed parameters of behaviours and levels of quality are also promoted as transparent acts, again suggesting that the more recent prescriptive practices (backward design and rubric-driven assessment) are *progressive* and not traditional.

The irony is that progressives embracing backward design and rubrics, for example, are embracing practices that move us farther away from empowerment for students than even traditional classrooms 40 years ago. As I will discuss later, these practices are most corrosive for literacy, notably for the writing programs

> I like being human because I know that my passing through the world is not predetermined, preestablished. That my destiny is not a given but something that needs to be constructed and for which I must assume responsibility. I like being human because I am involved with others in making history out of possibility, not simply resigned to fatalistic stagnation. Consequently, the future is something to be constructed through trial and error rather than an inexorable vice that determines all our actions. (Freire, 1998, p. 54)

For critical educators, the open-ended nature of learning and living along with the inherently collaborative essence of being fully human grounds all that we seek and offer in classrooms. Yet, public education in the U.S. has embraced cultural norms honouring fixed perceptions of learning and living along with human performances in isolation. That our schools seek and endorse standardisation (with a recent call for national standards and increased national testing) and isolation is a reflection of cultural faith in analysis, a linear understanding of existence, and rugged individualism.

Freire's challenge to "fatalistic stagnation" is muted by the powerful momentum of Western ideas about existence that feeds a prescriptive and authoritarian approach to schooling. Many progressive and critical educators have confronted the reality of public education—the pursuit of discipline and control over empowerment and understanding.

Further, the critical embracing of "scientific" rejects the distorted view of "scientific" found in popular discourse and even federal legislation—No Child Left Behind, the National Reading Panel, What Works Clearinghouse. Popular and political calls for scientific is envisioned as a fixed capturing of fact and truth, a belief that we simply can and should codify knowledge in order to instill that knowledge into passive students. For critical educators, knowledge and truth are relative things, shifting perceptions of reality based on the ever-evolving world in which we live. Science, for critical educators, is a recursive and ongoing pursuit of knowledge that values the pursuit and recognises "there is no finish line."

We must not ignore, as well, that Americans believe the rugged individual myth, expecting human performances to be in isolation (testing, for example) and assuming that direct causational relationships exist between each human and any outcomes associated with that person. Foundational to critical thought is a recognition that to be human is to be contextualised, to be in tandem with other humans and the world; further, critical scholars remain highly skeptical of any simple correlations, valuing the human behaviours, beliefs, and outcomes as the result of dozens or even hundreds of influences that may or may not be within our grasp to identify.

As I will examine later, the writing curriculum and how we assign, respond to, and assess writing have been profoundly impacted—and corrupted—by the "fatalistic stagnation" of prescription and learning/performing in isolation.

> Education does not make us educable. It is our awareness of being unfinished that makes us educable. . . .Another kind of knowledge necessary to educational practice. . .is the knowledge that speaks of respect for the autonomy of the learner. . . .[B]oth the authoritarian teacher who suffocates the natural curiosity and freedom of the student as well as the teacher who imposes no standards at all are equally disrespectful of an essential characteristic of our humanness, namely, our radical (and assumed) unfinishedness, out of which emerges the possibility of being ethical. (Freire, 1998, pp. 58–59)

My discussion above sits far too close to the edge of suggesting that dualities exist; instead, I would argue that seeing the world in dualities is a flaw and that political power often grows from leaders manipulating the popular tendency to function within false dualities. But one of the most popular and powerful charges against public schools is the suggestion that two types of teachers exist (and only these two)—the authoritarian (preferred by our cultural norms) and the permissive.

Those teachers labelled *progressive*—and more rarely *critical*—are often stereotyped as "postmodern," and thus without any standards, without any desire to be rigorous, challenging, or evaluative. But as Freire explains, this characterization is misleading since critical educators embrace neither authoritarianism nor permissiveness by teachers. The truly progressive and critical classroom pursues teachers and students seeking to be authoritative—having developed and exhibited a care for knowledge, truth, and respect for human agency that gives both the teacher and the students credibility.

And within that authoritative stance, the teacher and the students remain in a state of learning, rejecting the possibility of being finished. Also, at any moment of empowerment, of authoritative awareness, we find ourselves making claims of right and wrong, of best, better, and inferior. Again, as Freire states, the pursuit of teaching and learning is an ethical pursuit, one that must embrace and practice an awareness of human unfinishedness and the rigour necessary for the pursuit of knowledge and morality.

> [T]he school, which is the space in which both teachers and students are the subjects of education, cannot abstract itself from the sociocultural and economic conditions of its students, their families, and their communities. (Freire, 1998, p. 62)

The great trap of being an idealistic educator, for me, has been coming to terms with the paradox of teacher and school impact on children and our society. While I remain committed to the power of teachers and schools to affect students and our society, I have also come to understand that the impact is nuanced and difficult to measure.

As I stated earlier, *teaching, education, empowerment, and literacy are all intertwined for critical educators as elements of praxis, of radical change in the lives of individuals and in the realities of society.* Yet, decades of evidence suggest that the power of teachers and schools to change society is often stunted by the exact social forces of poverty and inequity that critical educators hope to overcome through education (Rothstein, 2010).

While I still promote classroom pedagogy that supports and models community and discourse (specifically through the writing program) as a contribution to critical citizenship beyond the walls of school, I must offer the caveat that cultural norms and societal realities are powerful influences on those classrooms regardless of what happens in school. In other words, I believe it is simplistic and naïve to believe that fostering community and democracy in the classroom will somehow transform a society stubbornly committed to rugged individualism, competition, and capitalism: "We are likely to find that the problems of housing and education, instead of preceding the elimination of poverty, will themselves be affected if poverty is first abolished" (King, 1967).

However, it is neither simplistic nor naïve to suggest that a classroom that "simply...reproduce[s] the dominant ideology" (p. 110), as Freire (1998) warns, is destined to fail our pursuit of radical empowerment. The classroom must be true to our ideals, but that classroom—and the teachers and students therein—must have broader social forces working in tandem with education to revolutionise a society that in 2010 *allows* 1 in 4 children to live in poverty (Adamson, 2007), *in* the wealthiest country in all of recorded history.

> The ideal, of course, is that, sooner or later, some mechanism whereby the students can participate in such an evaluation should be worked out.... (Freire, 1998, p. 63)

The most corrosive classroom dynamic is grading—that teachers evaluate and assign grades to student work and ultimately students themselves. Yet, to foster community and empower, the critical educator is faced with a dilemma in that traditional context:

> How do we instill in our students the ability to be effective judges over their own learning? Part of that process for me means supporting a shift in

> students' thinking about conventional, traditional ways of grading--the teacher keeps record of assignments completed and assigns a grade based on that criteria. . . .As we make this shift from the "I learn for you," to the existential "I learn for me; I am responsible for my own acts; I can make a difference," we support the activation of both the body and mind of the learner and empower them to help transform assessment practices. (Miller, 2008, pp. 160, 170)

> After all, our teaching space is a text that has to be constantly read, interpreted, written, and rewritten. . . .It is my belief that today the progressive kind of teacher needs to watch out as never before for the clever uses of the dominant ideology of our time, especially its insidious capacity for spreading that idea that it is possible for education to be neutral. This is an extremely reactionary philosophy, which uses the classroom to inculcate in the students political attitudes and practices, as if it were possible to exist as a human being in the world and at the same time be neutral. (Freire, 1998, pp. 89–90)

Possibly the most powerful force against which critical educators work is the expectation for and belief in the possibility of objectivity. Teachers-in-training and practising teachers are often reminded that they are to remain politically neutral. As critical educators, however, we must constantly remind those making claims for objectivity that objectivity is in fact a subjective stance—just as claiming to be politically neutral is a political stance: "Because curriculum is not a neutral entity, because it is always ideologically inscribed, educational purpose is *always* a political question" (Kincheloe & Weil, 2001, p. 16).

The critical classroom embraces that being fully human is existing in subjectivity (the only way to view and experience the world is through each of our senses and our consciousness), that being fully human is political since we are all engaged with each other in a perpetual negotiation of ideas, material goods, and space. Instead of denying or muting that which makes us human (our subjectivity and political reality), teachers should create classrooms in which teachers and students embrace their humanity in the pursuit of transparency, dignity, justice, and equity.

> Freedom becomes mature in confrontation with other freedoms, defending its rights in relation to parental authority, the authority of teachers, and the authority of the state. . . .It's in making decisions that we learn to decide. . . .Consequences are what make decision making a responsible process. (Freire, 1998, pp. 96–97)

All of education—formal learning within schools and the natural learning that comes through living—is about confrontation of the self with the other; for young people, this is a confrontation of empowerment with the many types of authority that surround them. Traditional schooling is driven by coercion and artificial rewards and punishments (from grades to corporal punishment to demerits and detention or suspension).

For critical educators, the classroom is a laboratory for students to make decisions, pitting their empowerment against the authorities that surround them, in order to experience the consequences with the teacher nearby to mentor—and even to monitor the results of those consequences (yes, the classroom can and often should provide some of the paternal safety nets that parents provide before children are set loose on the world as young adults).

> What ought to guide me is not the question of neutrality in education but respect, at all costs, for those involved in education. Respect for teachers on the part of school administrators, whether public or private. Respect among teachers and students. And respect between both. This respect is what I should fight for, without ceasing. . . .What is my neutrality, if not a comfortable and perhaps hysterical way of avoiding any choice or even hiding my fear of denouncing injustice. To wash my hands in the face of oppression. (Freire, 1998, p. 101)

The prescriptive classroom is driven by demonstrated *disrespect* for marginalised students (if not all students at a certain age). By determining the *what* and *how* of student learning, behaviour, and products *for* students (without having ever even met those students), we initiate a classroom of disrespect for the potentiality of each student. Traditional education is built upon such assumptions.

The critical classroom, by contrast, proceeds by honouring that all students can and must be allowed to determine their own world. Again, as Freire noted above, this does not mean there is no role for the teacher to shape and even guide students in their journey, but the journey must be the students'—and the journey must be one of mutual respect.

> The freedom that moves us, that makes us take risks, is being subjugated to a process of standardization of formulas, models against which we are evaluated. . . .We are speaking of that invisible power of alienating domestication, which attains a degree of extraordinary efficiency in what I have been calling the bureaucratizing of the mind. (Freire, 1998, p. 111)

Westerners, and specifically Americans, have embraced a narrow view of science: That meticulous care, the scientific method, can result in a final product (or state of being) that reduces all doubt, chance, risk, and thus, humanity. In schools, the bureaucratic narrowness of being "scientific" has evolved into prescriptive standards and high-stakes tests that remove all decisions from teachers and students while also shifting onto teachers and students a narrow accountability that corrupts the concept of being responsible—How is it ethical to hold someone responsible for that which she or he did not determine?

At the heart of the "bureaucratizing of the mind" is the systemic faith in behaviourism that instills in students and their teachers the pursuit of *avoiding* mistakes. The traditional classroom is one that demonises taking risks and punishes error. The critical educator sees risk and error as *essential* to learning—not something to be avoided, but something at the core of being fully human.

> In truth, I feel it is necessary to overcome the false separation between serious teaching and the expression of feeling. . . .Affectivity is not necessarily an enemy of knowledge or of the process of knowing. (Freire, 1998, p. 125)

The traditional classroom honours the cognitive while marginalising the affective, again seeking to dehumanise instead of embracing our full humanity. The critical classroom respects and even celebrates the whole child and the whole adult.

The Western bias toward the cognitive and the logical is a bias toward a masculine norm, one that the culture uses to marginalise women as emotional (thus lesser than rational men). Rationality, logic, and a narrow perception of science as fixed—all combine to remove *living* from the classroom, to reduce teaching and learning to a dust-covered tomb instead of the vibrant, growing, and evolving entities that they are when humans are at the center.

SCRIPTED COMPOSING, SILENT CHILDREN, CLOSED MINDS

The era of standards, testing, and accountability that began in the early 1980s with A Nation at Risk includes a tragic fate for writing instruction, which had made a turn for the better in the late 1970s with the rise of the National Writing Project (NWP) and a recognition of the importance of the writing process and authentic writing products for students as well as a writing life for teachers of composition. At first, the standards movement claimed only math and reading, signalled by the historic measuring of math and reading on the SAT and the rise of periodic tests of math and reading as part of the accountability machine within states.

The standards and accountability movement reached a peak in the early days of the 21st century with No Child Left Behind, but writing suffered its tragic fate a bit later. In short, if we purposefully designed education broadly and the writing curriculum narrowly to stifle expression and mute a sense of community, we could not have created a system better suited than the one we have now. For writing, the shift away from the promise of the NWP and toward the very worst warning from Freire (1998)—"The freedom that moves us, that makes us take risks, is being subjugated to a process of standardization of formulas, models against which we are evaluated" (p. 111)—occurred throughout the rise of the accountability movement, but was codified around 2003–2005 with the addition of the writing section of the SAT.

A national call for a focus on writing (Harvey, 2006), which grew out of the College Board that not-so-coincidentally initiated the writing section on the SAT, predated the revised SAT that includes three sections, adding writing. The literacy field spoke out against this move (Ball et al., 2005), but the power of the SAT won. As a result, the writing curriculum now and traditionally includes the worst possible characteristics if we are pursuing student voice, empowerment, and expression—especially as critical citizens in a free society:

- *Prompted writing*—From state high-stakes assessments of writing to the SAT, students are evaluated from writing prompts. The great irony of this dynamic is that we know students struggle to write from prompts due to lack of interest in the topic, and we also know that surface features in prompted writing is often more problematic than in chosen writing (Thomas, 2005). Prompted writing contributes to coercive instruction, but prompts—which dictate topics, format, audience, and other elements of composing—remove from students some of the most important *choices* of being a writer. Essays produced from prompts, then, are likely to skew downward the data from those evaluations, and indirectly, the prompted nature of essay evaluations clearly deforms the writing curriculum of schools, again asking less of students, not more.

- *Isolation*—Formal assessments of writing, on high-stakes testing and even in classrooms, creates a tension with traditional views of evaluation. Best practice in writing supports composing as a collaborative journey (Thomas, 2005), but traditional views of evaluation and some narrow views of plagiarism and cheating require all evaluated work to be completed in isolation. Isolation is clearly not conducive to students developing a sense of community.
- *What counts as "composing"*—The SAT assessment of writing is an extreme example, but it highlights the very worst of the current high-stakes approach to writing. The SAT writing section allows only 25 minutes for the actual writing sample, thus it ignores the importance of process—the value of time, choice, and response emphasised by Atwell (1998)—as well as asking students to make the types of decisions all writers must make (see above). Further, the SAT writing test actually allows *more time* (35 minutes) for the multiple-choice section than for the composing section on a writing test. This is a powerful and corrosive aspect of high-stakes testing that honours correlations for authentic performances over the performances themselves.
- *Rubrics*—Like prompts, rubrics drive what students write on assessments, but those rubrics also drive what labels we place on student writing and the students themselves. Again, it is disturbing that the evidence on the impact of rubrics is as damning as the impact of prompts on student writing (Kohn, 2006; Mabry, 1999; Newkirk, 2005; Thomas, 2005; Wilson, 2006b, 2007). When high-stakes assessment of writing grew from state assessments to the SAT, writing programs embraced fully prompted essays, rubric scoring guides, and anchor papers, reducing the composing of students to filling-in-the-blanks through exposition instead of choosing A, B, C, or D.
- *Surface features and characteristics over content*—Despite decades of evidence that writing instruction should focus primarily on content over surface features (LaBrant, 1946, 1953, 1957; Thomas, 2005; Weaver, 1996), the rise of high-stakes assessment of writing has refuelled a focus on surface features since they are easier to score; some states have experimented with computer-graded essay evaluation (Hurwitz, 2004). Again, as a result of the focus on surface features and the inclusion of a multiple-choice section on the SAT writing section, classrooms are returning to isolated grammar exercises, stealing precious time from composing by students and further dampening students' interest in writing.

Before examining briefly how to reform writing practices in the classroom to fuel critical citizenship among teachers and students, let's look at two vivid examples of the corrupting influence of high-stakes testing on writing. First, Wilson (2006a) took "My House" from Sandra Cisneros's *House on Mango Street* and scored it using a program from the Educational Testing Service (ETS). Once Cisneros's work was evaluated, Wilson rewrote the piece using the suggestions from the program.

The result was a longer piece by 270 words—longer is better according to ETS—and the piece was magically transformed to a standard five-paragraph essay. This experiment by Wilson (2006a) exposes the folly of rubric-driven assessment of writing as well as the norms of essay writing that have been honoured in traditional schooling for over a century: What testing and English classes demand for writing is, in fact, worse than what professional writers produce; ironically, the texts we choose to teach in those same English classes are the exact examples that refute what the test demands.

This raises a key question for education. Do we want students who write formulaic essays that score high on assessments, or do we want students to write works that speak for the empowerment of all people like the work of Cisneros?

And the SAT writing section is proving to be just as corrosive as the ETS process above. A 14-year-old, Milo Beckman, recently took the SAT for a second time and was surprised to find that his writing score rose. When he saw the higher score and weighed that against his own belief that he had not written as well the second time, Beckman became suspicious that his higher score was the result of his writing a *longer* essay; and with some detective work and research, he has shown that this hypothesis proves true: The SAT rewards longer essays (Milo Beckman, 2010).

WRITING AS EMPOWERMENT: CRITICAL CITIZENSHIP IN SCHOOL AND LIFE

"The individual voice is the communal voice," writes Joyce Carol Oates (2003), continuing, "The regional voice is the universal voice" (p. 1). Another writer, Adrienne Rich (2001), presents a damning recognition about our schools that stands in stark contrast to Oates's belief in voice:

> Universal public education has two possible—and contradictory—missions. One is the development of a literate, articulate, and well-informed citizenry so that the democratic process can continue to evolve and the promise of radical equality can be brought closer to realization. The other is the perpetuation of a class system dividing an elite, nominally "gifted" few, tracked from an early age, from a very large underclass essentially to be written off as alienated from language and science, from poetry and politics, from history and hope—toward low-wage temporary jobs. The second is the direction our society has taken. The results are devastating in terms of the betrayal of a generation of youth. The loss to the whole of society is incalculable. (p. 162)

As we end the first decade of the 21st century, Rich is right, but critical educators recognise the essence of Oates's direct and simple faith in "individual voice" as a part of "communal voice." The West, specifically the U.S., is a people dedicated to rugged individualism, suspect of community and collaboration. And our public schools broadly, along with our approaches to writing, narrowly reveal these commitments and suspicions.

We are not a critical community, not a critical citizenry dedicated to radical democracy; we are instead competing workers worshipping a fickle consumerocracy—and our schools are perpetuating the true ideals that drive our culture. If we are to become an empowered people, however, public schools must change, and at the heart of that change must be a new vision of writing. That new vision of writing must embrace the following:

- Writing/composing is inherently an act of collaboration, not a solitary act. The myth of the rugged individual is exactly that, a myth. To be fully human is to collaborate with other humans, with one's environment, with one's self, and with other acts of human expression. Writing is a stark example of community that is routinely misrepresented in schools as a solitary act. At the very least, the writer requires an audience for the final text composed. But the collaboration is much greater than that in reality. The writing programs in schools and classrooms must embrace the full range of composing as collaboration, composing as the negotiation of meaning through expression. Some of the elements of that embracing include peer and teacher conferencing during the composing process, public sharing of drafts and final products (including publishing in a variety of contexts and formats), and placing student original writing against a wide variety of texts, such as peer texts, published texts, and model texts.
- Classroom texts must reflect the formats and genres of writing that exist in the work of empowered writers. Templates for writing have long dominated writing instruction in formal education, most notably the five-paragraph essay. Ask any group of college students to list those things they *cannot* do in their writing along with what they *must* do in their writing, and the responses are telling: Introductions with a thesis sentence as the last sentence, 6–8 sentences per paragraph, no "I," don't use contractions, conclusions that restate the introduction. When I ask students to compare these "lessons" about writing with authentic text, we always discover that they fall apart because professional writers, *empowered writers*, rarely conform to the templates of school writing. If public schooling and the pursuit of writing in those schools are to support critical citizenship, we must replace moribund and inauthentic templates for writing with students exploring rich examples of writing for expanding their awareness of how we express ourselves as free and empowered humans.
- The creation of text must be the choice of those students writing/composing. As I noted above, most of what professional writers decide is prescribed for students—prompt, genre, content, format, and audience. The writing program must shift the responsibility for decisions about composing to the students. Writers are driven by choice and purpose—both of which are qualities of empowerment. Students, however, are guided by correctness and the paralyzing pursuit of avoiding error—characteristics of oppressed humans.

- The writing process of each student must be a process she/he discovers and refines through authentic experiences with literacy, and we must acknowledge that the writing process is idiosyncratic and chaotic (Weaver, 1996). Traditional approaches to writing and behavioural assumptions about learning have reduced an authentic concept—the writing process—to a script, *the* writing process. As I have visited schools over the past decade, I have witnessed innumerable classrooms with the writing process captured in posters over the marker boards in classrooms—laminated pencils numbered, "1. Prewriting," "2. Drafting," "3. Revision," "4. Editing," "5. Publishing." The writing process, then, simply becomes yet another script students seek to fulfill, with composing lost in the meantime. We need instead to offer students ample experiences searching for, discovering, and then revising their own writing processes, not as an act of conformity but as an act of empowerment and expression.
- Writing is the pursuit of craft, of art and not science. Many of the problems I have identified so far can be tied to our misguided concept of "scientific" and "rigorous." We have pursued for over a century capturing human existence and human performances in neat and linear formulas, disregarding that existence perpetually shows us that there are no templates. Instead of a formula for writing, our students need a dedication to craft, recognizing that expression is both innate and something that deserves the polish and care of craft. Empowerment is not license, but the responsibility of agency that must not be squandered or trivialised. For far too long, public schools and writing in those schools have squandered and trivialised our most precious human gift, expression. Critical citizenship cannot thrive without every person having access to the art and craft of human expression.
- Composing is occasionally an avenue of learning, and not always the pursuit of product. While our writing programs must honour expression, we must also help students embrace the act of composing as a process toward discovery and understanding, an act that supersedes any product.

Writing in her introduction to *The Faith of a Writer*, Joyce Carol Oates (2003) explains about the tension between expressing her views on writing while avoiding offering a manual for how others *should* pursue writing:

> The spirit of [the book] is meant to be undogmatic, provisional. More about the process of *writing* than the uneasy, uncertain position of being *writer*. In my life as a citizen as in my life as a writer I have never wished to raise any practice of mine into a principle for others. Underlying all these essays is my prevailing sense of wonderment at how the solitary yields to the communal. . . .We begin as loners. . . .; if we persevere in our art, and are not discouraged in our craft, we may find solace in the mysterious counter-world of literature that transcends artificial borders of time, place, language, national identity. Out of the solitariness of the individual this culture somehow emerges, variegated, ever-alluring, ever-evolving. (p. xiii)

REFERENCES

Adamson, P. (2007). *Child poverty in perspective: An overview of child well-being in rich countries.* Innocenti Report Card (7). United Nations Children's Fund Innocenti Research Centre. Florence, Italy. Retrieved February 14, 2011, from http://www.unicef-irc.org/publications/pdf/rc7_eng.pdf

Atwell, N. (1998). *In the Middle: New understanding about writing, reading, and learning* (2nd ed.). Portsmouth, NH: Boyton/Cook.

Ball, A., Christensen, L., Fleischer, C., Haswell, R., Ketter, J., Yageldski, R., & Yancey, K. (2005, April 16). The impact of the SAT and ACT timed writing tests. Urbana, IL: National Council of Teachers of English. Retrieved February 14, 2011, from http://www.ncte.org/library/NCTEFiles/Resources/Positions/SAT-ACT-tf-report.pdf

Freire, P. (1993). *Pedagogy of the oppressed* (M. B. Ramos, Trans.). New York: Continuum.

Freire, P. (1998). *Pedagogy of freedom: Ethics, democracy, and civic courage* (P. Clarke, Trans.). Lanham, MD: Rowman and Littlefield Publishers, Inc.

Freire, P. (2005). *Teachers as cultural workers: Letters to those who dare to teach* (D. Macedo, D. Koike, & A., Oliveira, Trans.). Boulder, CO: Westview Press.

Greene, M. (1995). *Releasing the imagination: Essays on education, the arts, and social change.* San Francisco: Jossey-Bass.

Harvey, J. (2006, May). *Writing and school reform, including the neglected "R": The need for a writing revolution.* National Commission on Writing for America's Families, Schools, and Colleges. New York: The College Board. Retrieved February 14, 2011, from http://www.collegeboard.org/prod_downloads/writingcom/writing-school-reform-natl-comm-writing.pdf

Hooks, B. (1994). *Teaching to transgress: Education as the practice of freedom.* New York: Routledge.

Hooks, B. (1999). *Remembered rapture: The writer at work.* New York: Henry Holt and Company.

Hurwitz, S. (2004, May 19). Indiana essays being graded by computers. *New York Times.* Retrieved May 19, 2004, from: www.nytimes.com.

Kincheloe, J. L. (2005). *Critical pedagogy primer.* New York: Peter Lang.

Kincheloe, J. L., & Weil, D. (2001). *Standards and schooling in the United States* (Vols. 1–3). Denver, CO: ABC-CLIO.

King, Jr., M. L. (1967). Final words of advice. *Wealth and Want.* Retrieved February 11, 2011, from http://www.wealthandwant.com/docs/King_Where.htm

Kohn, A. (2006, March). The trouble with rubrics. *English Journal, 95*(4), 12–15.

Kohn, A. (2008, Spring). Progressive education: Why it's hard to beat, but also hard to find. *Independent School.* http://www.alfiekohn.org/teaching/progressive.htm

LaBrant, L. (1946). Teaching high-school students to write. *English Journal, 35*(3), 123–128.

LaBrant, L. (1953). Writing is learned by writing. *Elementary English, 30*(7), 417–420.

LaBrant, L. (1957). Writing is more than structure. *English Journal, 46*(5), 252–256, 293.

Mabry, L. (1999, May). Writing to the rubric: Lingering effects of traditional standardized testing on direct writing assessment. *Phi Delta Kappan, 80*(9), 673–679.

Miller, sj. (2008, Summer) Liberating grades/liberatory assessment. *International Journal of Critical Pedagogy, 1*(2), 160–171. The Paulo and Nita Freire International Project for Critical Pedagogy. McGill University, Montreal, Quebec, Canada. Retrieved August 20, 2009, from http://freireproject.org/ojs/ index.php/home/article/view/69/40

Milo Beckman, New York teen, discovers the secret to scoring highly on the SAT test. (2010, November 5). Retrieved November 8, 2010, from http://www.huffingtonpost.com/2010/11/05/milo-beckman-new-york-tee_n_779722.html

Newkirk, T. (2005, November). The new writing assessments: Where are they leading us? *English Journal, 95*(2), 21–22.

Oates, J. C. (2003). *The faith of the writer: Life, craft, art.* New York: Ecco.

Rich, A. (2001). *Arts of the possible: Essays and conversations.* New York: W. W. Norton and Company.

Rothstein, R. (2010, October 14). *How to fix our schools* (Issue Brief 286). Washington, DC: Economic Policy Institute. Retrieved February 14, 2011, from http://www.epi.org/publications/entry/ib286
Thomas, P. L. (2005). *Teaching writing primer*. New York: Peter Lang USA.
Weaver, C. (1996). *Teaching grammar in context*. Portsmouth, NH: Boynton/Cook Publishers.
Wilson, M. (2006a, Spring). Apologies to Sandra Cisneros. *Rethinking Schools, 20*(3), 42–46.
Wilson, M. (2006b). *Rethinking rubrics in writing assessment*. Portsmouth, NH: Heinemann.
Wilson, M. (2007, March). Why I won't be using rubrics to respond to students' writing. *English Journal, 96*(4), 62–66.

P. L. Thomas
Associate Professor of Education,
Furman University (Greenville, SC, USA)

MAY AL-FARTOUSI AND DOLANA MOGADIME

MEDIA REPRESENTATIONS OF MUSLIM WOMEN WEARING THE BURKA

Criticism and Implications

INTRODUCTION

This chapter provides a critical analysis of 30 local and international online newspaper articles and focuses on the common language used in the latter sources to represent certain Muslim women living in the West. More specifically, the paper outlines a debate corresponding to media representations of the Muslim Association of Canada's request to ban the burqa (transliterated henceforth as burka). In October 2009, the Muslim Canadian Congress (MCC) called upon the country's federal government to prevent Muslim women from covering theMore..ir faces in public (Lewis, 2009), ostensibly due to incidents involving burka-wearing bank robbers, in addition to the negative images and stereotypes associated with Muslim women's cultural use of the garment. Most notably, the decision made by the late Sheikh Mohammed Sayyed Tantawi, the then Grand Imam of Cairo's al-Azhar University (the chief centre of Arabic literature and Sunni Islamic learning in the world), to ban women from wearing the burka or face veil encouraged the MCC to adopt a similar position with regard to establishing a ban on the public use of burkas (Worthington, 2010).

The study was undertaken by two researchers. The first is May Al-Fartousi, a Canadian Middle Eastern educator whose interest in the topic stems from her role as a Muslim scholar striving for social justice and equity underpinned by Islamic principles. Al-Fartousi favours an Islamic school of thought whose practices do not include the use of the burka. However, Al-Fartousi addresses the issues related to banning the burka in a Western context wherein the political, cultural, and social aspects differ completely from those in Islamic countries such as Saudi Arabia and Afghanistan. Moreover, Al-Fartousi's interest in this issue is inspired by her own schooling experiences as an Arab Muslim female student who has lived in the Middle East as well as in Canada, and who has faced the pressures of social differences and racism. As a child wearing the hijab (i.e., head scarf) in the Middle East, her school experience was not positive—she was home-schooled in Grades 11 and 12 due to a secular policy that prevented female students from observing hijab in regular classrooms. Similar to the recent debate on banning the burka, Al-Fartousi argues that this decision may isolate some Muslim women and prevent them achieving certain basic rights.

The second author is Dolana Mogadime, a professor of sociocultural studies whose research interests in critical sociology, social justice, equity, and feminist theories motivated her to make a contribution to critiquing the problem of belief manipulation and the manufacturing of consent among the media in relation to Muslim women. Furthermore, Mogadime (2005) has previously undertaken critical analysis of media discourse regarding the implementation of equity policy in society, a widely debated issue in the popular press.

Both authors focus on revealing the relationships that characterize racial oppression and seek to foster multiple viewpoints in order to shed light upon the social construction of reality. Specifically, they hope to elaborate on the exclusionary social and political discourses which may contribute toward discriminatory stereotypes levelled at the Muslim female in North American everyday life. In this paper, the authors pay particular attention to the gender and religious argumentation that manufactures a monolithic interpretation of Muslim women wearing the burka.

Yosso and Solórzano (2002) explain that educators cannot group all women's experiences together. Zine (2008) and Cooke (2008), in turn, confirm that Muslim women have complex layers of identity, which includes racialized and religious identities. Accordingly, Muslim women have multiple identities and their experiences transform their identities (Bullock, 2002; Hamdan, 2006). A Muslim woman's identity, then, is continually constructed and reconstructed in the context of interacting both within and across differences. Indeed, the function of Islamic dress represents a significant means of communicating social and religious values (Clarke, 2003). As a form of social communication, there are multiple meanings associated with the veil that vary historically, culturally, and politically (Bullock, 2000, 2002; Hamdan, 2007; Zine, 2002). For example, although the Muslim dress may correspond to positive attributes of modesty and privacy in an Islamic context, the practice has entered into Western societies as a symbol of fundamentalism and extremism; the Western media often essentializes or misrepresents Muslim women as veiled figures and discusses veiling "as an expression of the general backward[ness] of the culture and all the cultural customs and norms [that] need to be cast away and replaced by Western lifestyle" (Skalli, 2004, p. 47).

METHOD: CRITICAL DISCOURSE ANALYSIS

We refer to critical discourse analysis as a means of challenging the hegemonic power and social inequality that emerge from media discourses. The discourse touches upon inequality corresponding to meso and macro levels such as organizations and institutions and the micro level through daily conversations and social interactions. The discourse represents social structures that reflect through the media certain meanings and social representations that make the dominance and social inequality seem natural (Blommaert & Bulcaen, 2000; van Dijk, 1993). Van Dijk (1993) refers to this method as

> a systematic discourse analysis of the genres or communicative events that play a role in the reproduction of racism, such as everyday conversations,

novels, films, textbooks, lessons, laws...or any other discourse genre that may be about ethnic groups and ethnic relations. (p. 28)

He describes such undertakings as interdisciplinary. We use the critical discourse analysis as a means to dissect the discriminatory hidden messages that may stereotype certain Muslim women. In this respect, this method is perceived as a social practice in which the dialectical relationship is framed by situations, institutions, and social structure (Fairclough & Wodak, as cited in Titscher, Meyer, Wodak, & Vetter, 2000).

A database search was conducted for recent articles appearing in international and local newspapers—the keywords "ban the burka" and "Muslim women wearing burka in Canada" were inputted in the Google search engine. Consequently, 30 online newspaper articles were coded and analyzed to arrive at an understanding of common language used to represent certain Muslim women wearing the burka. The themes garnered from reading these articles touched on the following points that are emblematic of certain Muslim women: controversy; associating the burka with the hijab and extremism; gender equality, freedom of choice, and harems; and religious rights (see Table 1). In the following sections, each theme will be analyzed in order to demonstrate the different layers that contribute to negatively representing some Muslim women in Canada.

Themes: Controversy

Various logical formations within Islam proceed from the same epistemological foundations. These foundations are based on a combination of revealed sacred knowledge in the form of the Holy Qur'an, historical narratives based on narrations of prophetic knowledge and wisdom (Hadith), and hermeneutic interpretations of these sources, from which Islamic Systems of jurisprudence (fiqh) are derived. A large proportion of Islamic epistemology is based on hermeneutic processes that may differ from one Islamic sect to another. It is within these hermeneutic spaces that possibilities for alternative readings of these primary epistemological sources exist. The authors argue that the differences in interpretations contribute to the complexities related to banning the burka. For example, according to policy related to al-Azhar University in Egypt, niqab/burka is a cultural practice not founded in Islam, while for Salafists wearing the burka is part of Muslim religious practice. This discrepancy between the two groups was described by the CBC news agency in 2010: "Salafists, who actively promote their creed, sometimes funded by wealthy patrons in Saudi Arabia, are opposed to Al-Azhar's theological teachings" or "they can't use that religious argument to defend a cultural practice that is harmful to women" (al-Atrush, 2009, para. 21). The process of different textual interpretations provided different understandings to the importance of wearing the burka, thus contributing to incompatible philosophical views.

Another example with this incompatibility can be represented by different interpretations of the concept of modesty, which is an important ideology within Islam. Modesty is achieved in Islam by following certain standards for both behaviour and dress. Secular and faith-based Muslim feminists negotiate modesty differently (Hamdan, 2007; Zine, 2004). In other words, some faith-based feminists believe in the truth of the Qur'an's message and find the veil to be a very modest form of dress (Denny, 2006); however, not all faith-based feminists consider veiling to be a religious requirement (Zine, 2006a). According to secular Muslim feminists, faith-based Muslim feminists frame their identities in accordance with patriarchal doctrine that is organized on racist and classist hierarchies (Zine, 2004). On the other hand, faith-based feminists view secular feminists somewhat as White women's movements that failed to address racism and classism in their social and political activism. The lack of solidarity between the two groups has contributed to the marginalization of Muslim women's voices in the setting of policy agendas.

Briefly, the differing opinions held by Muslims creates an urgently contested public debate that effectively brings to light both the complexity of this issue and the need for further research as a means to identify the implications for some Muslim women living in the West. For instance, cultural and historical contexts associated with wearing the burka and the aforementioned decision made by the head of the al-Azhar University in Egypt (Sunni Islam's foremost spiritual authority) that niqab/burka is a cultural practice not founded in Islam contradicted the sectarian Salafists, who support wearing the burka as part of Muslim religious practice and thus oppose al-Azhar's theological teachings. Consequently, this debate is interwoven with complicated issues related to controversial sectarian differences.

Themes: Associating the Burka with Hijab and Extremism

Although there were explicit statements that banning the burka is not linked to the hijab, both local and international online newspaper articles linked the ban on the burka with France's decision in 2004 to prevent Muslim women from wearing the hijab, and this may give the public who are not familiar with hijab and burka the impression that banning the hijab needs to be considered too. For instance, in one of the undergraduate courses that Al-Fartousi instructed, she used to hear some discriminatory comments from certain undergraduate students that associated her hijab to the burka. Similarly, in 2003 the French government banned the wearing of the veil in public institutions, to the alarm of the Muslim community members who saw it as an obvious act of religious discrimination. Two teenaged sisters were expelled from their high school in the Paris suburb of Aubervilliers for refusing to take off their headscarves. Many young Muslims felt uneasy about the arguments over secular beliefs and viewed the position against wearing the hijab as hostile and discriminatory (Hamdan, 2007). The young Muslims felt that Islam was being singled out because of a fear of fundamentalism. Domestically, Canada recognizes and promotes multiculturalism as a fundamental characteristic of Canadian heritage and identity (Department of Justice Canada, 2009). However, a controversial incident happened when young Muslim schoolgirls were expelled for wearing the hijab to school in Quebec (Zine, 2006a, 2006b). In sum, what happened in Quebec can be seen as an example of the idea that extended into the 20th century from the colonial period, of the backwardness of the East as opposed to the enlightened attitudes of modern secular nations. Many researchers assert the need to challenge the negative stereotypes of the veil as oppressive, especially for those Muslims who live in the West (Bullock, 2002). Moreover, in some newspaper articles, the word "veil" is used interchangeably with "burka," thus contributing to generalizing various Muslim women's dress as tools for "degrading" and "oppressing" women (Lewis, 2009).

Many of the newspaper articles associate wearing the burka with extremism. In his book, *What Went Wrong?* Lewis (2002) elaborates how the West has undertaken double standards by claiming to support democracy but at the same time planning for ultimate control over the oil resources of the Middle East. No doubt, Al-Qaeda is a self-confessed enemy to the West. As such, it provides a rationale (correct or not) for the West to insert its legitimized presence in the Middle East for the sake of democracy and protecting the countries from terrorism. In this respect, the media discourses play a significant role in establishing the need for the West to fight Al-Qaeda. This can be seen through the negative images that represent Muslim women as a single homogeneous group regardless of their diverse ethnic and racial backgrounds, and through language that is used to stereotype Muslim women who wear the burka as "medieval and misogynist symbols of extremism with no basis in Islam" ("Muslim Lobby Group," 2009, para. 1). In sum, the war on terror was linked to wearing the burka and provides a reason for banning the cultural garment in order to ensure security and protection. It is also interesting to discover that the burka is associated with extremism by both Western as well as Muslim critics; many Muslim leaders and politicians agree that wearing the burka is related to extremism, which thus supports the decision to ban the burka.

Themes: Gender Equality, Freedom of Choice, and Harems

The themes associated with gender equality, freedom of choice, and harems demonstrate different interpretations. Most authors reported that the burka, which again is associated with extremism, disadvantages women by decreasing their chances of getting employment and encourages a distorted practice of Islam. Some of the negative terms associated with Muslim women included "prisoners behind netting," "deprived of identity," and "degrading" ("Sarkozy: Burkas not Welcome," 2009). Further, most of the arguments are related to women who are being forced to wear the burka by their husbands, thus supporting Western media discourses that construct the Muslim woman as an oppressed, marginalized other who lacks voice and agency and is (albeit at worst) a hallmark of an Islamic society that is in opposition to the so-called Western civilized world. The newscaster ("Sarkozy: Burkas not Welcome," 2009) relates this view of harmed women presented by the media to oriental backwardness (Said, 1979). In this regard, we refer to Said (1997) who touches upon "the idea of European identity as a superior one in comparison with all the non-European peoples and cultures" and observes that, "There is in addition the hegemony of European ideas about the Orient, themselves reiterating European Superiority over Oriental backwardness" (p. 46).

Consequently, many complicated issues contribute to the development of negative stereotypes of the veil, affecting Muslim women's identities.

However, other authors (including one Western male and two female Muslims) defended the choice of some Muslim women to wear the burka, and referred to U.S. President Barack Obama's words that it is "important for Western countries to avoid impeding Muslim citizens from practising religion as they see fit for instance, by dictating what clothes a Muslim woman should wear" ("President Barack Obama's Speech to the Muslim World," 2009, para. 5). Other online newspaper articles reported the belief of some Muslim and Western scholars that wearing the burka constitutes a religious right.

Themes: Religious Rights

While the *Canadian Charter of Rights and Freedoms* (Department of Justice Canada, 2009) promotes the notion that every individual possesses freedom of religion, the MCC says the Charter should not apply in the case of the niqab because it is not a requirement of the faith. Quebec Premier Jean Charest has proposed enacting Bill 94 which, if approved by the National Assembly of Quebec, would deny essential government services, public employment, educational opportunities, and health care to people who wear facial coverings. Most of the newspaper articles reported that the province will hold public hearings on the draft legislation. In opposition to this bill, Muslim women in Manitoba critique the proposed legislation in Quebec that may limit the wearing of the burka; the article describes how Muslim women gathered in Winnipeg to educate others about Islam and veiling ("Manitoba Muslim Women decry veil limits," 2010). Due to the different viewpoints related to wearing the burka, religious rights are interwoven with these complicated controversial issues. In any case, we support the need to consider the consequences associated with banning the burka, as some women may be isolated from getting access to education and health services, thus creating many tensions for these women.

Themes: Implications for Education

The veil is one of the most provocative forms of dress and is underpinned by multiple meanings that have been generated by historical, cultural, and political factors (Bullock, 2000, 2002; Zine, 2002). Differing opinions within a variety of Muslim sects create an urgently contested public debate that effectively brings to light both the complexity of this issue and the need for further research as a means to identify the implications for young Muslim students. Such studies would likely identify the variety of experiences and help to overcome the stereotypes existing in the West.

Despite the country's reputation as a multicultural society, Canada has a range of social and political issues that contribute to negative racial stereotypes concerning Muslim females that, in turn, have direct consequences for students' school experiences. Some exclusionary social and political discourses used by some Western media contribute to discriminatory stereotypes levelled at the young Muslim female in North American schools today. For example, the Muslim schoolgirls who were expelled for wearing the hijab in the Quebec school system signal the problem of racial and religious discrimination with wearing the hijab (Geaves, 2005).

Muslim students in Canada face many challenges, such as pressures to assimilate, identity dilemmas, school drop-out rates, feelings of alienation, and the predicament of Islamophobia (Collet, 2007; Khalema & Wannas-Jones, 2003; Zine, 2001). Islamophobia is woven into Muslim students' daily lives and targets their religious, ethnic, and gendered identities (Fournier & Yurdakul, 2006; Kepel, 1997; Skalli, 2004; Zine, 2001). For instance, Mogadime, Ramrattan Smith, and Scott (in press) discuss how Muslim youths are routinely represented as a threat to national security throughout the Western world and how the popular press is a vehicle for reproducing assumptions about Muslim youths as potential terrorists. Furthermore, Bill 94 influences not merely Muslim women wearing the burka but extends more broadly to include Muslim youth in the West. From the decision made to ban burkas and from the themes around terrorism and stereotypes, it is easy to anticipate that Muslim youth will continue to struggle in terms of negotiating their religious and ethnic identities. The media's discourses and representations of Muslim women place many Muslim youth, especially those whose religious identities are visible, in vulnerable situations in terms of knowing how to how to position themselves and protect their religious identities (Sensoy & Stonebanks, 2009). In many contexts, the media inaccurately represents Muslim females as one homogeneous group. Muslim females do not experience wearing the veil in the same way. The political and the religious contexts of Muslim females wearing the burka differ totally from Muslim women wearing the burka in the West. Many of the Taliban's rules do not adhere to basic Islamic laws, especially those relating to women; for instance, Islam did not specify a certain type of hijab (Hamdan, 2007). Thus, any dress that covers the body except the face and the hands is considered as acceptable hijab, regardless of its relation to any other nationality.

On the other hand, some Muslim women in the West associate their observance of the burka with freedom of choice and religious rights that are prominently mentioned in many reports about human rights (Mcquigge, 2009). In this respect, it is important to examine the implication of banning the burka with the acknowledgement of the right of Muslim youth to exercise their religious rights. From the report of the Senate Standing Committee on Human Rights (2007) *Children: the Silenced Citizens*, the rights of religion have been manifested in many various contexts. For instance, the report's Article 20(1) indicates that for a child who is deprived of a family due to abuse, alternative care must consider the child's own ethnic, religious, cultural, and linguistic background. The report's articles that address the needs of migrant children (Chapter 11, Articles 7, 9, 10, 11, 21, 22, 35) indicate that regular contact from friends, relatives, religious, social and legal counsel, and guardians need to be addressed. The report's Chapter 12 (Early Childhood Development, Articles 12, 18, and 29) indicates that the preparation of the child in a free society must consider the understanding and the acceptance of friendship among all peoples, ethnic, national, and religious groups and persons of indigenous origin; Article 30 is more specific, outlining the importance of religion by considering the right of a minority child to enjoy his or her own culture and to practice his or her own religion. However, as a community member, Al-Fartousi discovered in her conversation with some women wearing the burka that their children faced challenges in their schools. Many of these kids experience racial and religious harassment due to their mothers' outfits. Al-Fartousi noticed that some mothers prefer to stay home to avoid any kind of harassment as a result of the decision to ban the burka, and some women even preferred to move to a more diverse setting to be safer.

In classroom settings, teachers can play an advocate role in addressing cross-cultural awareness by assisting students toward cultural competencies. Hanvey's discussion (1975, as cited in Bennett, 2007, p. 354) on cultural consciousness provides two different perspectives on cross-cultural awareness. The former deals with *ethnocentrism* in which one cultural group from the same ethnicity views the world through their own cultural perspective. The latter is related to *cross-cultural awareness* in which the diversity of ideas is recognized and the limitations of the ethnocentrism are acknowledged through critical examination. Proponents of cultural diversity such as Bennett (2007) argue that attainment of higher levels of cross-cultural awareness can only develop if children are supported through critical thinking processes (e.g., toward critiquing their cultural assumptions and evaluations). However, we assert that before fostering the cross-cultural awareness, teachers need to simultaneously take into consideration both students' cultural backgrounds, as well as their own. In other words, an acquired deep understanding regarding students' cultural knowledge basis is necessary regardless of whether classrooms are located in monocultural or diverse settings. Through media literacy, students can be introduced to diversity issues that best ensure that the world views of a diverse population of learners are respected and valued. Teachers are encouraged to think of promoting and preparing critical citizens by asking such questions as: What are the advantages and disadvantages of engaging students in critical thinking around diversity and social justice? Examinations of the language used in the media discourses can be implemented in order to promote students' awareness of issues related to discrimination or misrepresentation in society. With this method, students will develop an understanding of diversity and global awareness in education such as understanding the hidden curriculum, hegemony, and Eurocentric ideology in the media, including TV programs.

CONCLUSION

Muslim females may share Islam, but they come from a wide variety of class-based, racial, and ethnic backgrounds. Accordingly, Muslims interpret the meaning of veiling differently, and their interpretations related to wearing the burka need to be respected and acknowledged as part of human rights and personal choice. Discussion and differences of opinions among Muslims are no less than the differences that exist among Western women; thus more study of the actual conditions of Muslim youth are needed to demonstrate the variety of Muslim experiences and to help overcome the stereotypes existing in the West.

Many researchers assert the need to challenge the negative stereotypes of the veil as oppressive, especially for those Muslims who live in the West (Bullock, 2002). As scholars in the area of social justice and equity, we believe that new models for understanding the relationship of religion and education must be developed, ones that perhaps respond to the underlying direction to keep religion out of Canadian schools (Lupu, Masci, & Tuttle, 2007; McLaren, 2003). Many incidents of anti-Muslim hate crimes have been reported since the events of 9/11 (Lynch, 2007). A number of Muslims feel that some Westerners act in a prejudicial way toward them due to their religious affiliation, country of origin, or physical appearance. Normalizing a cultural or religious practice means trying to make it seem like it is a part of everyday life. For instance, girls should not be harassed for wearing headscarves. As Taylor and Whittaker (2003) state, "a lesson that encourages students to critically examine the social pressures to follow current clothing trends juxtaposed against the freedom some Muslims experience by wearing a head covering avoids normalization" (p. 262). This paper is intended to provide insights into the complex political, religious, and cultural factors that may affect the representation of Muslim women's identities. We hope from this paper that readers will develop a better understanding of the role the media can play in representing certain Muslim women.

REFERENCES

al-Atrush, S. (2009). Al-Azhar chief 'should resign over veil remark.' Retrieved from http://www.google.com/hostednews/afp/article/ALeqM5iPvlRmtd5rKQ7eL4vF1xFKURT2aA.

Bennett, C. I. (2007). *Comprehensive multicultural education theory and practice* (6th ed.). New York: Pearson.

Blommaert, J., & Bulcaen, C. (2000). Critical discourse analysis. *Annual Review of Anthropology, 29*, 447-466. doi:10.1146/annurev.anthro.29.1.447.

Bullock, K. (2000). The gaze and colonial plans for the unveiling of Muslim women. *Studies in Contemporary Islam, 2*(2), 1-20.

Bullock, K. (2002). *Rethinking Muslim women and the veil.* Herndon, VA: International Institute of Islamic Thought.

Clarke, L. (2003). Hijab according to the Hadith: Text and interpretation. In S. S. Alvi, H. Hoodfar, & S. McDonough (Eds.), *Muslim veil in North America: Issues and debates* (pp. 214–286). Toronto: Women's Press.

Collet, B. A. (2007). Islam, national identity and public secondary education: Perspectives from the Somali diaspora in Toronto, Canada.*Race, Ethnicity and Education, 10*(2), 131–153.

Cooke, M. (2008). Deploying the Muslim woman. *Journal of Feminist Studies in Religion, 24*(1), 91–99.

Denny, F. M. (2006). *An introduction to Islam.* Upper Saddle River, NJ: Pearson Prentice Hall.

Department of Justice Canada. (2009). *Canadian charter of rights and freedoms.* Retrieved from http://laws.justice.gc.ca/en/charter/1.html

Fournier, P., & Yurdakul, G. (2006). Unveiling distribution: Muslim women with headscarves in France and Germany. In M. Bodemann & G. Yurdakul (Eds.), *Migration, citizenship, ethnos* (pp. 167–184). New York: Palgrave Macmillan.

Geaves, R. (2005). *Aspects of Islam.* Washington, DC: Georgetown University Press.

Hamdan, A. (2006). Arab women's education and gender perceptions: An insider analysis. *Journal of International Women's Studies, 8*(1), 52–64.

Hamdan, A. (2007). The issue of hijab in France: Reflections and analysis. *Muslim World Journal of Human Rights, 4*(2), 1–29.

Kepel, G. (1997). *Allah in the West: Islamic movements in America and Europe*. Stanford, CA: Stanford University Press.

Khalema, N. E., & Wannas-Jones, J. (2003). Under the prism of suspicion: Minority voices in Canada post-September 11. *Journal of Muslim Minority Affairs, 23*(1), 25–39.

Lewis, B. (2002). *What went wrong? Western impact and Middle Eastern response*. New York: Oxford University Press.

Lewis, C. (2009, October 8). Muslim group calls for ban on the burka. *National Post*. Retrieved from http://www.faithandmedia.org/articles/show/1647

Lupu, I. C., Masci, D., & Tuttle, R. W. (2007). *Religion in the public schools*. Washington, DC: The Pew Forum on Religion and Public Life. Retrieved from http://pewforum.org/uploadedfiles/Topics/Issues/Church-State_Law/religion-public-schools.pdf

Lynch, S. N. (2007). *Police find Gilbert teen innocent in bomb scare*. Retrieved from http://www.highbeam.com/doc/1G1-164301931.html

Manitoba Muslim women decry veil limits. (2010, May 7). *CBC News*. Retrieved from http://www.cbc.ca/news/canada/manitoba/story/2010/05/07/mb-head-coverings-meeting-1057.html

McLaren, P. (2003). A pedagogy of possibility. In A. C. Ornstein, L. S. Behar-Horenstein, & E. F. Pajak (Eds.), *Contemporary issues in curriculum* (3rd ed., pp. 26-35). Boston: Allyn & Bacon.

Mcquigge, M. (2009). Muslim organization urges Ottawa to ban burkas, niqabs in public. *MSN News*. Retrieved fromhttp://news.ca.msn.com/top-stories/cbc-article.aspx?cp-documentid=22128929

Mogadime, D. (2005). Elite media discourses: A case study of the transformation of the administrative judiciary in South Africa. *Journal of Black Studies, 35*(4), 155–178.

Mogadime, D., Ramrattan Smith, S., & Scott, A. (in press). The problem of fear enhancing inaccuracies of representation: Muslim male youths and Western media. In A. Abdi (Ed.), *Decolonizing philosophies of education*. Rotterdam, Boston & Taipei: Sense Publishers.

Muslim lobby group urges Ottawa to ban burkas, niqabs. (2009, October 7). *Toronto Star*. Retrieved fromhttp://www.thestar.com/news/canada/article/706989--muslim-lobby-group-urges-ottawa-to-ban-burkas-niqabs

President Barack Obama's speech to the Muslim world (2009, June 4). *Time News*. Retrieved from http://www.time.com/time/politics/article/0,8599,1902738-6,00.html

Said, E. (1979). *Orientalism*. New York: Vintage Books.

Said, E. (1997). Orientalism. In A. Gray & J. McGuigan (Eds.), *Studying culture: An introductory reader* (2nd ed., pp. 42–53). London: Arnold.

Sarkozy: Burkas "not welcome" in France. (2009, June 22). *CBS News*. Retrieved from http://www.cbsnews.com/stories/2009/06/22/world/main5103076.shtml

Sensoy, O., & Stonebanks, C. D. (2009). *Muslim voices in school: Narratives of identity and pluralism*. Rotterdam, the Netherlands: Sense.

Skalli, L. (2004). Loving Muslim women with a vengeance: The west, women, fundamentalism. In J. L. Kincheloe & R. Steinberg (Eds.), *The miseducation of the west: How schools and the media distort our understanding of the Islamic world* (pp. 43–58). Westport, CT: Praeger.

Senate Standing Committee on Human Rights. (2007, April). *Children: The silenced citizens. Effective implementation of Canada's international obligations with respect to the rights of children*. Retrieved from http://dsp-psd.pwgsc.gc.ca/collection_2007/sen/YC32-391-1-01E.pdf

Taylor, L. S., & Whittaker, C. R. (2003). *Bridging multiple worlds: Case studies of diverse educational communities*. Boston: Pearson Education.

Titscher, S., Meyer, M., Wodak, R., & Vetter, E. (2000). *Methods of text and discourse analysis*. London: Sage.

van Dijk, T. A. (1993). *Elite discourse and racism*. London: Sage.

Worthington, P. (2010). Quebec's burqa ban is not racist. *Toronto Sun.* Retrieved fromhttp://www.torontosun.com/ news/columnists/peter_worthington/2010/03/29/13400986.html

Yosso, T., & Solórzano, D. (2002). Critical race methodology: Counter-storytelling as an analytical framework for education research. *Qualitative Inquiry, 8*(1), 23–24.

Zine, J. (2001). Muslim youth students in Canadian schools: Education and the politics of religious identities. *Anthropology and Educational Quarterly, 32*(4), 399–423.

Zine, J. (2002). Muslim women and the politics of representation. *American Journal of Islamic Social Sciences, 19*(4), 1–22.

Zine, J. (2004). *Staying on a critical path: A critical ethnography of Islamic schooling in Ontario.* Unpublished doctoral dissertation. University of Toronto, Toronto, Canada.

Zine, J. (2006a). Creating a critical faith-centered space for antiracist Feminism. *Muslim World Journal of Human Rights, 3*(1), 167–187.

Zine, J. (2006b). Between orientalism and fundamentalism: The politics of Muslim women's feminist engagement. *Muslim World Journal of Human Rights, 3*(1), 1–25.

Zine, J. (2008). Lost in translation: Writing back from the margins. A roundtable response to Miriam Cooke's "The Muslimwoman." *Journal of Feminist Studies in Religion, 24*(1), 110–116.

APPENDIX

Table 1. Emerging themes—banning the burka

Article no.	Unknown Author	Muslim Author	Western Author	A	B	C	D	E	F	G	H
1		√		√		√	√	√	√	√	
2		√		√		√			√		√
3	√			√	√	√	√	√	√	√	
4	√			√	√	√	√	√	√	√	
5	√			√	√	√	√	√	√	√	
6	√			√	√	√	√	√	√	√	√
7	√			√	√	√	√	√	√	√	√
8	√			√	√	√	√	√	√	√	
9	√			√	√	√	√	√	√	√	
10	√			√		√	√	√	√	√	
11	√			√	√	√	√	√	√	√	
12	√			√	√	√	√	√	√	√	
13	√			√	√	√	√	√	√	√	
14	√			√	√	√	√	√	√	√	
15	√			√	√	√	√	√	√	√	
16	√			√	√	√	√	√	√	√	√
17	√			√	√	√	√	√	√	√	√
18		√		√	√				√		√
19	√			√	√	√	√	√	√	√	√
20	√			√	√	√	√	√	√	√	
21	√			√	√	√	√	√	√	√	
22	√			√	√	√	√	√	√	√	
23	√			√	√	√	√	√	√	√	
24	√			√	√	√	√	√	√	√	
25	√			√	√	√	√	√	√	√	
26	√			√	√	√	√	√	√	√	
27	√			√	√	√	√	√	√	√	
28	√			√	√	√	√	√	√	√	
29	√			√	√	√	√	√	√	√	
30	√			√	√	√	√	√	√	√	

Note. A = association of burka with hijab; B = negative images; C = political and religious controversy; D = association of burka with harem; E = gender equality; F = differing interpretations of religious rights; G = burka as feature of extremism; H = freedom of choice.

May Al-Fartousi
Faculty of Education,
Brock University, Ontario, Canada

Dolana Mogadime
Faculty of Education,
Brock University, Ontario, Canada

SHANNON A. MOORE AND RICHARD C. MITCHELL

TRANSDISCIPLINARY APPROACHES TO YOUNG PEOPLE'S CITIZENSHIP

From Bystanders to Action

ABSTRACT

These are unprecedented times for democratic traditions as world society drifts almost rudderless towards neo-liberal capitalist collapse without many alternative visions coming into view (Hyslop-Margison & Thayer, 2009). As a response, the authors present thematic and theoretical findings from a case study utilising grounded theory analytical procedures to look at aspects of active child and youth citizenship in Ontario, Canada. Their investigation focused on events associated with a youth rally hosted by Nobel nominee and children's rights activist Craig Kielburger, and a heuristic model illustrating key findings is included to further contextualise this emergent global assemblage (Sassen, 2008) of childhood citizenship vis-à-vis adult power. The main argument from the research concerns the adoption of the United Nations Convention on the Rights of the Child (UNCRC, 1989) as a transdisciplinary framework for critical citizenship education since the treaty cuts across orthodox knowledge silos to do with 'childhood', 'youth' and 'citizenship' (see also Mitchell, 2010; Doek, 2009). Although marginally implemented in Canada, previous contentions in that country over whether children have rights at all are being replaced with ongoing monitoring of this treaty and young people's rights to participate more fully in society (UN Committee on the Rights of the Child, 1995, 2003). It is clear from the study that global phenomena associated with the Kielburgers' international non-governmental organisation *Free the Children* offer a critical entry point into contemporary expressions of active, inclusive citizenship for tens of thousands of young people throughout the world.

Keywords: UN Convention on the Rights of the Child, critical citizenship education, transdisciplinarity, grounded theory.

INTRODUCTION

In the eyes of many observers, history has been kind to Canada with an apparently stable social democracy where many of its citizens enjoy comparatively high levels of prosperity, the rule of law through its courts and judiciary, enviable protection for many minorities, freedom of the press, freedom of speech, of religion, of peaceful assembly, along with the rights to vote and strike, and publicly funded education and healthcare. In response, the authors present a case study investigating child and youth citizenship during a period of creeping suppression of the rights of young people, described by the nation's upper house as "silenced citizens" (Senate of Canada, 2007)[1]. The study was framed by the research question: 'What are some of the critical issues for young people as they attempt to exercise their rights to participatory citizenship in Canada and beyond?'[2]

From the standpoint of critical pedagogy espoused by 20th century Brazilian educator Paulo Freire (1970), the main argument here contradicts UK educator Dina Kiwan's (2005) contention that human rights and citizenship are conceptually distinct, and that conflating the two notions is "incoherent" and "may actually obstruct the empowerment and active participation of individuals" (p. 37). The investigation builds on Canadian sociologist Daiva Stasiulis' (2002a, 2002b) earlier analysis of children's rights and citizenship that similarly theorised the work of Craig Kielburger, co-founder of the international non-governmental organisation, *Free the Children* as an alternative to traditional citizenship models. With programs in 4,000 North American schools, the Kielburger brothers (older brother and Harvard-educated lawyer Marc is his co-founder/co-director) have built more than 500 schools in 16 countries, and employ more than 100 people in their Toronto-based charity (Kielburger & Kielburger, 2006). In 2009 they took in nearly $16 million in donations along with $8 million more in the US as part of what they identify as "the world's largest network of children helping children through education". Throughout their evolution and growth from an elementary school and home-based initiative, they have also quietly challenged the foundations of Canadian tax law related to charitable fundraising through their somewhat radical approach to social enterprise (Wingrove, 2010).

Here we draw upon both theory and empiricism to uncover new intersections among and between children's human rights, citizenship and pedagogy with findings elicited from a partnership with Mr. Kielburger and key informants involved in a 2009 youth rally he hosted in Ontario, Canada (Brock University Press, 2010).

Echoing Kiwan's (2005, 2007) sentiments, UK-based researcher Matthews (2001) declares the "concept of citizenship relates to the relationship between individuals and the state" as well as the "conditions required for social participation", and not so much to any one philosophical underpinning (p. 299). It is clear from the literature, however, that many theorists integrate notions of democratic citizenship with experiences of human rights or their violation (Donnelly, 2008; Douzinas, 2006; Hawkins, 2009; Mitchell, 2010; O'Byrne, 2003), and our investigation was premised on similar assumptions that the two are linked through human relationships, however beneficial or insidious. Despite an abundance of millennial rhetoric associated with implementing such "principles and provisions" from Article 42 of the United Nations Convention on the Rights of the Child (herein CRC, 1989), young people are less represented in Canada's educational, legal, policy or legislative arenas than is the case for their contemporaries in many UK and European settings (Mitchell, 2003; Senate of

Canada, 2007; Osler & Starkey, 2005). Their position in Canada is consistent with Henry Giroux's (2010b) analysis of the lack of critical citizenship in the US:

> Imposed amnesia is the modus operandi of the current moment. Not only is historical memory now sacrificed to the spectacles of consumerism, celebrity culture, hyped-up violence and a market-driven obsession with the self, but the very formative culture that makes compassion, justice and an engaged citizenry foundational to democracy has been erased from the language of mainstream politics and the diverse cultural apparatuses that support it (para. 2).

Findings from this study also appear consistent with Hyslop-Margison and Thayer's (2009) contention that contrary to the "reproductive model of citizenship education, a citizenship education based upon [Freirean] critical pedagogy considers society and citizenship as dynamic, fluid and contestable constructs where fundamental social change is both imaginable and practically possible" (p. 2). A heuristic model built upon grounded theory analysis of findings is included that illustrates the key themes from the study leading to its "theoretical code" (Glaser, 2005).

LOCAL/GLOBAL ASSEMBLAGES AND CRITICAL CITIZENSHIP

Similar to globalisation, democracy is still a highly contested and localised term (Vrasti, 2009), and with the ongoing collapse of "vulgar capitalism" decried by Hyslop-Margison and Thayer (2009) the increasing interdependence of "world society" (Luhmann, 1997) points to a "multitude of transformations and challenges across and despite borders" (Vrasti, 2009, p. 4). An increasingly complex "global assemblage" (Sassen, 2008) of both childhood and human rights has emerged that can no longer be solely encompassed or understood through the lens of the nation-state since the world can no longer be reduced "into mutually exclusive sovereign units" (Vrasti, 2009, p. 1). In this local/global nexus, active citizenship continues to become uncoupled from traditional geopolitical borders, notwithstanding Kiwan's position (2005). Similar to Turner (2006), and to Isin and Turner's (2007) notions of "invigorating" the discourse through continued re-theorising, we agree with their understanding of an emergent "global citizenship" (pp. 12–13). We further agree with Sen's (2004) straightforward observation that to understand contemporary developments in human rights law, policy and practice, a more integrated framework is called for, and it is clear in the literature that this re-theorising is underway. O'Byrne (2003) has gone a considerable distance with his integration of a 'sociology of human rights', as has Turner (1993, 1997) before him.

As researchers with a standpoint grounded in professional practice with young people, we've observed many to be very active in their attempts to redefine world society described by theorists such as Luhmann (1997), Beck and Lau (2005), and Isin and Turner (2007). One of us has previously theorised the movement of CRC texts into domestic legislation and practice throughout the world as an example of "social autopoiesis" after Luhmann's (1997) systems theory (Mitchell, 2005; 2007; also UK childhood theorists King, 1994, and Moss and Petrie, 2002, p. 65). We re-emphasise Giroux's (2003) point here that "educators need to develop a politics and pedagogy that combine the modernist legacy of social justice, equality, freedom, and rights with late modern concerns with difference, plurality, power, discourse, identities and politics ...elements of a *democratic postmodernism*" (p. 54, emphasis added; see also Dahlberg, Moss, & Pence, 1999).

Our contention is that the CRC offers educators one such an overlooked opportunity – see Hawkins (2009) for one such omission in Canada and Matthews (2007) in the US – one that embeds the consciousness of critical citizenship into their human rights curricula. This could come about naturally as a reflection of democratic institutions in a time of crisis characterised by UK-based sociologist Zygmunt Bauman (2000) as 'liquid modernity'. Mehmoona Moosa-Mitha (2005) takes her theorising of youth citizenship in Canada in a similar direction arguing for a "difference-centred alternative" based upon her research with sexually exploited youth. Like Giroux (2003, 2010a, 2010b), she contends that rights-based discourses need to "take a more fluid and pluralist approach to citizenship that is situated in a politics of solidarity, a transversal politics where citizens occupying multiple subject positions such as class and gender and race come together in solidarity to resist a common oppression" (p. 372). Her approach reflects an alternative to the traditional, top-down orientation towards civics and citizenship pedagogies that stifles political participation in its cradle (Hyslop-Margison & Thayer, 2009). These latter authors further aim for pedagogues to re-create "thick democracy...[since] our role in education is not to prepare students for a new economic reality designed by others, but to prepare them to shape social reality in more progressive and socially just sorts of ways" (pp. x, xvii). They echo Hannah Arendt's (1970) earlier arguments for an understanding of education that is linked to democracy, but one that holds power to prepare children to take up real responsibilities in the renewal of a common world (as cited in Giroux, 2010a, p. 1).

Clearly, there exist deep inequities in the globalised capitalist system wholly incongruent with human rights theory, law, policy and practice under all present regimes. Yet democratic political systems still represent the best systems to promote and protect human rights, however arguably (Howard-Hassmann, 2005; see also Farrow, Kielburger, & Davidson, 2010). Notwithstanding, democracy only works if citizens are politically engaged and trusting in government, contend Morgan and Streb (2001). Stronger voice and fuller direct participation in education, politics and the economy offer a more organic episteme for a generation connected by social media, social networking and social capital. Active, participatory expressions of democracy - such as youth environmental protesters climbing onto Canada's parliament buildings (China View News, 2009) or peaceful demonstrators during the 2010 Toronto G-20 Summit - fundamentally challenge industrial-age thinking about democracy, politics, law and the production of knowledges (see also Kincheloe and McLaren's, 2005 trenchant reflections).

Education, however, is still a cornerstone for understanding and experiencing citizenship rights (Moore, 2008; Moore & Mitchell, 2008; Tomaševski, 2006) since basic knowledge of civic, social and political rights is the most basic human right of all (Arendt, 1970; Freeman, 2007). From the standpoint of Freirean pedagogy, a critical discussion of children's human rights in the classroom offers new potential to enact the dynamics of citizenship, one that is at the same moment a formal political status as it engages in democratic teaching and learning relations (Ben-Arieh & Boyer, 2005; Devine, 2002; Stasiulis, 2002a, 2002b; Tomaševski, 2006). Moosa-Mitha (2005) takes this analysis a step further:

> Children's difference from the adult 'norm' assumed of citizens in liberal models of citizenship results in overlooking children's citizenship rights through a construction of children as "not-yet-citizens". Alternative models of citizenship that centre on 'difference' of social identities such as gender, race sexuality, class, and so on, offer possibilities of defining citizenship in ways that take their rights and status as citizens seriously on the basis, rather than the exclusion, of their identity as children. (pp. 369–370)

Such criticality allows for the uncovering of citizenship through institutional power relations associated with young people's lesser maturity and adults in authority. Educational sites, particularly for young people, have emancipatory potential, and the pedagogue a potential midwife of autonomy, political agency and social change. Nevertheless as Giroux (2003) argues:

[M]any educators have failed to take seriously Italian Marxist Antonio Gramsci's insight that '[e]very relationship of *hegemony* is necessarily an educational relationship' with its implication that education as a cultural pedagogical practice takes place across multiple sites as it signals how, within diverse contexts, education makes us both subjects of and subject to relations of power. (p. 64)

In line with UK law professor Michael Freeman (2007) and Canadians Mitchell and McCusker (2008), and in contrast to US-based Matthews (2007), we argue here that in theory and practice critical citizenship education – particularly within states with publicly-funded education regimes – should begin with the CRC. This international legal and policy framework provides a set of organizing principles for active citizenship that has been ratified by 193 states; its Article 42 obliges each one to simply inform young people they possess a unique set of human rights. Indeed, during a 2002 interview with one of the treaty's 1979–1989 non-governmental negotiators, Mitchell (2005) found this same text was conceived by consensus and added in late going as an "international compliance indicator" (pp. 324–325). It represents the document's least ambiguous text: "States Parties undertake to make the principles and provision of the Convention widely known, by appropriate and active means, to adults and children alike" (UNCRC, 1989; see also UN General Assembly, 1994). As Freeman (1992) observed, "[m]uch of the world has as much chance of implementing the Convention as sending its citizens to the moon", and indeed he notes many states would choose the latter over the former (p. 41). In the same piece, though, Freeman emphasises how it will remain important to recognise and associate children's rights "with other rights movements (women, civil rights etc.) ... [since] 'rights' enables one to talk in terms of 'entitlements' " (p. 31).

EPISTEMOLOGICAL FRAMEWORK

In Canada, traditional approaches to citizenship pedagogies adopt a top-down, cognitive and developmental psychology orientation towards civics curricula – see Howe and Covell (2005, p. 123), Morgan and Streb (2001) for a US example, and also Woodhead (1999) for one UK analysis – with implicit ideological assumptions of creating the type of 'docile citizen' decried by Raby (2005). This study's epistemology appears congruent with Stasiulis' theoretical concerns (2002a, 2002b) since we also started with top-down policy reviews along with bottom-up alternative perspectives, in this case with Mr. Kielburger himself as a key informant along with seven student activists who worked for 18 months to host him. Our research continues the move away from tiresome arguments to do with 'universalism' premised upon intractable ontological debates towards those to do with epistemology and new human rights knowledge (Mitchell, 2005, 2010).

Previously, Canadians enjoyed an international reputation as human rights champions by being among the founding members of the United Nations (United Nations International Children's Emergency Fund [UNICEF], 2009) and early promoters of the CRC (Mitchell, 2000, 2005). This claim is no longer tenable since the current political dynamics in the nation and the actual experience of citizenship for those under 18 clearly reflect ideological interpretations by successive governments violating its terms (Howe & Covell, 2005, 2007; UN Committee on the Rights of the Child, 1995, 2003). Generalised fears of young people in Canada have been coupled with "dominant Western notions of childhood that fetishize innocence and attribute passivity and incompetence to children" (Stasiulis, 2002b, p. 507) as they propel adultist institutions to favour power and control over participation (Moore & Mitchell, 2009; Mitchell, 2010; see also Scraton, 1997 in the UK). Although still widely misunderstood by childhood academics and advocates alike, serious efforts to implement the CRC in Canada could still have a...

> ...profound impact on real children's lives...children's rights are being pushed to the side and even violated....one only needs to take a brief survey of the issue of child poverty, or the situation of Aboriginal or special needs children to realize that this is true. (UNICEF, 2009, p. 14).

Noted Canadian scholars Howe and Covell (2005) also observe "the enjoyment of rights is basic to citizenship" but currently children's citizenship is consistent with core human rights principles "only in part" (p. 63; see also Howe, 2005; Hill, Davis, Prout & Tisdall, 2004; Scraton, 1997 for UK analyses. In a recent discussion of CRC "miseducation" [sic], Howe and Covell (2010) rightly point out that while 'rights and responsibilities' may be a common link pedagogically and in the literature, "there is no mention of children's responsibilities in the Convention" (p. 91). In fact, the responsibilities of the state are paramount and adults in institutional and political authority are most at fault when it comes to the lack of rights-based citizenship experiences for young people (Senate of Canada, 2007). Stasiulis (2002a) contends this attitude of "inequality and exclusion" of young people from important policy and pedagogical debates is endemic and reflective of the "unsettling of the nation-state", the "decline of social rights" and the "hegemony of neo-liberal governance" in Canada, and even more broadly as transformations associated with globalisation (p. 365).

As critical theorists reconstructing the pedagogical as political and the political as pedagogical, we chose to investigate these concerns for young people's participatory citizenship directly through numerous disciplinary and professional lenses identified in the literature as "transdisciplinary" (Nicolescu, 1999, 2002). Transdisciplinarity concerns emergent new thinking, new ways of accessing old ways of thinking, construction of new ways of knowing, and praxis in order to transcend tired, dichotomous critiques that recognise multiple new sites and forms of knowledge creation (Kincheloe & McLaren, 2005; Moore & Mitchell, 2008).

It is acknowledged here, however, that contested notions relative to a just and more inclusive 'citizenship' for Aboriginal peoples across Canada must remain bracketed as separate but integrally related investigations clearly transcending the exploratory scope of this study (Canadian Aboriginal News, 2009). In this, we concur with Kincheloe's (2008) observations that the vast majority of North Americans...

...are absolutely unaware they are using Native land – it is just not part of Western consciousness – that we are on Native land....It seems rather obvious (even though nobody seems to think about it) that a central dimension of any critical pedagogy has to deal with the subject of indigeneity, and it is something very few critical scholars are aware of or interested in. (pp. 153–154)

Stasiulis (2002a) outlines the contours of this national amnesia and its harvest of contested notions of citizenship inherited from Canada's colonial past through to its present-day "treaty federalism and treaty citizenship" (pp. 369–370). She deconstructs citizenship from this historical standpoint while translating the analysis to the status of the nation's children (2002b). Her reflections also include discussion of tensions between child protection ideologies and democratic participation rights for young people underpinning the 2002 UN General Assembly Special Session on Children alongside the work of Canadian youth activist Craig Kielburger. Her observations of this local/global connection for children's citizenship pointed us implicitly to outcomes from the 2002 Special Session listed in the policy framework *A Canada Fit for Children* (Government of Canada, 2004), and to Mr. Kielburger's work, each providing empirical entry points for our investigation. Additional legal and historical analyses were provided by the Senate Standing Committee on Human Rights study of CRC implementation (Senate of Canada, 2007). Their three-year comparative analysis investigated domestic and international responses to the treaty and, similar to Stasiulis, the Committee completely rejects any notion of participatory citizenship for children most clearly through expert testimonies from dozens of young people.

Widely noted in the international and domestic press, perhaps the most egregious example of this exclusionary approach to Canadian citizenship is that of 15-year-old child soldier Omar Khadr, shot in the back and partially blinded during a 2002 Afghanistan firefight with US marines, who languishes in military prison at

Guantanamo Bay, Cuba at time of this writing (Mitchell, 2010; Shephard, 2008). We maintain that "transdisciplinarity" offers a useful framework for understanding such interconnected phenomena, and this is defined by Nicolescu (2002), Russell (2000) and others as moving beyond traditional epistemological expressions of scholarship towards a way of knowing "that will be essential in the 21st and later centuries" (Koizumi, 2001, p. 219). Nicolescu (2002) explains:

> Multidisciplinarity concerns studying a research topic not as just one discipline but in several at the same time...it brings a plus to the discipline in question [but this plus] is in exclusive service to this discipline...Interdisciplinarity concerns the transfer of methods from one discipline to another...like multidisciplinarity, interdisciplinarity overflows the disciplines, but its goal still remains within the framework of disciplinary research...transdisciplinarity concerns that which is between disciplines, across the different disciplines, and beyond all disciplines. (pp. 42–44)

Somerville and Rapport (2000, pp. 6–7) emphasise similar distinctions between transdisciplinary approaches to law, education, science, politics and cultural studies of media and the arts that sharply contrast multi- or even inter-disciplinary methodologies since the former is fundamentally associated with critique. The authors' epistemological standpoint in the investigation was also informed by transdisciplinary approaches to childhood studies which have shaped how we understand and act in the academy. This transition in thinking came about before entering academic life after three collective decades of front-line counselling with young people in British Columbia within mental health, education, youth justice and foster care settings.

METHODOLOGICAL FRAMEWORK

Brock University student plans for a local conference entitled *Be the Change: Youth Leadership Conference on Global Citizenship* offered a clear opportunity to collect various data in response to Kiwan's (2005, p. 37) critique that child rights scholars argue only rhetorically for "human rights as the theoretical underpinning of citizenship and citizenship education". The investigation adopted an exploratory, inductive methodology that reflects the uncertainty found within related discourses and the call for continued re-theorising. As noted, our research question 'What are some of the critical issues for young people as they attempt to exercise their rights to participatory citizenship in Canada and beyond?' framed the study. The one-day conference was conceived by a campus-based, student-led *Free the Children Action Group*. This unique university chapter of the international non-governmental organisation co-founded by the Kielburger brothers embarked upon a two-year funding drive which included collaboration with 15 local high-school students employed by the Niagara Regional Public Health Authority (REACT, 2010). The May, 2009 event was attended by over 500 elementary, high-school and university-aged delegates motivated to hear Mr. Kielburger speak and to participate in workshops on themes of global citizenship and activism with and for young people (Brock University Press, 2010).

As researchers we set about designing a case study that utilised inductive, grounded theory methods to address theoretical gaps in the literature by eliciting experiential dimensions of participatory, democratic citizenship with the cohort of young people involved in the Kielburger conference. As critical educators we also participated directly in the university- and community-based systems that offered rich data collection opportunities. Thus, the aim and design of the inquiry focused upon the following: discovering and representing substantive theory derived from in-person, open-ended interviews with key stakeholders; documentary analyses of domestic and international legal and policy texts; and constant comparison of these data with each other and with reviews of a transdisciplinary body of literature. The study was also congruent with Strauss and Corbin's (1998a) arguments for adopting grounded procedures explicitly to generate new theory and doing social science research as the same process.

> Although we do not create data, we create theory out of data. If we do it correctly, then we are not speaking for our participants but rather are enabling them to speak in voices that are clearly understood and representative. Our theories, however incomplete, provide a common language (set of concepts) through which research participants, professionals and others can come together to discuss ideas and find solutions to problems. (p. 56)

Grounded theory was chosen as the most congruent analytical and procedural approach since this approach has been established for over 40 years in the social and traditional sciences as a cogent guide to initial understanding of phenomena within qualitative or quantitative paradigms (Glaser, 2005; Glaser & Strauss, 1967; Strauss & Corbin, 1998a, 1998b). Grounded theory provides a set of inductive methods that lead the research team from studying concrete realities into a rendering of new conceptual understanding (see Charmaz, 2006 for constructivist approaches). This is achieved through development of a theoretical statement or representation illustrating conceptual dimensions found in the data that address the research question. The inductive entry point to the study was marked as one of us responded formally to a student request to participate as a faculty mentor in development of a campus-based chapter of *Free the Children*. As noted, the Kielburgers established *Free the Children* in 1995 (when Craig was 13 years of age) and the organisation has become internationally renowned. It epitomises the principles of social entrepreneurship noted by Trivedi (2010) as a type of activism driven by innovation to create economic benefits for solving social problems, not as a means to drive profits (p. 68). Today *Free the Children* "is the world's largest network of children helping children having improved the lives of over one million young people through education" (Kielburger & Kielburger, 2006; also *Free the Children*, 2011). As brother and co-founder Marc Kielburger (as cited in Wingrove, 2010) confirms, their philosophy is straightforward:

> [I]f we can give people the opportunity to make choices that support a more sustainable lifestyle, it is possible to do and generate profits…in fact, that classic win-win is the very cornerstone of the entire social economy. (p. F-2)

Co-construction of knowledge with young people in relationship as co-researchers/co-authors is an example of this critical approach that steps outside traditional knowledge silos since all research subjects are 'insiders' and experts in their own lives (Charmaz, 2006; Kincheloe & McLaren, 2005; Kellett & Ward, 2008). In light of this dimension of experiential citizenship, we included views from four senior elementary school students who attended the conference (three females and one male) as co-authors of a separate research paper (Moore, Gegieckas, Marval, McCauley, & Peloquin, 2011). Eight additional key stakeholder interviews were conducted over a period of six months – three females and five males – and each was transcribed, coded and analysed using grounded theory procedures over a 12-month period. Informed consent was given by all participants to include their own names with published interview excerpts if they chose this option. Our analysis also includes collation of memoing and other notes taken during 10 participant observations by the researchers during student, faculty and professional planning sessions held at the university and in community-based offices of the Niagara Health Region.

DISCUSSION OF KEY THEMATIC FINDINGS

Selected findings presented in this section were described, compared, and then reinterpreted through open coding of texts and theoretical development relative to the emergence of the study's "theoretical code" argued by Glaser (2005) for all grounded theory studies. Moreover, Strauss and Corbin (1998b) emphasise the reflexive nature of grounded theory research stipulating that "interpretations must include the perspectives and voices of the people whom we study" (p. 160). However, these latter authors further caution: "We are naïve if we think we can 'know it all' but even a small amount of understanding can make a difference" (Strauss & Corbin, 1998a, p. 56).

Building upon our previous investigations, we were also cognizant of the ongoing ideological schism between the two originators of grounded theory, and thus, we chose the 'Glaserian' approach to coding and analysis (Glaser, 2005; Mitchell, 2005, 2007; Mitchell & McCusker, 2008; Moore & Mitchell, 2010; for contrasts see Strauss & Corbin, 1998a, 1998b). The three thematic findings identified in the following sections were most salient for theory generation, and are presented with supporting interview excerpts from the larger dataset to show movement across levels of abstraction to concept discovery and, finally, arrival at the study's theoretical code.

These data include excerpts from Mr. Kielburger's interview as well as from a university student partner (acronym MH) and a Niagara Regional health promotion professional who served as co-organiser/co-facilitator of the conference (acronym HR). Figure 1.1 below illustrates our grounded analysis and results with 'transdisciplinarity' as the main theoretical finding; the heuristic model conceptualises how young people acquire knowledge of human rights; the local/global dimensions of young people's contemporary citizenship experiences; and associated experiential outcomes in the shift from passive bystander to active citizen. A discussion of these results takes place following the model and analysis of interview data.

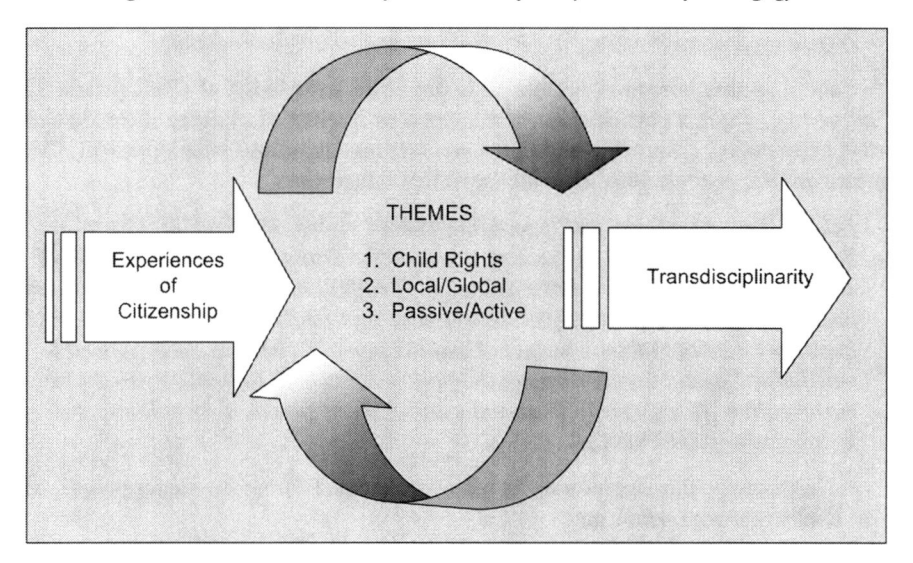

Figure 1. 1 - Heuristic Model for Transdisciplinary Citizenship Pedagogy.

The model is derived from thematic findings to illustrate movement across levels of abstraction to concept discovery and emergence of the study's theoretical code. The themes were identified as: Child Rights Knowledge; Local/Global Nexus; and the shift from Passive to Active Citizens.

Human Rights Knowledge

It is consistent and documented for over two decades that the majority of Canadian students of any age know little to nothing about their human rights as articulated within the CRC (Senate of Canada, 2007; Howe & Covell, 2005; Mitchell, 2005, 2010). Since most Ministries of Education have not chosen to make the teaching of the CRC compulsory throughout their provincial curricula – a clear violation of CRC Article 42 as well as key elements of the right to education found in Articles 28 and 29 (UN Committee on the Rights of the Child, 1995, 2003) – many young people hear about their Convention rights for the first time in institutional venues other than the classroom. The following interview excerpts show evidence of the theme of human rights knowledge – the first from Mr. Kielburger:

> *We teach young people at a very young age that they should wait, that they're too young to participate, that the problems of the world are too large,*

that they should wait until they get a good job, reach a position of influence, become an adult, turn eighteen, run for office, become a C.E.O. and then they can influence things.

For Canadian young people basic rights of citizenship are enshrined in the CRC–these rights are both often fulfilled and often not. For instance, the basic right to education- our country, obviously, is extraordinary when it comes to providing opportunities, yet still shortcomings are evident regarding federal funding for First Nations and Aboriginal schools.

Central to this human rights theme is the basic knowledge of CRC Article 12 and young people's participation in matters that interest or concern them. In this way, community, citizenship and rights are interconnected and interdependent. Key informant HR provides further evidence of this integration:

I think that experience and expressing human rights are directly related to being a citizen, and giving back to community: You need to be an engaged citizen in order to have a full expression of rights. And if you want to make changes in your community you soon realise that politics are actually a very important part of making change. ..I wanted to make changes but I realised I was limited unless I went through the political route and it was important to make policy. In university I started getting more involved in politics, and keeping myself informed...

Unfortunately, this opportunity is often not created for or by young people, as Mr. Kielburger also points out:

But young people, kids particularly in elementary school, aren't given this permission. For some reason adults in authority, and educators, think they need to wait until they've reached some golden age. As a result young people can become bored or disempowered.

*The most interesting right in the CRC is the right children have to participate in the protection and fulfilment of those rights, **and** to be aware of those rights. In Canada, there is a shortfall when it comes to government protection and government fulfilment, and that's where I think a lot of young people are stepping up themselves. That's where I think it gets more interesting because in Canada the voting age is eighteen, and we have no Children's Commissioner or federal representative for children.*

The closest thing we have to a federal representative for children are the Senate Committees on various topics and these are not very inclusive in their involvement of youth voices. Canada needs an independent federal representative for children that is able to introduce legislation, speaking on behalf of children and review legislation on behalf of children – serving as a check and balance.

In Canada, like many countries that have ratified the CRC, power relations due to young people's lesser maturity impede young people from active engagement as critical citizens capable of enacting solutions. These power relations are impacted further by adultist ideologies of childhood – standardised developmental trajectories; child as future investment; child and young person as incompetent, innocent, vulnerable or deviant. We have observed each of these to promulgate docility or boredom as common responses. There are four "principles" obliged in CRC Article 42: Article Two and rights to freedom from discrimination; Article 3 and rights for decisions to be taken in their best interests; Article 6 and the right to maximum healthy development; and the key human rights text for this study, Article 12 and rights to participate and express views freely. Clearly by any interpretation of Article 12, young people must now themselves be primary sources for adult information needed to interpret the other three principles.

Local/Global Nexus

Young people often seek opportunities to experience how local initiatives can contribute to meaningful change – a change that starts with the community for many through small acts, as key informant MH explains:

To change anything you have to first change yourself, change the things you do, as in Mahatma Gandhi's words "Be the change you wish to see in the world". So to me Free the Children reflects this principle – Free the Children says that if you want to stop child labour don't start by targeting corporations or governments, start with yourself. Start by buying clothing that's child labour free …little steps …and understand that small actions can have a big impact.

Mr. Kielburger also discusses impediments to Canadian application and understanding of CRC principles through the case of Omar Khadr's imprisonment, reinforcing the contention that his detainment and trial are being discussed throughout the world:

Omar Khadr's situation is far more than a citizen question for me—it's a basic human rights and CRC question for me. Omar's case sets a very dangerous precedent, not only in North America, but in the countries where we work primarily in parts of Africa, where you need societies to be willing to recognise that young people under duress were forced to extreme actions and who are victims themselves.

And in many societies that we work in…where they have very elaborate reconciliation processes built in at a communal level to welcome child soldiers back in, to forgive and welcome them back as members of a society, and to understand that this was an extraordinary force that brought them into those circumstances.

Why not in Canada… do we not recognise something that the most basic communities in parts of Africa recognise through healing ritual and reconciliation? For me it's a basic child's rights question and Omar's situation although widely talked about elsewhere has been severely overlooked here.

Young people often yearn to see their participation in civil society translate into action, and that the 'personal' is often times 'political', and that boundaries between the local/global are being redefined. MH offers an example of this point:

Even small contributions to local community can have a ripple butterfly effect into the rest of the global community...and this idea of real change engages youth---they are craving change...young people need to make a effort but also politicians need to make an effort as well.... Seeing change gives young people hope and that is the best way to combat apathy.

Responding to the desire that many children and young people articulate to be more active contributors is possible through creative engagement within current educational curricula. A pedagogy that incorporates critical citizenship – highlighted in both the literature and the policy and legal documents – has real potential to shape this transformation, as MH explains:

I noticed a lot of high school students were doing their forty hours of community service – that's the requirement – and many were doing meaningless hours they had to fulfill. I wanted to inspire and instill a sense of community by engaging them in meaningful activities so that not only are you benefiting yourself, but you are benefiting your community in a much greater way...and so that's global citizenship on a local scale. I also wanted to inspire them, in telling them about global citizenship, that we all have a responsibility not just for our own community and not just our own nation, but actually for our whole world. Because of globalisation we are all interconnected.

From Passive to Active Citizenship

We have observed CRC implementation in our own context (and elsewhere) being impeded by disciplinary constraints that dissolve its constituent principles by isolating them from its interdependent provisions (Mitchell, 2000, 2005, 2010; Moore & Mitchell, 2009, 2010). While educators, sociologists, physicians, nurses, psychologists, legal theorists and legislators, practitioners and activists debate outcomes of the CRC, each typically does so from their own disciplinary or professional perspective. This tendency frequently results in a "tower of babble" when trying to establish common pedagogical or professional interventions (Moore & Mitchell, 2009, p. 30). Such myopic 'cutting and pasting' of constituent treaty texts occurs without holistic integration of law, policy or practice, and has thus far truncated implementation compared with other social democracies (Mitchell, 2005; Senate of Canada, 2007; see also Matthews, 2007). The challenge remains to shift assumptions about the capacity of individual children and young people, as Kielburger explains:

Personally, I believe we should lower the voting age. I think it should be lowered to sixteen, but I think you need at the same time to bring with that a mandatory and true participation within education programs in elementary and high schools.

The biggest impediment to developing a sense of global citizenship is the social norms around the role of young people...so often parents- and well-intentioned parents have this belief that they need to protect children from all the violence and suffering in this world, and so when we talk about the participation of children, we often hear parents say, 'I'd love to get my kids involved with volunteerism, but I don't want to expose them to all of that negativity.' My response is: 'Listen, kids know what's happening in this world. I don't care how young a child is. They know there's a war in Iraq, they see it on the news. They know there's bullying in the schoolyard, so you can't tell them to close their eyes to it.

We live in an extraordinary age where most often children are seen as adults in waiting, but by doing that, they define their self-worth by the peer group that they belong to, and we segregate peer groups in our society, by the music they listen to, the clothes they wear, instead of the contribution they make to society, which not only are we now lacking that valuable contribution, but this has a negative impact on young people themselves.

Taking the point further by emphasising young people as active change agents, Kielburger declares underage citizens need to be taken seriously by adults in authority:

*What makes a Canadian citizen for me? The rights **and** responsibilities associated with being a citizen? I think one of the things that makes Canada extraordinary is that we do enshrine those rights through our Charter of Rights and Freedoms, but I think where we fall short is also in the responsibilities that all have, including **adults,** - and those responsibilities need to be – I'm trying to think of the right term to look for – almost inoculated, or shared with the youngest of ages including in school.*

Reinforcing a similar point that this approach to citizenship is dynamic, experiential and must be mentored within emancipatory adult relationships, key informant HR expressed the following:

When you're a child growing up you learn by watching those around you. I think it starts with role-modelling in the home and outside—that's how we learn what service to community might be...So I think in terms of nurturing it starts as early as possible. If it's in terms of volunteering, do your parents do it? What do they do on Saturday and Sunday afternoons? Do they bring you along with them? You can find opportunities to participate meaningfully; you make space for young people... young people want to be engaged but if they do not find or create positive engagement opportunities they will find negative ones...

Key informant MH added this important caveat:

In school I was repulsed by the politics. I held the same belief almost every young person has: politics are corrupt and when you see a politician it's corruption. That was the association that I used to make. My perception of politics is changing and this began when I started to immerse myself in my community and then look at it with an open mind and explore politics a bit more.

The first step to addressing retrograde adultist perspectives constraining the participation of young people is to realize that citizenship experiences may begin at the earliest ages. Key stakeholder HR explains this in the following:

Because there's that innate need to be part of a group, to be part of something bigger than yourself and hopefully those will be positive experiences, but it's been my observation from some of the places I've been and the things I've seen that if you don't fill that void, there are negative players out there that will step in and fill that void. Participation is inspiring and empowering. If you empower the youth to believe that they can then they will end up making their own opportunities and it will come to the point where you don't even have to make them for them anymore. That's right. I truly believe it's innate, that they want to give back.

As noted in our literature and policy reviews, children and young people have been largely silenced from Canadian civil society engagement and curriculum development, as Mr. Kielburger also rightly observes:

One thing we do lack is that mandatory responsibility for young people where so often youth are seen as passive bystanders. I had the honour to attend a conference a handful of years ago with thirty individuals locked in a room for a week including the Dalai Lama ... About four or five days into it because, when you have a week to talk about this topic you have to go deeper, that consensus emerged and it was built around a phrase the Dali Lama had said.

*He said: "The greatest challenge of our time is we're raising a generation of passive bystanders". We know how to solve poverty, we know how to solve global climate change, we know how to address the root causes, but the problem is we're not educating children in a means that encourages them to become **active citizens** to enact these solutions. And by telling them to wait, you know, children don't suddenly turn eighteen and develop a social conscience. They have to be nurtured through that process including the process of active citizenship, and the process of social responsibility by exercising it through freedom of speech, freedom of religion, freedom of the press.*

So how do students grow up being global citizens? Well, to a certain extent, they're thrust into it! They're thrust into it in the diversity of cultures and traditions and in questions that are posed in Canada, but that's the passive part. That's the part where you happen to be sitting next to someone in your school who speaks a different language than you do or comes from a different country of origin. The active part is where often we've been lacking and I think that that has been fulfilled in a way by a lot of grass roots....So the question is, "Why should an organisation like Free the Children have to exist when in fact, this should already be part of the education process and embedded within the global education process?"

Similar to our finding that multiple theoretical and methodological perspectives are creating new knowledge, the Kielburger brothers and *Free the Children* have stepped outside the box through their approach to social entrepreneurship challenging outdated assumptions about young people's apathy. It is also apparent throughout the data that key informants have articulated various conceptual properties of our three themes within most of the excerpts above. This common approach to responses further illustrates the interconnectedness of these dimensions with experiences of active citizenship at many levels. The basis for this claim is also evidenced by the collaborative partnerships among university students, high school students employed in regional health promotion, and elementary students – all of whom attended a citizenship conference framed by their human rights (CRC Articles 12, 13). Once again, Nicolescu (1999) succinctly articulates the phenomenon:

The emergence of a new culture, capable of contributing to the elimination of tensions menacing life on our planet will be impossible without a new type of education which takes into account all the dimensions of the human being. (p. 4)

Multilateral international negotiations leading to the UN Convention on the Rights of the Child (1989) are another example of broad based, global initiatives undertaken in this fashion. As a result the treaty became the first legally binding convention to be embraced throughout the entire world. To this day, the treaty's monitoring process exerts ongoing impacts on international agenda-setting (Doek, 2009, p. 772; Freeman, 2007; Editorial [*The Lancet*], 2010). Yet such developments are still not proportional to the demographic changes across the globe (UNICEF, 2009, p. 63).

Since CRC ratification by the UN in 1990 there have been 1.8 billion new humans, each now just more than 20 years of age and encompassing the first and largest cohort in history interconnected by global communications technologies. In light of our analysis of interviews and additional data collected in this study, we reiterate our argument that a transdisciplinary appreciation and application of the CRC allows divergent and contradictory viewpoints from social work, education, law and mental health to impact the debate relating to child citizenship in Canada and beyond her borders.

CONCLUSION

This findings reported in this chapter are premised on the assumption that knowledge of human rights is integral to experiences of local and/or global citizenship for young people at any educational level. Our challenge as the study unfolded was to uncover alternative models for critical citizenship that might be working within or beyond the classroom, and in so doing transdisciplinarity emerged as the theoretical code underpinning our analysis. As the study closes, we argue that the CRC offers a potential new approach towards teaching and learning democratic practices as a transdisciplinary human rights framework for citizenship pedagogy and an alternative to current neo-liberal models. Clearly, the notion has had little traction in our own political spaces to date (Mitchell, 2010; Moore, 2006; Moore & Mitchell, 2009; Moosa-Mitha, 2005; Senate of Canada, 2007).

The fluidity of our times and the unprecedented electronic evaporation of geopolitical borders allow us to strengthen the argument for transdisciplinarity potentially leading towards the democratic postmodernism Giroux (2003) envisions. Transdisciplinarity has an inherently critical stance towards the status quo in any specific discourse or type of research, and could more adequately address young people's citizenship in the context of globalisation. Change and permanent interrogation are focal points of transdisciplinarity, and through these lenses we take the additional perhaps controversial stance that human populations are being reoriented towards interconnectedness notwithstanding their residential status in any sovereign state. In fact, processes that might begin to address humanity's collective concerns are emerging within new types of dialogue among citizens and this point is reinforced by our analysis (see also Rosling, 2006).

Guantanamo prisoner Omar Khadr is another Canadian exemplar of the fluidity of citizenship and the permeability of geopolitical borders. Captured in Afghanistan but not Afghani, held by the American military for war crimes, he is a child of the globe and not solely of a particular state. While local experiences shaped Khadr's citizenship they were also global, just as the global is retained in his current local within the glare of international legal, political and media reaction. As Mr. Kielburger noted, child soldiers such as Khadr are victims of war and singular disciplinary, legal or even multidisciplinary lenses are simply inadequate to address these complex issues, just as they are no longer the sole concern of two nations at war.

In stark comparison, both Khadr and Kielburger are Canadian by birth and began their activism as school children in Toronto-area classrooms. By virtue of differentiated adult relations, both have become global citizens just as each became poster children for the times noted by Bauman (2000), Sassen (2008), and Vrasti (2009). Each demonstrates profoundly different life trajectories with one stretching to the current Afghan war and at least one high court ruling (Supreme Court of Canada, 2010 SCC 3), the other to a Nobel nomination and rock star status among children, young people and his peers well beyond his native land. In light of their seminal early experiences and subsequent emergence to global status, previous theoretical notions of how citizenship rights are constituted appear inadequate at best. This study demonstrates why we can no longer analyse citizenship within the binaries of state or statelessness, legal or illegal, just or unjust, citizenship or rights – or even 'me to we' as the Kielburgers (2006) have written.

NOTES

[1] While a 'western' basis for citizenship is frequently understood and sometimes argued relative to a particular geopolitical space or nation-state (see Kiwan, 2005, for example), the United Nations Convention on the Rights of the Child has nonetheless become an international framework for child citizenship in a reconstruction of the discourse over the past two decades. The positive changes in domestic legislation to do with genital cutting in the 'non-western' states of Kenya, Senegal, Sudan, Egypt and Ethiopia offer only the most recent evidence of this conceptual and political shift in defining childhood locally and globally (Editorial, 2010, *The Lancet*, p. 1800). These outcomes are representative of ongoing international efforts to curb dangerous forms of child labour, to halt the child sex trade, and to repatriate former child combatants – each of which are odious practices that exploit and damage individual young people by stultifying their experience as child 'citizens' in any political or cultural context.

[2] This study was reviewed by Brock University Research Ethics Board (Moore/Mitchell 08-289) and preliminary findings were presented at the *International Journal of the Arts and Sciences Conference* in Aix-en-Provence, France June 11, 2010. The authors would like to express gratitude for generous, astute and respectful feedback on an earlier iteration from Professor Engin Isin.

REFERENCES

Arendt, H. (1970). *On violence*. New York: Harcourt Brace and Co.

Bauman, Z. (2000). *Liquid modernity*. Oxford: Blackwell Publishers Ltd.

Beck, U., & Lau, C. (2005). Second modernity as a research agenda: Theoretical and empirical explorations in the 'meta-change' of modern society. *British Journal of Sociology, 56*(4), 525–557.

Ben-Arieh, A., & Boyer, Y. (2005). Citizenship and childhood: The state of affairs in Israel. *Childhood, 12*(1), 33–53.

Brock University Press. (2010, November 30). *Brock hosts 'Be the Change' Conference*. Retrieved July 25, 2011, from: http://media.www.brockpress.com/media/storage/paper384/news/2010/04/06/News/Brock.Hosts.be.The.Change.Conference-3900468.shtml

Canadian Aboriginal News. (2009, September 14). Discrimination Against first Nations Filed in the Human Rights Commission. Retrieved July 25, 2011, from: http://www.canadianaboriginal.ca/index.php?option=com_content&task=view&id=49&Itemid=9

Charmaz, K. (2006). *Constructing grounded theory – A practical guide through qualitative analysis*. London: Sage Publishers Ltd.

China View News. (2009, December 7). *Canadian environment protesters climb onto parliament buildings*. Retrieved July 25, 2011, from: http://news.xinhuanet.com/english/2009-12/07/content_12607631.htm

Dahlberg, G., Moss, P., & Pence, A. (1999). *Beyond quality in early childhood education and care: Postmodern perspectives*. London: Routledge/Falmer.

Devine, D. (2002). Children's citizenship and the structuring of adult-child relations in the primary school. *Childhood, 9*(3), 303–320.

Doek, J. (2009). The CRC 20 years on: An overview of some of the major achievements and remaining challenges. *Child Abuse and Neglect, 33*(11), 771–782.

Donnelly, J. (2008). Human rights: Both universal and relative. *Human Rights Quarterly, 30*(1), 194–204.

Douzinas, C. (2006). Postmodern just wars and the new world order. *Journal of Human Rights, 5*(3), 55–75.

Editorial. (2010, November 27). Female genital mutilation and social change. *The Lancet, 376* (9755), p. 1800. [online]. Retrieved July 25, 2011, from: http://www.thelancet.com/journals/lancet/article/PIIS0140-6736 10 62149-6/fulltext

Farrow, M., Kielburger, C., & Davidson, D. (2010, December 22). How the world can help Haiti. *The Globe and Mail*, pp. 10–11. Retrieved July 25, 2011, from: http://m.theglobeandmail.com/news/world/americas/how-the-world-can-help-haiti/article1846652/?service=mobile andtabInside_tab=0 andpage=3

Free the Children. (2011). *FTC – Children helping children through education*. Retrieved July 25, 2011, from: http://www.freethechildren.com/

Freeman, M. (1992). The limits of children's rights. In M. Freeman & P. Veerman (Eds.), *The ideologies of children's rights* (pp. 29–46). Dordrecht, Netherlands: Kluwer Academic.

Freeman, M. (2007). Why it remains important to take children's rights seriously. *The International Journal of Children's Rights, 15*, 5–23.

Freire, P. (1970). *Pedagogy of the oppressed*. New York: Herder and Herder.

Giroux, H. A. (2003). *The abandoned generation*. New York: Palgrave Macmillan.

Giroux, H. A. (2010a, 15 February). Democracy and the threat of authoritarianism: Politics beyond Barack Obama. *Truthout/OP-ED*. Retrieved July 25, 2011, from http://www.truthout.org/democracy-and-threat-authoritarianism-politics-beyond-barack-obama56890

Giroux, H. A. (2010b, November 16). Living in the age of imposed amnesia: The eclipse of democratic formative culture. *Truthout/OP-ED*. [online]. Retrieved July 25, 2011, from: http://archive.truthout.org/living-age-imposed-amnesia-the-eclipse-democratic-formative-culture65144

Glaser, B. (2005). *The grounded theory perspective III: Theoretical coding*. Mill Valley, CA: Sociology Press.

Glaser, B., & Strauss, A. (1967). *The discovery of grounded theory – Strategies for qualitative research*. Chicago: Aldine.

Government of Canada, 2004. *A Canada Fit for Children – Canada's plan of action in response to the May 2002 United Nations Special Session on Children*. Retrieved July 25, 2011, from: http://www.hrsdc.gc.ca/eng/cs/sp/sdc/socpol/publications/2002-002483/page01.shtml

Hawkins, C. (2009). Global citizenship: A model for teaching universal human rights in social work education. *Critical Social Work, 10*. Retrieved July 25, 2011, from: http://www.uwindsor.ca/criticalsocialwork/global-citizenship-a-model-for-teaching-universal-human-rights-in-social-work-education

Hill, M., Davis, J., Prout, A., & Tisdall, K. (2004). Moving the participation agenda forward. *Children & Society, 8*(1), 77–96.

Howard-Hassmann, R. E. (2005). The second great transformation: Human rights leapfrogging in the era of globalization. *Human Rights Quarterly, 27*(1), 1–40.

Howe, R. B. (2005). Citizenship education for child citizens. *Canadian and International Education, 34*(1), 42–49.

Howe, R. B., & Covell, K. (2005). *Empowering children – Children's rights education as a pathway to citizenship*. Toronto: University of Toronto Press.

Howe, R. B., & Covell, K. (2007). *A question of commitment – Children's rights in Canada*. Waterloo, ON: Wilfrid Laurier University Press.

Howe, R. B., & Covell, K. (2010). Miseducating children about their rights. *Education, Citizenship and Social Justice, 5*(2), 91–102.

Hyslop-Margison, E. J., & Thayer, J. (2009). *Teaching democracy – Citizenship education as critical pedagogy*. Rotterdam, Boston, & Taipei: Sense Publishers.

Isin, E. F., & Turner, B. S. (2007). Investigating citizenship: An agenda for citizenship studies. *Citizenship Studies, 11*(1), 5–17.

Kellett, M., & Ward, B. (2008). Children as active researchers: Participation and power sharing. In S. A. Moore & R. C. Mitchell (Eds.), *Power, pedagogy and praxis: Social justice in the globalized classroom* (pp. 91–103). Rotterdam, Boston & Taipei: Sense Publishers.

Kielburger, C., & Kielburger, M. (2006). *Me to we: Finding meaning in a material world*. Toronto: Wiley and Sons.

Kincheloe, J. (2008). The past, present, and future of critical pedagogy: With Joe Kincheloe. In C. S. Malott (Ed.), *A call to action: An introduction to education, philosophy, and Native North America* (pp. 153–162). New York: Peter Lang Publishers.

Kincheloe, J., & McLaren, P. (2005). Rethinking critical theory and qualitative research. In N. K. Denzin & Y. S. Lincoln (Eds.), *The Sage Handbook of Qualitative Research* (3rd ed., pp. 303–342). Thousand Oaks, CA: Sage Publishers Ltd.

King, M. (1994). Children's rights as communication: Reflections on autopoietic theory and the United Nations Convention. *Modern Law Review, 57*(3), 385–401.

Kiwan, D. (2005). Human rights and citizenship: An unjustifiable conflation? *Journal of Philosophy of Education, 39*(1), 37–50.

Kiwan, D. (2007). Uneasy relationships? Conceptions of 'citizenship', 'democracy' and 'diversity' in the English citizenship education policymaking process. *Education, Citizenship and Social Justice, 2*(3), 223–235.

Koizumi, H., 2001. Trans-disciplinarity. *Neuroendocrinology Letters, 22*, 219–221.

Luhmann, N. (1997). Globalization or world society: How to conceive modern society? *International Review of Sociology, 7*(1), 67–79.

Matthews, H. (2001). Citizenship, youth councils and young people's participation. *Journal of Youth Studies, 4*(3), 299–318.

Matthews, S. H. (2007). A window on the "new" sociology" of childhood. *Sociology Compass, 1*(1), 322–334.

Mitchell, R. C. (2000). Implementing children's rights in British Columbia using the population health framework. *The International Journal of Children's Rights, 8*(4), 333–349.

Mitchell, R. C. (2003). Ideological reflections on the DSM-IV-R (or Pay no attention to that man behind the curtain, Dorothy!). *Child and Youth Care Forum, 32*(5), 281–298.

Mitchell, R. C. (2005). Postmodern reflections on the UNCRC: Towards utilising Article 42 as an international compliance indicator. *The International Journal of Children's Rights, 13*(3), 315–331.

Mitchell, R. C. (2007). Grounded theory and autopoietic social systems: Are they methodologically compatible? *Qualitative Sociological Review, 3*(2), 5–18.

Mitchell, R. C. (2010). Who's afraid now? Reconstructing Canadian citizenship education through transdisciplinarity. *The Review of Education, Pedagogy, and Cultural Studies, 32*(1), 37–65.

Mitchell, R. C., & McCusker, S. (2008).Theorising the UN Convention on the Rights of the Child within Canadian post-secondary education: A grounded theory approach. *The International Journal of Children's Rights, 16*(2), 159–176.

Moore, S. A. (2006). Transdisciplinary approaches to critical multicultural pedagogy in Canadian higher education. In D. Zinga (Ed.), *Navigating multiculturalism: Negotiating change* (pp. 126–139). Newcastle, UK: Cambridge Scholars Press.

Moore, S. A. (2008). Social justice and education in a world fit for children? In J. A. Kentel & A. Short (Eds.), *Totems and taboos: Risk and relevance in research on teachers and teaching* (pp. 17–29). Rotterdam, Boston & Taipei: Sense Publishers.

Moore, S. A., Gegieckas, T., Marval, L., McCauley, H., & Peloquin, S. (2011). Constructing critical citizenship with young people: Alternative pedagogies. *International Journal of Child, Youth and Family Studies, 2*(3/4), 494–509.

Moore, S. A., & Mitchell, R. C. (Eds.). (2008). *Power, pedagogy and praxis: Social justice in the globalized classroom*. Rotterdam, Boston & Taipei: Sense Publishers.

Moore, S. A., & Mitchell, R. C. (2009). Rights-based restorative justice: Evaluating compliance with international standards. *Youth Justice, 9*(1), 27–43.

Moore, S. A., & Mitchell, R. C. (2010). Theorising rights-based restorative justice: The Canadian context. *The International Journal of Children's Rights, 19*(1), 81–105.

Moosa-Mitha, M. (2005). A difference-centred alternative to theorization of children's citizenship rights. *Citizenship Studies, 9*(4), 369–388.

Morgan, W., & Streb, M. (2001). Building citizenship: How student voice in service-learning develops civic values. *Social Science Quarterly, 82*(1), 154–169.

Moss, P., & Petrie, P. (2002). *From children's services to children's spaces – Public policy, children and childhood*. London: Routledge/Falmer.
Nicolescu, B. (1999, April). *The transdisciplinary evolution of learning*. Paper presented to the Symposium on Overcoming the Underdevelopment of Learning held at the Annual Meeting of the American Educational Research Association, Montreal, Canada.
Nicolescu, B. (2002). *Manifesto of transdisciplinarity*. New York: State University of New York Press.
O'Byrne, D. J. (2003). *Human rights – An introduction*. London: Pearson Education.
Osler, A., & Starkey, H. (2005). *Changing citizenship – Democracy and inclusion in education*. London: Open University Press.
Raby, R. (2005). Polite, well-dressed and on time: Secondary school conduct codes and the production of docile citizens. *Canadian Review of Sociology and Anthropology, 42*(1), 71–92.
REACT. (2010). *Smoke free movie night*. [online]. Retrieved July 25, 2011, from: http://www.niagararegion.ca/news/default.aspx
Rosling, H. (2006). "Debunking third world myths with the best stats you've ever seen". [online]. *Ted Talks - Ideas Worth Spreading*. Retrieved July 25, 2011, from: http://www.ted.com/talks/hans_rosling_shows_the_best_stats_you_ve_ever_seen.html
Russell, W. (2000). Forging new paths: Transdisciplinarity in universities. [online]. *Wisenet Journal – Australia's Women in Science Inquiry Network*, Issue 53. Retrieved July 25, 2011, from: http://www.wisenet-australia.org/issue53/contnt53.htm
Sassen, S. (2008). *Territory, authority, rights: From medieval to global assemblages*. Princeton, NJ: Princeton University Press.
Scraton, P. (Ed.). (1997). *"Childhood" in "crisis"?* London: Routledge.
Sen, A. (2004). Elements of a theory of human rights. *Philosophy and Public Affairs, 32*(4), 315–356.
Senate of Canada. (2007). *Children: The silenced citizens*. Ottawa: Standing Senate Committee on Human Rights, Government of Canada. Retrieved July 25, 2011, from http://www.parl.gc.ca/39/1/parlbus/commbus/senate/Com-e/huma-e/rep-e/rep10apr07-e.htm
Shephard, M. (2008). *Guantanamo's child: The untold story of Omar Khadr*. Mississauga, ON: John Wiley & Sons, Canada, Ltd.
Somerville, M. A., & Rapport, D. J. (2000). *Transdisciplinarity: reCreating integrated knowledge*. Oxford: EOLSS Publishers Co. Ltd.
Stasiulis, D. (2002a). Introduction: Reconfiguring Canadian citizenship. *Citizenship Studies, 6*(4), 365–375.
Stasiulis, D. (2002b). The active child citizen: Lessons from Canadian policy and the children's movement. *Citizenship Studies, 6*(4), 507–538.
Strauss, A., & Corbin, J. (1998a). *Basics of qualitative research: Grounded theory procedures and techniques* (2nd ed.). London: Sage Publications Ltd.
Strauss, A., & Corbin, J. (1998b). Grounded theory methodology: An overview. In N. K. Denzin & Y. S. Lincoln (Eds.), *Strategies of qualitative inquiry* (1st ed., pp. 158–183). London: Sage Publications Ltd.
Supreme Court of Canada. (2010). Canada (Prime Minister) v. Khadr, 2010 SCC 3, [2010] 1 S. C. R. 44. Retrieved July 25, 2011, from: http://scc.lexum.umontreal.ca/en/2010/2010scc3/2010scc3.html
Trivedi, C. (2010). Towards a social ecological framework for social entrepreneurship. *The Journal of Entrepreneurship, 19*, 63–80.
Tomaševski, K. (2006). *The state of the right to education worldwide – Free or fee*. 2006 global report. Retrieved July 25, 2011, from: http://www.katarinatomasevski.com/
Turner, B. S. (1993). Outline of a theory of human rights. *Sociology, 27*(3), 489–512.
Turner, B. S. (1997). Citizenship studies: A general theory. *Citizenship Studies, 1*(1), 5–18.
Turner, B. S. (2006). Classical sociology and cosmopolitanism: A critical defense of the social. *The British Journal of Sociology, 57*(1), 133–151.
United Nations Committee on the Rights of the Child. (1995). *Concluding observations/ comments: Canada*. Geneva: United Nations.

United Nations Committee on the Rights of the Child. (2003). *Concluding observations/ comments: Canada*. Geneva: United Nations.
United Nations Convention on the Rights of the Child. (1989). New York, Geneva: United Nations.
United Nations General Assembly. (1994, December). Resolution 49/184. *United Nations decade for human rights education 1995–2004 and public information in the field of human rights – No. 1*. New York: United Nations.
United Nations International Children's Emergency Fund. (2009). *Not there yet: Canada's implementation of the general measures of the Convention on the Rights of the Child*. Florence, Italy: Innocenti Research Centre and UNICEF Canada.
Vrasti, W. (2009). The politics of globalization studies: From the problem of sovereignty to a problematics of government. *Institute of Globalization and Human Condition: Working Papers Series, 9*(5), 1–21.
Wingrove, J. (2010, March 20). Marc and Craig Kielburger's do-gooding social enterprise. *The Globe and Mail* (pp. F1–F6). Retrieved July 25, 2011, from http://www.theglobeandmail.com/news/national/marc-and-craig-kielburgers-do-gooding-social-enterprise/article1506256/
Woodhead, M. (1999). Reconstructing developmental psychology – Some first steps. *Children & Society, 13*(1), 3–19.

Shannon A. Moore,
Richard C. Mitchell
Brock University, Canada

AUTHOR BIOGRAPHY

Richard C. Mitchell is an Associate Professor in the Child and Youth Studies Department of Brock University, Ontario, Canada, and holds a Ph.D. in Sociology and Social Policy from the University of Stirling, Scotland. He has written theoretically and empirically on the United Nations Convention on the Rights of the Child across the social sciences concerned with both individual children and the nature of contemporary childhoods. He is loving partner to Shannon, and doting father to Finn and Siobhán.

Shannon A. Moore is Director of Women's Studies and an Associate Professor in the Dept. of Child and Youth Studies at Brock University, Ontario, Canada. Shannon holds a Ph.D. in Counselling Psychology and her scholarship emphasises community-based implementation of UN human rights and justice instruments. Guided by a standpoint in critical pedagogy, Shannon integrates feminist and indigenous epistemologies with emphasis on transformational justice. As a clinical counsellor, Dr. Moore has practiced within educational, social service, mental health and correctional service contexts in Canada and the UK.

Wangbei Ye is a lecturer in the department of politics, at the East China Normal University. She teaches undergraduate and graduate students majoring in Ideology and Politics Education. She has published articles and presented papers in the fields of citizenship education and politics of curriculum studies. She received her Bachelor of Arts degree from Beijing Normal University and her Doctor of Philosophy degree from the University of Hong Kong.

Sandra J. Wolf is an Assistant Professor in the Faculty of Education at Lakehead University. She currently teaches courses within the Aboriginal Honours Bachelor of Education program and Aboriginal-perspective graduate classes. Sandra has been a classroom teacher and educational program administrator for Native children and adults for over thirty years.

Emery Hyslop-Margison is a Professor in the Faculty of Education at the University of New Brunswick, Fredericton, Canada. He has published extensively in the areas of critical work studies and philosophy of education. His forthcoming text, Capitalism, Post Neo-liberalism and Revolutionary Pedagogies, explores the effects of current economic trends on education and considers how teachers might resist their undemocratic impact.

Josephine L. Savarese is an Associate Professor in the Department of Criminology and Criminal Justice, St. Thomas University, Fredericton, New Brunswick. She has published in a variety of legal and social science journals. Her research focuses on criminal law, the Charter of Rights and Freedoms as well as sentencing and Aboriginal justice.

AUTHOR BIOGRAPHY

Gaysu R Arvind is Professor in Elementary and Social Education in Department of Education at University of Delhi. Her academic and research interests include study of the marginalized, cultural studies, understanding indigenous knowledge systems, pedagogy of sciences and cognitive psychology. She was the Post-Doctoral Commonwealth Fellow at the University of Manchester and Post-Doctoral UGC Research Fellow at the University of Delhi. Her works has been published in the *Journal of Cultural Historical Psychology, International Journal of Social Science, Journal of Research in Rural Education, Psicologia and Sociedade, Perspectives in Education* and also appear as chapters in *Routledge Handbook of Asian Education* and various other international books.

Keith Heggart has been an educator for more than a decade, working in independent, systemic and public schools in both the United Kingdom and Australia. During that time, he has worked as a Senior Leader in two schools, and started his doctoral studies, which are focused on popular education inspired approaches to civics and citizenship education in the Australian context. Keith is a firm believer that schools have a social purpose, and as such, must be greenhouses for the flowering of democracy and social justice, and that this should be the primary aim of educational systems. To this end, Keith has written widely on education from a critical theory perspective, and trialled a number of different programs in schools aimed at improving equality within the school context.

Lee Jerome is Principal Lecturer in Education at London Metropolitan University, where he manages the secondary initial teacher education programme and also contributes to the MA Education course. His research interests are related to citizenship education and the relationship between history and citizenship. Before working in universities he taught history and sociology in secondary schools in London.

Hugh Starkey is Reader of Education at the Institute of Education , University of London , and founding co-director of the International Centre for Education for Democratic Citizenship. He is programme leader for online MA in citizenship and history education by distance learning. He has acted as a consultant on language teaching and on human rights education for the Council of Europe, UNESCO, European Commission and the British Council. He is co-author with Audrey Osler of Teachers and Human Rights Education (Trentham Books, 2010).

Sam Mejias is a researcher at the Institute of Education, University of London specializing in the fields of human rights education and international educational development. He has worked as a project manager and curriculum specialist for human rights NGOs in the United States and England for the past decade and is currently completing doctoral research on Amnesty International's global education programs.

Helen Trivers recently completed a Masters in Citizenship Education at the Institute of Education. She began her career as a teacher through the Teach First programme and went on to work in the area of citizenship education and human rights education for organisations including Amnesty International and the British Institute of Human Rights. She is currently a teacher in a primary school in London.

P. L. Thomas, Associate Professor of Education (Furman University, Greenville SC), taught high school English in rural South Carolina before moving to teacher education. He is currently a column editor for *English Journal* (National Council of Teachers of English) and series editor for *Critical Literacy Teaching Series: Challenging Authors and Genres* (Sense Publishers). Follow his work at http://wrestlingwithwriting.blogspot.com/ and @plthomasEdD.

May Al-Fartousi is a PhD. Candidate at Brock University. She worked as an instructor at the elementary and postsecondary levels in the Middle East as well as in Canada. Her research interests include: diversity issues in schools, Islamic studies, disability and culture. Her doctoral dissertation addresses various cultural and religious aspects pertaining to female Shi'i-Muslim Canadian students wearing hijab within the context of homogeneous public elementary schools.

Dolana Mogadime, Ph.D., is an Associate Professor in the Faculty of Education at Brock University, Ontario, Canada. From 2005- to the present she served on the Executive of the Canadian Association for the Study of Women in Education (CASWE) as President-Elect, President and Past-President and the Equity Issues Representative. She has published her research in international journals such as The International Journal of Diversity in Organisations, Communities and Nations; Urban Education; Journal of Black Studies; Canadian Women's Studies; Canadian feminist anthologies as well as Canadian anthologies on Black feminisms.